The Real Charlie Kirk

The Real
Charlie Kirk

DICK MORRIS

Humanix Books

The Real Charlie Kirk

Humanix Books, P.O. Box 20989, West Palm Beach, FL 33416, USA
www.humanixbooks.com | info@humanixbooks.com

Cover & Interior Design: Ben Davis

ISBN: 978-1-63006-351-1 (paperback)
ISBN: 978-1-63006-352-8 (ebook)

Printed in the United States of America

10 9 8 7 6 5 4 3 2 1

CONTENTS

INTRODUCTION ... XIII

CHAPTER 1: THE DAY THE MEGAPHONE FELL SILENT ... 1

CHAPTER 2: AMERICAN BEGINNINGS ... 13

CHAPTER 3: FROM CAMPUS TO THE WHITE HOUSE ... 25

CHAPTER 4: TURNING POINT ON CAMPUS — CHARLIE KIRK'S REVOLUTION ... 37

CHAPTER 5: FOR CHARLIE, CHRIST WAS EVERYTHING ... 49

CHAPTER 6: CHARLIE'S FIGHT FOR LIFE, HIS WAR ON TRANSGENDER ... 61

CHAPTER 7: HIS FINAL CHAPTER YET TO BE WRITTEN ... 75

CHARLIE KIRK TIMELINE ... 87

ABOUT THE AUTHOR ... 111

INTRODUCTION

The Voice That Changed History Will Change the Future

CHARLIE KIRK WAS NOT JUST A POLITICAL ACTIVIST. He was a movement, a force of nature, and in many ways, a prophet for our time.

His voice was one of reason, conviction, and clarity in an age of noise, fear, and manipulation. Like Socrates in ancient Athens, Charlie deployed questions, logic, and relentless clarity to expose falsehood and hypocrisy.

And like Jesus Christ, Gandhi, and Martin Luther King Jr., Charlie's life was cut short—yet his death only magnified his influence.

Tertullian once wrote, "The blood of martyrs is the seed of the Church." So too with Charlie Kirk.

His martyrdom has become the seed of a movement that will shape America for generations to come.

Charlie's greatest impact came in the 2024 election—a contest that reshaped the course of American history.

Donald Trump, written off by elites and establishment forces, stormed back to defeat Kamala Harris. I was an adviser to President Trump for his comeback campaign in 2024.

I can tell you that at the center of this turnaround was the tireless work of Charlie Kirk. His organizing, his connection with young people, his relentless defense of Judeo-Christian values—all helped spark a political earthquake.

The 2024 Youth Earthquake

For decades, Democrats had claimed young voters as their own. But in 2024, something unprecedented happened.

A surge of support among young Americans went to Trump—and the credit belongs to Charlie Kirk. Through Turning Point USA, his media presence, and his sheer personal energy, Charlie made conservatism not only acceptable, but exciting to a new generation.

He spoke directly to their frustrations: the cancel culture that suffocated free thought, the economic burdens of student debt, and the hollow promises of "woke" ideology.

Charlie showed them that conservatism was not a relic of the past, but a vibrant philosophy rooted in truth, freedom, and opportunity. His ability to reach young Americans—on campuses, online, and in their communities—was decisive.

The election results for 2024 showed that the same younger voters (ages 18-30) that overwhelmingly supported Joe Biden in 2020 moved dramatically to favor Donald Trump.

Trump would capture roughly 46% of the youth vote, compared to just 36% in 2020, according to the AP VoteCast survey.

And among men under 30, the shift was especially pronounced: In 2024, young men favored Trump by an 11-point margin (54% to 43%), a dramatic swing from 2020 when many young men had leaned toward Biden.

That swing of young voters to Trump in 2024 was the single most underreported story of the election. Without it, Trump would not have returned to the White House. Charlie made it happen.

Evangelicals, Latinos, and the Defense of Life

But Charlie's work was not limited to youth. He forged a powerful alliance between evangelicals and Latino voters—a coalition that proved fatal to the Democrats' chances.

For years, the Left assumed Latinos would be their permanent base. But Charlie understood their values: family, faith, and life. He recognized their anger at the cultural radicalism that had overtaken the Democratic Party.

Charlie spoke directly to these concerns. He reminded evangelicals and Latinos alike that the sanctity of life was not negotiable.

He championed the unborn. He defended family values. He stood against the tide of transgender ideology, teaching that biology is not bigotry, and that protecting children from irreversible harm is not "fascism" but common sense.

This message resonated deeply. Latino voters—Catholic, Protestant, evangelical—saw in Charlie a leader who understood their concerns. And evangelicals found in him a champion unafraid to fight the battles too many Republicans had abandoned.

Charlie's work benefited Donald Trump. In 2020, exit polling showed Joe Biden winning about 65% of the Latino vote to Trump's 38%.

But in 2024, Trump's share of Latinos rose significantly, with some polls showing 48%. No modern Republican presidential candidate had pulled this level of support from Latino voters.

The result: a new GOP coalition that delivered the decisive blow to the Democrats in 2024.

A Nuclear Explosion in History

Charlie lived only a relatively short life, but his impact was like a nuclear explosion in history. Few individuals have so transformed the political landscape in so brief a time.

Yet both the Left and the Republican establishment recognized the danger he posed to their stranglehold on power. The Left despised him because he exposed their hypocrisy, dismantled their narratives, and won over their voters.

Establishment Republicans feared him because he proved that real conservatism—rooted in cultural truth, not watered-down compromise—could win.

It was no accident that Fox News banned him. Just as they had tried to silence other strong Trump supporters after the 2020 election, they hoped to sideline Charlie and protect their brand of "controlled opposition."

But Charlie refused to be silenced.

With the help of Newsmax, his radio program, his podcasts, and his social media reach, Charlie broke through the media blockade. He showed the nation that the old gatekeepers could be bypassed—and defeated.

Tragically, Charlie's enemies determined that silencing his words was not enough.

Like the martyrs before him, Charlie's death sparked a movement. His blood became the seed of a new conservative awakening.

Just as Socrates was forced to drink hemlock, and Jesus was nailed to the cross, Charlie too was cut down with a gunshot to his head. His public assassination shocked the nation, but in death, he became even greater than in life.

The Left had spent years stoking fear, convincing vulnerable communities that conservatives were "fascists" out to destroy them. They whipped the transgender movement into a frenzy, portraying Charlie as an existential threat simply because he defended women's sports, opposed the mutilation of children, and stood for biological truth.

When his assassin pulled the trigger, the Left celebrated—revealing the very hatred Charlie had warned against.

But the result was not the silencing of his message. Quite the opposite.

Like the martyrs before him, Charlie's death sparked a movement. His blood became the seed of a new conservative awakening.

Global Movement of Faith and Freedom

The aftermath of Charlie's death revealed the depth of his impact. Young people, once skeptical of politics, rallied to his cause.

Evangelicals redoubled their commitment to cultural engagement. Law-abiding Americans—tired of lawlessness, censorship, and corruption—found new courage in Charlie's example.

And beyond America, Charlie's influence spread. His words, his vision, and his example ignited believers across the globe.

Just as the message of Jesus spread through the Apostles, and the legacy of Gandhi inspired movements of freedom worldwide, Charlie's message continues to echo far beyond our shores.

His death became not an end, but a beginning—a resurrection of purpose for millions.

Charlie Kirk Playbook

Charlie's legacy is not only spiritual but also practical. He provided the Republican Party with a political playbook for years to come. That playbook rests on two pillars:

1. **Stay consistently conservative on economic policy.** Resist the temptations of big government, runaway spending, and fiscal

irresponsibility. Uphold free markets, limited government, and economic opportunity.

2. **Engage fully in the culture war.** Refuse to surrender the issues of life, family, faith, and freedom. Stand for Judeo-Christian values, defend the unborn, and reject the radical left's assault on identity, biology, and truth.

This two-part formula is the road map to long-term conservative victory. Charlie proved it in 2024, and his legacy ensures it will endure.

Both the Left and the Republican establishment tried to stop Charlie, but neither succeeded. They mocked him, banned him, censored him, and ultimately killed him. Yet in each case, their efforts backfired.

Fox News' ban only highlighted the courage of networks like Newsmax who gave him a platform. Social media censorship only made his words spread faster through alternative channels. And his assassination only magnified his influence, transforming him into a martyr whose name will be remembered alongside the greatest leaders of history.

Charlie Kirk taught us that truth cannot be silenced.

Charlie Kirk has died. But Charlie Kirk's message is risen. His life was brief, but his impact eternal. He gave young people courage, he gave evangelicals and Latinos a voice, and he gave conservatives a road map for victory.

In the years to come, his influence will only grow. Like Jesus, like Socrates, like Martin Luther King Jr.,

Charlie's work will continue to bear fruit long after his death.

His voice will echo through history, reminding us that faith, freedom, and truth can never be destroyed.

And so, as we reflect on his life and his legacy, we know this: Charlie Kirk is coming again—through the movement he inspired, through the millions he awakened, and through the timeless truths he lived and died for.

PROVE ME WRONG

1

The Day the Megaphone Fell Silent

IT WAS A CLEAR WEDNESDAY MORNING ON SEPT. 10, 2025 when the news broke: Charlie Kirk, conservative leader, commentator, and founder of Turning Point USA, had died suddenly.

The headlines cascaded across every news app and television chyron in the nation within minutes. Some reports emphasized the abruptness, others the irony—that a man who made a career out of telling America to “wake up” had slipped, without warning, into the eternal sleep.

For millions of his followers, the shock was not only personal—it was political. It was also a religious moment for many.

First and foremost, Kirk was a Christian.

He was also a prominent Christian leader on par with evangelicals who have had an impact on American life.

In the polarized theater of American politics, Kirk had been a megaphone, amplifying youthful energy for the right, a voice that seemed both reckless and indispensable to a certain generation of conservatives.

To the left, he was a provocateur; to the right, a culture warrior; to many outside politics altogether, he was a meme factory. But death has a way of stripping away caricature. On that morning, when phones buzzed with push notifications—"Charlie Kirk, conservative activist, dies at 31"—the question was not only how he died, but what would die with him.

Shockwaves Through a Movement

For young conservatives, Kirk was more than a pundit. He had built a campus-based empire, making Turning Point USA a cultural juggernaut. He filled stadiums with students waving red caps and chanting slogans. He sat in the green rooms of Fox News, whispering sound bites that would ricochet across the digital ecosystem within hours.

His death, sudden and unanticipated, created a vacuum. The right had no shortage of voices—Tucker Carlson still spoke nightly, Ben Shapiro commanded a sprawling media company, President Donald Trump remained a looming figure—but Kirk's particular lane was unique.

He was the bridge between a college freshman attending their first conservative conference and the machinery of Washington power. His genius had been packaging ideology into viral content: Instagram posts, fiery speeches, TikTok snippets. He made politics feel like a concert tour.

When such a figure disappears, movements often fracture. Who would inherit the students, the meme pages, the donors, the microphone? Within hours of his death, that was the whispered conversation in hotel bars where conservative strategists were gathered for conferences, in Slack channels of political operatives, and in the dorm rooms of Turning Point's chapter leaders scattered across American campuses.

His death raises questions about what happens next for the conservative youth movement. Do they double down on Kirk's free-wheeling style? Or does his absence create space for a less Christian, less pro-Trump leadership?

The Politics of Martyrdom

Death in politics often confers a kind of sainthood. Martin Luther King Jr.'s assassination solidified him as a moral prophet. John F. Kennedy's sudden end froze his presidency in eternal youth.

Even opponents hesitate, in death's aftermath, to speak ill. For Kirk, the calculus was complicated. He was polarizing in life; could he be sanctified in death?

The early hours told the story. Liberal commentators, cautious not to appear ghoulish, offered restrained condolences while reminding followers of Kirk's record of divisive rhetoric. Conservatives, meanwhile, painted him instantly in heroic terms: a warrior felled too soon, a truth-teller silenced in his prime.

His face began to appear on hastily designed graphics with biblical verses, shared across Instagram stories.

For years, Kirk had warned his audiences that the left wanted to silence them, that conservative voices were under siege on campuses, online, and in culture.

Now, many of his followers folded it into that larger story: a fighter, gone too soon, because the world was too hostile to his truth. In that sense, his death might galvanize more than his life did.

Generational Shifts

Kirk represented a specific generational moment in conservatism. He was born in 1993, the same year Bill Clinton entered the White House. He came of age not during the Reagan Revolution, but in the era of George W. Bush, Barack Obama, and the culture wars of social media. His political style was not white papers and think tanks—it was Instagram stories, podcasts, viral debates with "liberal snowflakes."

His death raises questions about what happens next for the conservative youth movement. Do they double down on Kirk's free-wheeling style?

Power Vacuums and Opportunists

Politics abhors a vacuum. Within days of Kirk's passing, speculation surged: Who would take over Turning Point USA? Would it merge with another organization? Could someone replicate his personal charisma?

Names floated quickly. Influencers on the right who had built large online followings suddenly hinted at their willingness to "carry Charlie's torch."

Established figures like Shapiro and Carlson, though already dominant in their own domains, eyed the strategic value of absorbing Turning Point's infrastructure.

Even Trump, always sensitive to the energy of youthful crowds, issued a statement that sounded a clarion call for action: "Charlie believed in America. We will honor him by continuing to fight."

The Coming Transformation

The death of a political figure rarely changes politics overnight. But it can alter trajectories. Kirk's passing highlighted deeper questions already simmering in American life:

1. THE PERSONALIZATION OF POLITICS

Charlie Kirk's career demonstrated how much movements now rely on personalities rather than institutions. His absence exposes the fragility of that model. Without him, can Turning Point USA sustain momentum? Or does it prove that personality-driven movements are inherently unstable?

2. THE BATTLE FOR YOUTH

Both parties understand that young voters will define the next decades Democrats invested heavily in climate and social justice appeals. Now, with the messenger gone, both sides may recalibrate. Democrats might press their advantage; Republicans might scramble to reframe youth outreach.

3. THE DIGITAL BATTLEFIELD

Kirk's legacy is digital. He showed how politics could be won—or at least shaped—through TikTok and Instagram reels, through podcasts more than policy briefs.

His death raises the question: Who will inherit that digital battlefield? Politics may not be transformed by who wins Congress, but by who dominates the algorithm.

Echoes in History

History offers precedents. When conservative firebrand Andrew Breitbart died suddenly in 2012, many feared his media movement would collapse. Instead, it metastasized—his website became more radical, more influential, and helped shape the Trump era. Could Kirk's death spark a similar dynamic? His absence might not cool the flames but fan them.

Alternatively, movements can sputter when their figurehead disappears. Ross Perot's Reform Party disintegrated after his withdrawal. The Tea Party lost coherence without charismatic leadership. The question is whether Kirk's infrastructure—Turning Point's conferences, its fundraising lists, its digital assets—can outlast the man himself.

The First 48 Hours

By the second day after the announcement, the politics of mourning had crystallized. Newsmax and Fox News ran tribute segments, airing archival clips of Kirk jousting with opponents on college campuses. Liberal media outlets framed his death as "the end of an era in youth conservatism." Social media was a battlefield: tributes and taunts colliding in algorithmic chaos.

But beneath the noise, operatives were already strategizing. Conferences that week included emergency sessions. Donors asked: Should we keep giving?

Chapter leaders asked: Who is in charge? Activists asked: What now?

In those first 48 hours, the transformation had already begun.

A Nation Watching

Kirk's death may not shift America's electoral map overnight. But it could mark the beginning of a new chapter in American politics.

For years, he embodied a certain mode of conservatism—brash, digital, youth-oriented, and undeniably effective in shaping culture. His absence now forces a reckoning.

What happened on the day Kirk died was not only the silencing of a voice. It was the opening of a question mark over the future of American politics.

2

American Beginnings

SOMEONE ONCE SAID ALL GOOD THINGS IN AMERICA start in the Midwest.

Such was the case when Charlie Kirk was born on Oct. 14, 1993, in Arlington Heights, Illinois, a quiet suburb northwest of Chicago.

His arrival did not come with the fanfare that would later define his public career. He grew up in a middle-class family grounded in hard work, patriotism, and faith.

His father, Robert Kirk, was an architect known for designing projects across the Midwest. His mother, a homemaker and a steady presence in his life, cultivated the rhythms of family and faith that would anchor him in later years.

The Kirks were not political dynasts or wealthy patrons of American conservatism. They were ordinary suburbanites, comfortable but not extravagant, proud of their work ethic, and eager to see their children succeed. Their neighborhood was defined by tree-lined streets, church communities, and high-achieving schools. To many, it was the picture of the American dream.

From his earliest days, Kirk absorbed a love of country. His father emphasized respect for service and sacrifice, even though he never served in uniform himself. Dinner-table conversations often touched on American history and the responsibilities of citizenship. The Kirk household leaned conservative in outlook, supportive of limited government and personal responsibility, but it was not overtly political.

Charlie Kirk grew up in an era when America itself seemed in transition. The optimism of the 1990s—booming markets, technological innovation, a sense of post-Cold War triumph—framed his early years. Yet the events of 9/11, which he experienced as a young boy, left an indelible mark. Like many of his generation, he learned early that America's place in the world was contested, that threats could come suddenly, and that national strength mattered.

Kirk attended Wheeling High School, a large public school in a working-class district. It was not the polished environment of elite preparatory academies that produced many political leaders. Instead, it was diverse, bustling, and competitive, a place where Kirk began to notice the cultural divides in American life.

He was a bright student, but not an academic standout. By his own admission, he struggled with mathematics but thrived in history and political science classes. Teachers recalled a boy who was outspoken, curious, sometimes restless. He joined the Boy Scouts, achieving the rank of Eagle Scout, where he honed leadership skills and a sense of civic duty.

Basketball was another passion. At 6-foot-5, Kirk played for his high school team. Though he dreamed of going further, the limits of his athletic abilities eventually forced him to reconsider. The disappointment of not excelling in sports became a formative moment. It redirected his energies toward public speaking and political debate, arenas where height and physical skill mattered less than conviction and articulation.

Kirk's first real taste of politics came not in Washington, but in his own backyard. As a teenager, he volunteered for local Republican campaigns in Illinois. He stuffed envelopes, knocked on doors, and handed out flyers. What struck him most was the disconnect between the grassroots energy he saw and the professional, often jaded political class. Even at a young age, he began to suspect that American conservatism needed a new style, one that spoke not in policy white papers but in cultural clarity.

In 2010, as a 17-year-old, he became involved in a campaign for Illinois Sen. Mark Kirk (no relation). Though the race was bruising, it introduced Charlie to the mechanics of campaigning: messaging, mobilization, and the role of young volunteers. That experience solidified his desire to pursue politics not as a sideline, but as a vocation.

The Turning Point: A Speech That Changed Everything

The pivotal moment came in 2012. Kirk, then just 18, wrote an essay for Breitbart News criticizing liberal bias in high school textbooks. The piece caught the attention of conservative media figures and gave him his first national exposure. In 2012, he networked with donors like Foster Friess at the Republican National Convention in Tampa. In 2016, he addressed the RNC, and again in 2020.

There, he met Bill Montgomery, a retired marketing executive and Air Force veteran. Montgomery was impressed by the teenager's passion and articulation. Over coffee, the two sketched an idea that would change both their lives: a youth organization designed to energize conservatives on high school and college campuses. Montgomery would provide the wisdom and connections; Kirk would bring the energy and charisma. Turning Point USA was born.

Perhaps the most unconventional choice of Kirk's early life was his decision to forgo college. He had been accepted into Baylor University, a respected Christian school in Texas. But at the last minute, he chose not to attend. Instead, he committed himself full time to building Turning Point.

This decision was radical, especially for a young man with a background where higher education was often considered nonnegotiable. For Kirk, however, it was philosophical as much as practical. He believed that universities had become indoctrination centers for liberal ideology.

By rejecting the traditional college path, he lived out the critique he would later articulate so often: that success and fulfillment did not require four years of academia.

His parents were supportive though uncertain. It was a gamble—eschewing stability for a fledgling idea. Yet it was precisely this leap of faith that gave Turning Point its edge. Kirk could speak authentically to students about resisting the pressure to conform to liberal norms because he had personally rejected the institutional path laid before him.

By the time he turned 20, Kirk was no longer just a restless teenager. He was a young entrepreneur of ideas, building an organization that would become one of the most influential conservative youth movements in America.

Building Turning Point USA

In its infancy, Turning Point was little more than Kirk, a few volunteers, and a folding table at community events. He traveled the country in a beat-up car, visiting campuses, hosting small events, and recruiting students. His pitch was simple: Young Americans should embrace free markets, limited government, and individual liberty.

The early years were grueling. Kirk crisscrossed the Midwest, often staying in cheap motels or on

supporters' couches. He would hand out copies of the U.S. Constitution, debate professors, and organize small gatherings in classrooms. His youthful energy—and willingness to listen to peers rather than preach—earned him credibility among students who might otherwise have ignored conservative politics.

Fundraising was a constant challenge. But Kirk proved adept at networking, cultivating donors who believed in his vision. His background gave him both a sense of discipline and an appreciation for self-reliance. He was unafraid to ask for help but equally unafraid to work without it.

Kirk's upbringing shaped his political style in subtle but profound ways.

- **Middle-Class Roots:** Coming from a family that worked for its success, Kirk absorbed the ethos of meritocracy. He believed opportunity should be earned, not given, and this belief permeated his speeches.
- **Public School Experience:** Seeing firsthand the ideological tilt of public education, he became convinced that the left dominated the classroom. His later crusades against liberal academia were rooted in his teenage frustrations
- **Faith and Family:** Growing up in a stable, faith-oriented household, Kirk valued tradition, church, and community. These formed the cultural backbone of his conservative worldview.
- **Athletic Disappointment:** His shift from basketball dreams to political ambition taught him resilience. Failure in one arena became fuel for success in another.

By the time he turned 20, Kirk was no longer just a restless teenager. He was a young entrepreneur of ideas, building an organization that would become one of the most influential conservative youth movements in America.

What drove Kirk was not merely ambition, but a sense of mission. He was convinced that the left had mastered the art of cultural influence—through

Hollywood, academia, and media—and that conservatives were perpetually playing defense. Turning Point, in his mind, was the conservative counterattack.

He was not yet a household name. He was, however, already a force—a tall, energetic young man with a microphone in his hand, a message on his lips, and a sense of destiny in his stride. Everything in his life had converged to prepare him for this role.

For Charlie Kirk, the journey had only just begun.

3

From Campus to the White House

THE ELECTION OF DONALD J. TRUMP IN NOVEMBER 2016 sent shockwaves across the American political landscape. To the establishment, it was a once-unimaginable upset; to the grassroots right, it was vindication. For one young conservative entrepreneur—Charlie Kirk—it was something else entirely: opportunity.

Kirk had already founded Turning Point USA (TPUSA) in 2012 with the intention of mobilizing conservative students on college campuses. By 2016, TPUSA had been steadily expanding its influence, establishing chapters across universities, and staging events designed to counter the overwhelmingly liberal bent of academia. Yet despite its progress, TPUSA was still more of a fledgling organization than a household name. Trump's surprise victory changed that overnight.

The rise of Trump gave TPUSA both validation and momentum. What was once considered fringe—an unapologetic defense of nationalism, populism, and free-market conservatism—suddenly became mainstream. And Kirk, barely in his 20s, positioned himself and his organization to ride this wave.

One of the most consequential developments for TPUSA was Kirk's cultivation of a close relationship with the Trump family. While many establishment Republicans were slow to embrace the new president, Kirk recognized that Trump represented the future of conservative politics. He built bridges not only to the president but also to Donald Trump Jr., who quickly became an outspoken supporter of TPUSA.

Trump Jr.'s involvement cannot be overstated. His charisma, social media reach, and fiery defense of his father's agenda resonated with young conservatives. At TPUSA conferences, Trump Jr. became a star

attraction, drawing crowds and lending legitimacy to the movement. For Kirk, the Trump family's support was a powerful endorsement, transforming TPUSA from a scrappy student outfit into an organization with direct ties to the White House.

Trump himself also acknowledged TPUSA's work. Whether through public praise, retweets, or appearances at TPUSA-affiliated events, the president's recognition elevated Kirk and his organization far above other youth groups. Kirk carefully cultivated the image of TPUSA as the "Trump generation's" political hub.

Building the Campus Battlefield

Trump's election reframed the battleground for TPUSA. No longer content with merely hosting debates or passing out literature, the organization began casting its efforts as a direct counterattack against the progressive establishment.

TPUSA branded campuses as ideological war zones, with conservative students portrayed as embattled minorities fighting hostile professors and administrators. Trump's rhetoric about "fake news" and the "radical left" dovetailed perfectly with this message. TPUSA tapped into a growing sense of grievance among conservative youths and offered them not only a community but a mission: Defend Trump's America against the academic elite.

The annual Student Action Summit became a centerpiece of this strategy. These high-energy gatherings mixed politics with entertainment, offering a convention-style experience that rivaled the feel of a Trump rally. With appearances by Trump family members, high-profile Republican figures, and conservative media stars, TPUSA conferences became pilgrimage sites for young conservatives.

The Media Amplifier

While TPUSA built its foundation on campuses, its rise to national prominence would not have been possible without amplification from conservative media. Fox News and Newsmax, in particular, played pivotal roles.

Fox News, the dominant cable news network for conservatives, began featuring Kirk as a young face of the movement. His regular appearances on shows like *Hannity* or *Fox & Friends* gave him access to millions of viewers. Kirk was articulate, telegenic, and uncompromising—a perfect fit for an audience energized by Trump's insurgent presidency. Through Fox, TPUSA's brand extended well beyond college quads and into living rooms across America.

Newsmax, though smaller at the time, also became an important ally. Known for giving airtime to emerging conservative voices, Newsmax provided Kirk and his allies with a platform to reach grassroots activists often overlooked by mainstream outlets. Newsmax's tone was unapologetically pro-Trump, which aligned seamlessly with TPUSA's trajectory. Together, Fox and Newsmax legitimized TPUSA as not just a student movement, but a national force in conservative politics.

The relationship between Trump, TPUSA, and conservative media was symbiotic. Trump's victory gave TPUSA cultural momentum; TPUSA mobilized young conservatives who served as vocal defenders of the administration; and media outlets amplified the organization's efforts, ensuring its message reached millions.

Kirk's brilliance lay in recognizing and nurturing this ecosystem. He understood that students on campus needed to feel connected to something larger than themselves. By tying TPUSA to Trump's presidency and embedding it in conservative media circuits, he made young conservatives feel like soldiers in a historic cause.

This synergy also benefited Trump. For a president often accused of struggling with younger demographics, TPUSA served as a pipeline of youthful enthusiasm. Kirk's organization framed Trump not as a relic of an older America but as a fighter against the establishment—an image that resonated strongly with students eager to rebel against authority figures in academia.

By the late 2010s, TPUSA was no longer a scrappy startup —it had become one of the most critical hubs of conservative organizing in America.

Scaling Beyond Campuses

After 2016, TPUSA's ambitions expanded dramatically. No longer just a campus-based advocacy group, it began to act more like a national political movement.

Kirk launched TPUSA's media arm, producing podcasts, digital shows, and social media content aimed at younger audiences. The content blended political commentary with lifestyle branding, borrowing tactics from influencers and entertainment media.

Conferences expanded in scale and scope, drawing not only students but also donors, politicians, and activists from across the country. TPUSA also launched subsidiary efforts, such as Turning Point Action, to engage more directly in elections.

By the late 2010s, TPUSA was no longer a scrappy startup—it had become one of the most critical hubs of conservative organizing in America.

The organization's meteoric rise was not without critics. Liberals accused TPUSA of stoking division and promoting conspiracy theories. Even within conservative circles, some argued that Kirk leaned too

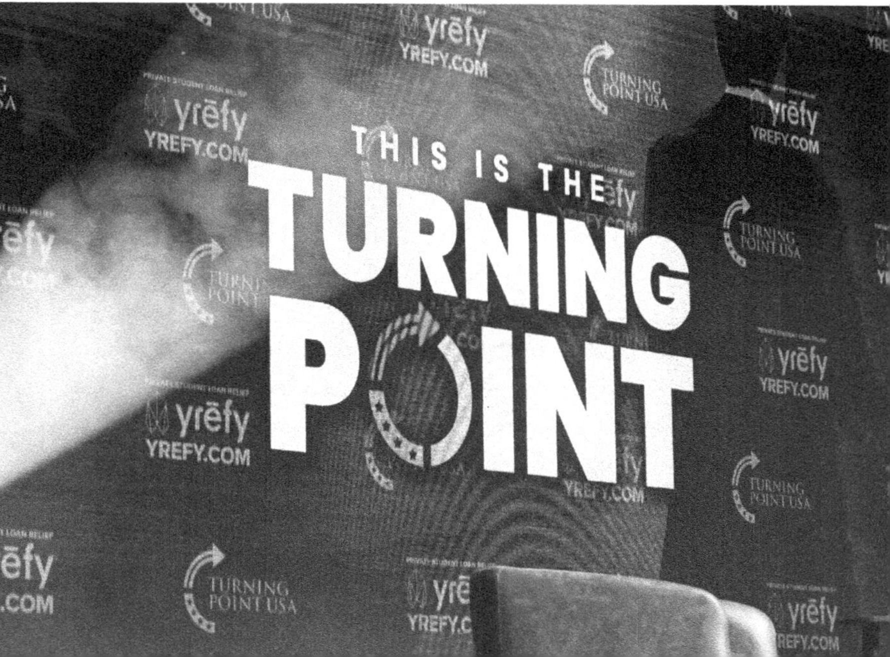

heavily on Trumpism at the expense of intellectual conservatism. Reports of internal management issues and controversial chapter leaders occasionally drew unwanted scrutiny.

Yet these controversies often fueled TPUSA's brand rather than hinder it. Within the conservative media ecosystem, criticism from the mainstream press was seen as validation. Every attack became proof that TPUSA was effective.

The Legacy of 2016

Looking back, the 2016 election was the inflection point. Without Trump's improbable victory, it is unlikely that TPUSA would have ascended so rapidly. Trump provided the movement's cultural energy, his family lent it credibility, and conservative media gave it national reach.

Kirk's skill was in connecting these dots. He turned TPUSA into more than just a student group—it became a central node in the Trump-era conservative movement. The success of TPUSA illustrates how quickly political organizations can scale in the digital age when aligned with the right personalities, causes, and media infrastructure.

TPUSA's journey after Trump's 2016 election demonstrates the importance of timing, relationships, and media in modern politics. The organization seized a political moment, leveraged high-level connections, and rode the currents of conservative media to national prominence.

In doing so, Kirk transformed himself from a college dropout with an idea into one of the most influential figures in the Republican Party. And while the Trump presidency is always identified for its tumult and controversy, its role in propelling TPUSA is undeniable.

What began as a campus movement has now become a major player in shaping America's political future. Without Trump's 2016 election—and the support of Trump Jr., conservative media outlets like Fox and Newsmax, and an energized base of young conservatives—TPUSA may never have grown beyond the margins. Instead, it stands today as a testament to how one political earthquake can create entirely new institutions of power.

AMERICA
THE GOLDEN AGE IS UPON US

4

Turning Point on Campus

Charlie Kirk's Revolution

FROM ITS INCEPTION IN 2012, TURNING POINT USA (TPUSA) was founded with a singular mission: to shift the political culture of America's college campuses.

Charlie Kirk, who never attended a four-year university, recognized early on that campuses were the battlegrounds where young Americans were not only educated but politically shaped. If the left dominated higher education, Kirk believed, the future of conservatism would be imperiled.

TPUSA's model was straightforward yet ambitious: establish student chapters on as many campuses as possible, provide training and resources, and encourage activism that promoted free markets, limited government, and patriotic values. By the time Donald

Trump won the presidency in 2016, TPUSA already had a foundation laid on dozens of campuses. Over the next decade, that network expanded into hundreds of chapters, making it the most visible conservative student organization in the country.

Kirk's strategy for growth was modeled less on traditional think tanks and more on grassroots organizing. TPUSA invested heavily in recruiting student leaders, often through large-scale conferences like the Student Action Summit. At these gatherings, students were trained in media engagement, activism techniques, and chapter-building strategies.

The organization also offered ready-made campaigns that students could replicate. Banners like "Big Government Sucks" or "Socialism Sucks" became iconic at campus tabling events. Rather than leaving each chapter to invent its own messaging, TPUSA provided polished materials, ensuring brand consistency and recognizable slogans nationwide.

Another cornerstone of TPUSA's expansion was digital media. Kirk and his team encouraged students to document their activism online, share videos of confrontations with administrators, and amplify incidents

of alleged bias against conservatives. This not only galvanized conservative students but also attracted donations from older conservatives eager to support "the next generation of fighters."

The financial backing was significant. With support from major donors and connections to conservative media, TPUSA could afford to provide travel stipends, free merchandise, and professional support to student leaders. This set it apart from underfunded student clubs that struggled to sustain themselves semester to semester.

The Liberal Landscape of Higher Education

To understand TPUSA's rise, one must also grasp the political climate of American universities in the 2010s and 2020s. Study after study confirmed that faculty leaned heavily to the left. At many elite institutions, conservative professors were rare, and student bodies often identified overwhelmingly as liberal or progressive.

This environment gave TPUSA a clear foil. At schools where left-wing activism was dominant—whether in the form of Black Lives Matter protests,

climate justice campaigns, or calls for expanded diversity policies—TPUSA positioned itself as the voice of the silenced minority. Students were told they were not alone, that conservatism still had a place on campus, and that they could be proud to defend their values.

In practice, the landscape varied widely. At large state schools in conservative-leaning states, TPUSA chapters often found robust support and even friendly faculty allies. At Ivy League and coastal institutions, however, chapters faced steep resistance from both students and administrators.

The presence of TPUSA on a campus rarely went unnoticed. At some universities, their tabling events were greeted with counterprotests. Activists accused the organization of being inflammatory, and in some cases, student governments attempted to deny TPUSA chapters recognition or funding.

The reaction from progressive students ranged from mockery to outright hostility . . . Ironically, this opposition often strengthened TPUSA's appeal . . .

Administrators often found themselves caught between competing pressures. On the one hand, they had to uphold principles of free speech and association; on the other, they faced demands from progressive students to limit what they viewed as harmful rhetoric. This tension produced high-profile battles over TPUSA events, with national media coverage often amplifying local disputes.

The reaction from progressive students ranged from mockery to outright hostility. Viral videos of students tearing down TPUSA posters or shouting down speakers became staples in conservative media outlets, feeding a narrative of campus intolerance. Ironically, this opposition often strengthened TPUSA's appeal, both to its student members and to donors who saw the group as bravely standing up to a hostile establishment.

Beyond the Quad: A National Platform

Even as it clashed with liberal student bodies, TPUSA leveraged every controversy into national attention. Appearances on Fox News, Newsmax, and other outlets ensured that small campus skirmishes were elevated into symbols of America's broader culture wars.

Kirk himself became a fixture on television, radio, and podcasts, often using campus incidents as evidence of the left's "war on free speech." By tying campus activism to national debates, TPUSA transformed itself from a student organization into a central pillar of the conservative movement.

This feedback loop was essential: Campus activism fed national exposure, which in turn drove more donations, which funded further campus expansion. No other conservative student group in modern history matched TPUSA's reach or recognition.

The Shock of Loss: After Charlie Kirk

When Kirk passed away unexpectedly, universities across America reacted in complex and often contradictory ways. On the one hand, Kirk had been a polarizing figure, and many campus communities that had clashed with TPUSA expressed relief or indifference. On the other hand, his death forced institutions to reckon with the movement's undeniable impact.

Some student governments issued statements acknowledging Kirk's influence while reiterating opposition to his politics. A few universities that had once tried to ban TPUSA events quietly reflected on whether such measures had been consistent with free expression. In academic circles, scholars began to publish analyses of TPUSA as a case study in modern political organizing, treating Kirk's work with the same seriousness as earlier student movements of the left.

Among conservative students, Kirk's death was met with grief and a renewed sense of mission. Vigils were held on campuses where TPUSA chapters had thrived. At conferences, speakers described him as a warrior who had given young conservatives permission to be bold in hostile environments.

Interestingly, some universities that had once battled TPUSA shifted their tone after his death. Campus administrators, mindful of his national prominence, issued carefully worded statements about free speech and the importance of dialogue across ideological divides. For institutions that had seen repeated clashes with TPUSA, acknowledging Kirk's legacy was a way to reset the narrative and avoid appearing intolerant in retrospect.

The long-term effect of Kirk's work is still debated. For critics, TPUSA left behind a culture of confrontation that exacerbated polarization on campus.

For supporters, it created a durable infrastructure for conservative students, ensuring that they would never again feel voiceless in academia.

Universities, too, were permanently shaped by the TPUSA era. The battles over recognition, funding, and free speech led many institutions to clarify or rewrite policies governing student organizations and guest speakers. In that sense, TPUSA forced higher education to grapple with the meaning of pluralism in an age of polarization.

Even after Kirk's death, the organization will continue under new leadership.

Kirk's TPUSA demonstrated the power of focused, well-funded activism in shaping national politics from the ground up.

Kirk's TPUSA demonstrated the power of focused, well-funded activism in shaping national politics from the ground up. By targeting universities, Kirk seized the symbolic heart of American intellectual life and inserted conservatism into spaces where it had long been marginalized.

The reactions he provoked—from outrage to admiration—were part of the strategy. TPUSA thrived on controversy, and in doing so, it exposed the ideological imbalance of higher education while building a generation of conservative activists.

JESUS
S MY GOD
MY KING
MY LORD
MY SAVIOR
MY HEALER
Will Walk with

For Charlie, Christ Was Everything

CHARLIE KIRK WAS NOT ONLY RECOGNIZED FOR HIS fiery speeches on college campuses and his influence among young conservatives, but also for his deep connection to Christianity.

To Kirk, politics and faith were inseparable; he viewed America's future as hinging on its moral and spiritual foundations. His public ministry became intertwined with his political advocacy, positioning him as one of the most outspoken defenders of evangelical Christianity in the modern American political landscape.

While firmly rooted in Protestant evangelicalism, Kirk also engaged with Catholic thought, finding common ground in moral and cultural issues that transcend denominational divides.

For Kirk, Christianity was not a personal footnote but the central axis of his worldview. Raised in a nominally Christian environment, his adulthood marked a deepening of his personal faith. He frequently cited the Bible as the ultimate authority on truth, morality, and human purpose. His theology emphasized:

- **The Authority of Scripture:** Kirk insisted the Bible is God's revealed word and the standard for both individual and collective life.
- **The Reality of Sin and Redemption:** Central to his message was that human beings need forgiveness through Christ, a message he tied closely to America's need for cultural renewal.
- **A Mission-Oriented Outlook:** Kirk viewed Christian evangelism not just as spiritual outreach but as cultural preservation, and believed that America's greatness depends on its adherence to biblical principles.

Kirk's style reflected the classic evangelical blend of personal piety and public engagement. Faith is not compartmentalized to private devotion but extends into every sphere of life, especially politics.

Founding Turning Point Faith

In recent years, Kirk pushed further into explicitly evangelical initiatives, most notably through Turning Point Faith, the religious arm of Turning Point USA.

This branch seeks to mobilize pastors, churches, and Christian youth into cultural and political activism.

The mission is clear: America cannot be saved politically unless it is first revived spiritually.

Kirk frequently spoke at churches across the country, framing political battles—over abortion, marriage, gender, and freedom of speech—as spiritual battles.

His message resonated with pastors who see their congregations under cultural pressure, and with young Christians looking for a political expression of their faith.

Turning Point Faith reflected Kirk's belief that the health of the republic is tied to the faith of its citizens. He often warns that secularism leads to moral decay, while a revival of Christianity restores civic order and national purpose.

For Kirk, separating religion from politics was impossible and undesirable. He frequently pointed out that America's Founding Fathers grounded the Constitution and the Declaration of Independence on Judeo-Christian values, particularly the belief in God-given rights. If rights are not given by God, Kirk argued, they can be taken away by the state.

Several Key Issues Demonstrated His Fusion of Politics and Faith:

1. ABORTION

Kirk was a staunch pro-life advocate. He framed abortion not simply as a political issue, but as a moral atrocity and national sin. He often cited Psalm 139, emphasizing that life is sacred from conception. In his speeches, he declared that a society that kills its unborn cannot sustain freedom.

2. RELIGIOUS LIBERTY

Kirk defended the right of Christians to live out their beliefs in public life, whether in business, education, or healthcare. He warned against government overreach that compels believers to act against their conscience, and framed such encroachments as steps toward tyranny.

3. MARRIAGE AND FAMILY

He viewed the biblical family structure—marriage between a man and a woman, raising children in faith, and moral discipline—as foundational to the health of civil society. He argued that political attacks on family values gradually weaken the moral fabric of the nation.

4. EDUCATION AND CULTURE

Kirk believed that secular progressivism had come to dominate higher education and public schools, steadily eroding the foundation of Christian values. Through Turning Point, he sought to counter this influence by equipping students with apologetics, sound political reasoning, and a firm biblical conviction.

Evangelical Work as Cultural Renewal

Kirk's brand of evangelicalism was activist at heart. His sermons and talks often echoed the tone of revival preaching—calling people to repentance, not just for personal sins but for national ones. His rallies at churches and universities often carried the fervor of revival meetings blended with the staging of political conventions.

Unlike some evangelical leaders who seek to stay out of politics, Kirk deliberately framed his work as culture war evangelism. He was not content with conversions in the private sphere, but insisted that Christians must reclaim cultural and political institutions. In his words, "If Christians don't engage, darkness will."

Kirk deliberately framed his work as culture war evangelism . . . insisting, "If Christians don't engage, darkness will."

This perspective resonates strongly with younger conservatives who see themselves as cultural outsiders in a secularized America. Kirk offered them not just political tools but spiritual ones.

Though firmly Protestant, Kirk showed a growing interest in Catholicism. He often engaged Catholic thinkers, attended Catholic events, and highlighted the church's intellectual and moral tradition. His admiration for Catholicism centered on several key areas:

1. PRO-LIFE LEADERSHIP

The Catholic Church's consistent and uncompromising defense of life was an inspiration to Kirk. He praised Catholic institutions for keeping the pro-life movement alive for decades, and often collaborated with Catholic leaders.

2. NATURAL LAW AND MORAL CLARITY

Kirk spoke favorably of Catholic philosophical traditions, especially natural law theory articulated by thinkers like Thomas Aquinas. He saw this intellectual heritage as a powerful counterweight to moral relativism.

3. CULTURAL CONSERVATISM

Catholic voices, ranging from Pope John Paul II to contemporary bishops, have long been allies in resisting secularization. Kirk readily acknowledged their central role in articulating a coherent vision of society rooted firmly in objective truth.

While Kirk himself remained evangelical, he viewed Protestants and Catholics as allies in a shared mission: defending life, liberty, and faith in the public square. This ecumenical respect showed Kirk's pragmatism and his recognition that cultural renewal requires a broad Christian coalition.

Kirk represented a new generation of evangelicals who refuse to separate their faith from their politics. For him, Christianity was not just personal salvation but public truth, meant to guide nations as well as individuals.

Kirk's blending of evangelical fervor with political messaging drew both admiration and criticism. Supporters laud him for boldly proclaiming the truth without apology. Critics, however, argue that he sometimes risked conflating the Gospels with partisan politics, reducing Christianity to a political agenda.

Others counter that Kirk simply carried on the tradition of American evangelicals—from Jonathan Edwards to Billy Graham—who saw national revival as inseparable from spiritual awakening.

Regardless of criticism, Kirk's influence is undeniable. He mobilized thousands of young believers, made churches central to political activism, and carved a space where evangelicalism openly shapes political identity.

Kirk represented a new generation of evangelicals who refuse to separate their faith from their politics. For him, Christianity was not just personal salvation but public truth, meant to guide nations as well as individuals.

Through his evangelical work, he built a movement that blends revivalist passion with political urgency, insisting that America's survival depends on its return to Christian foundations.

6

Charlie's Fight for Life, His War on Transgender

PASTOR LUCAS MILES SAID BLUNTLY, "CHARLIE KIRK died a martyr."

Miles was a close friend of Kirk's and ran his Turning Point Faith.

Just before Kirk died, he penned the foreword for Miles' new book, *Pagan Threat: Confronting America's Godless Uprising.*

Kirk walked the walk. He strongly opposed abortion and the radical transgender movement.

His views and his outspokenness may have cost him his life.

For more than a decade, Kirk had built a public identity around a simple set of commitments: a muscular, unapologetic conservatism; a fusion of faith and politics; and an unflinching moral language on social issues.

In the years before his death, those commitments—especially his relentless pro-life advocacy and forceful critiques of transgender ideology—became central to how he spoke, who followed him, and how opponents responded.

From the earliest days of Turning Point USA, Kirk placed abortion at the moral center of his public activism. He consistently framed abortion not as a private policy question or a matter of medical nuance but as a fundamental human rights issue—his language often borrowed from religious and juridical registers.

As he explained in his segments "Ask Charlie Anything," abortion was not just a religious issue.

"Even if I didn't believe in the Bible, there is no scientific justification for abortion," he said.

"There just isn't. If you believe that life is a human being, then as soon as that life is formed, that life is deserving and worthy of protection under the law."

Across speeches to student audiences, conservative conferences, and national media appearances, Kirk called for the legal protection of the unborn, arguing that scientific facts about conception, biblical understandings of life, and a republican commitment to the sanctity of human dignity all pointed toward a single moral conclusion: Life begins at conception, and society has an obligation to defend it.

Journalistic retrospectives and clips resurfaced after his death, highlighting earlier comments in which he described abortion in stark terms—equating it, in some viral clips, to a mass atrocity—and explaining that his position was informed by both faith and a literal reading of biological beginnings.

"We allow the massacre of a million and a half babies a year under the guise of women's reproductive health," Kirk argued.

"We are allowing babies to be taken away and discarded every single year, just saying they are not humans."

"You are using dehumanizing language, saying, 'Oh, it's an embryo'; no, that's a baby, made in the image of God, deserving protection," he added.

"It is never right to justify the mass termination of people under the guise of saying that they are unwanted. That's how we get Auschwitz, that's how we got the greatest horror of the 20th century."

More than once, he compared abortion to the Holocaust or worse.

When someone challenged him by asking if he was comparing abortion to the Holocaust, Kirk replied:

"Absolutely, I am. In fact, it is worse. It's worse."

Kirk's style was direct and rhetorical by design. In long-form interviews and rapid-fire campus debates, he often combined Scripture, science, and political argument—pointing to passages and what he characterized as the self-evident truth that a unique human genome emerges at conception.

He framed laws protecting life as a fulfillment of biblical teaching and a social contract that protects the vulnerable. To supporters—many drawn from church groups, conservative student networks, and pro-life organizations—his arguments felt like an integrated moral case that synchronized personal belief with public policy.

Kirk took the position that even in extreme cases, such as a very young child becoming pregnant by rape, the baby should still be delivered.

"For me . . . the answer is yes, the baby would be delivered."

Complementing his pro-life advocacy was an equally robust commitment to a traditional "pro-family" vision.

Kirk presented family—marriage between a man and a woman, stable parenting, and a faith-centered household life—as the bedrock institution for American flourishing.

Kirk presented family—marriage between a man and a woman, stable parenting, and a faith-centered household life—as the bedrock institution for American flourishing.

He argued that cultural decay followed when those institutions were devalued, and he repeatedly urged policy and cultural leaders to incentivize marriage and parental authority.

In speeches to Christian audiences, he paired appeals to Scripture with a political program: family as the natural school of virtue, family as a check on state power, and family as the place where future citizens are formed.

These lines—part pastoral, part political—helped him cement alliances with religious conservatives and with politicians who saw family policy as a core issue of cultural conservatism.

Kirk's opposition to the transgender rights movement was one of his most notable—and to some, polarizing—stances. He described what he saw as the radicalism of current transgender ideology not merely as a policy disagreement but as a cultural shift that, in his view, threatened the coherence of sex-based institutions and the rights of parents.

The Advocate reported Kirk as saying, "Trans people are a 'throbbing middle finger to God.'"

He used this language to express moral outrage at transgender activism, especially the idea of redefining biological sex and gender.

He believed males in women's sports with transgender athletes was "cheating."

Speaking at a Saving America Tour event regarding swimmer Lia Thomas, Kirk said:

"[Lia] Thomas has destroyed female sports as we know it . . . I want every human being to be able to flourish. But I also don't like cheaters, and you shouldn't either."

"You need to intervene," he said, according to Media Matters. "Get off the court, get out of the pool. It's not going to happen anymore."

In that same speech, he argued that male-born athletes have physical advantages (bone density, testosterone, musculature) over female competitors that cannot be fully mitigated by hormone suppression.

In debates and on his show, he criticized medical interventions for minors, questioned the expansion of gender-based legal categories, and warned of the social consequences of decoupling sex from biology.

His critics—radical LGBTQ advocates, civil rights organizations, and many left-wing journalists—accused him of dehumanizing rhetoric and amplifying fear of trans people.

Supporters of his stance viewed his positions as a principled defense of biological reality and parental authority. Either way, the language he used—framed in urgent, moral terms—made him both an influential voice and a frequent target.

In the same or similar contexts, Kirk argued that gender fluidity or transgender identity represents a challenge to biological reality, natural law, or what he saw as the traditional moral order.

"We must ban trans-affirming care—the entire country. Donald Trump needs to run on this issue," Kirk said.

He added that "there are only two genders" and transgenderism/gender fluidity are "lies that hurt people and abuse kids."

After Kirk's murder, investigators said they are exploring motive in ways that puts his public rhetoric under harsh new scrutiny.

Law enforcement officials and major news outlets reported that the suspect was identified as 22-year-old Tyler Robinson. Charging documents allege he had been living and romantically involved with a transgender woman at the time of the attack, and that he appeared to have been radicalized online and obsessed with Kirk.

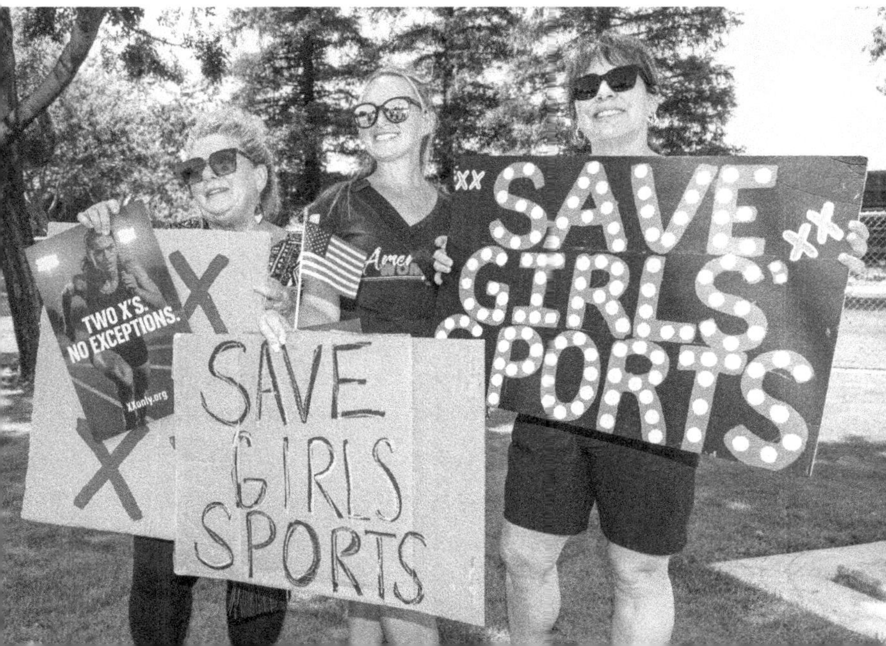

Federal investigators recovered forensic evidence tying Robinson to the scene, and said they were examining whether any communications or contacts connected him to people who had been publicly critical of Kirk.

Those details have been reported by multiple outlets and were described by the FBI as part of an active inquiry; authorities have not, however, drawn firm conclusions in public about a single, clear motive or about any conspiratorial link between organized groups and Robinson's actions.

Robinson faces several charges, including aggravated murder, and officials say they are seeking the dealth penalty.

Charging documents and investigators have alleged that his public positions—especially regarding transgender issues—may have been a factor; the case is ongoing.

The overlap between his political alliances and his cultural positions is also significant.

Kirk's anti-trans and pro-family arguments found common cause with President Donald Trump and with several Christian conservative organizations that had, before 2025, mobilized around similar themes: defending religious liberty, restricting transition-related medical care for minors, and prioritizing parental rights.

That alignment brought Kirk access to political platforms and a constituency that viewed cultural change as existential. It also invited fierce contestation from advocacy groups on the left.

After his death, leaders across the conservative movement—political and religious—invoked his words and framed his work as part of a broader struggle over America's moral horizon.

There is no question that Kirk's public stances and focus on abortion and transgender issues played a role in his death.

The investigation is ongoing, and while officials have disclosed elements—such as the suspect's relationship with a transgender partner and writings suggesting an ideological fixation—they have not issued a definitive motive that reduces a complex criminal act to a single cause.

The tragedy of his killing has prompted urgent conversations about the responsibilities of public figures, the volatile interplay of online radicalization and real-world violence, and the need for nonviolent channels for debating ideas.

What is indisputable, however, is that Kirk's words made him a visible symbol in a polarized public square: a standard-bearer for a set of moral claims that inspired deep loyalty and equally deep animus.

The tragedy of his killing has prompted urgent conversations about the responsibilities of public figures, the volatile interplay of online radicalization and real-world violence, and the need for nonviolent channels for debating ideas.

For historians of conservative media, and for readers trying to understand Kirk's place in 21st-century American life, the last chapter of his public life will be read against the backdrop of his core arguments.

He consistently urged a return to what he viewed as first principles—respect for nascent human life, reverence for family, and skepticism toward rapid cultural change—anchoring his case in a mixture of biblical citation, appeals to science, and partisan mobilization. Whether one agreed with him or not, he was unmistakably effective at turning moral conviction into organizational power. The aftermath of his death—both the criminal inquiry and the rhetorical ripples—has forced a national reckoning about the shape of political speech, the line between passionate advocacy and incendiary rhetoric, and how a democratic society preserves debate while protecting citizens from violence.

Charlie
CHARLIE KIRK
1993 - 2025
WE ARE
CHARLIE
WE ARE
CHARLIE

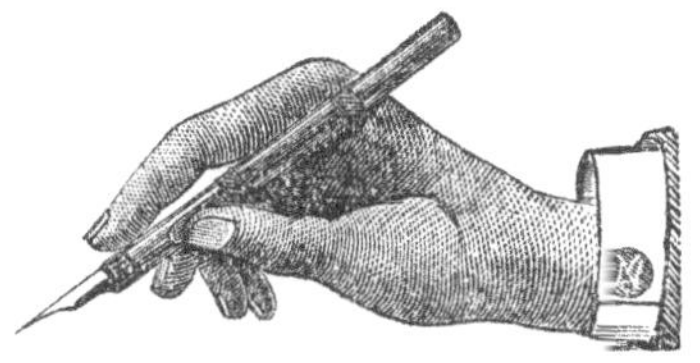

7

His Final Chapter Yet to Be Written

WHEN CHARLIE KIRK WAS FATALLY SHOT ON SEPT. 10, 2025 at a Turning Point USA event on the campus of Utah Valley University, the nation—already deeply fractured along political, cultural, and religious lines—found itself confronted with a moment that could not be ignored.

Kirk, a powerful and exceptionally influential figure in conservative youth politics and evangelical circles, did not die quietly.

His brutal assassination rippled outward fast, with grief, anger, criticism, fear, and uncertainty all spilling into the public square.

In the immediate days after the shooting, the atmosphere in America was electric and raw. Thousands turned out for memorials, vigils, and TV specials.

Political gatherings, church services, even secular spaces—town halls, campuses, civic centers—were filled with people recalling Kirk's speeches, quoting his slogans, and reflecting on what his work had meant.

- **Public Mourning:** People who disagreed with Kirk politically still expressed sorrow at the violent manner of his death. Many emphasized that no matter one's views, the idea of a public figure being gunned down politicized the very act of speech and gathering. Flags at federal buildings were flown at half-mast. President Donald Trump announced he will posthumously award Kirk the Presidential Medal of Freedom.

- **Evangelical Response:** The Christian evangelical community—and more broadly Christian leaders across denominational lines—cited Kirk's death as that of a martyr. Sermons compared his life and message to those of earlier Christian leaders who challenged secular or political power and faced persecution. Faith leaders urged calm but also called for greater resolve in defending religious liberty, life, and free speech.

- **Political Shock:** Both political parties expressed horror at what many described as the latest escalation in U.S. political violence. Republican leaders denounced the act, blamed rising rhetoric and intolerance, and called for investigations into ideological motivations. Democrat leaders also condemned the act, while warning about how any

> rhetoric from all sides can contribute to a climate of hostility.

A public death this charged also brought instant debate—and not only of the emotional kind, but of ideological responsibility.

Many critics asked whether the intensity of political, media, and religious rhetoric in recent years helped create a climate where violence became possible. Accusations flew: Conservatives warned that left-wing extremism and demonization of conservative activists had been escalating; liberals responded that far-right hate speech, conspiracy-driven claims, and attacks on marginalized groups had been pervasive. Questions poured in about whether speech on both sides had crossed the line.

Videos of the shooting, social media reactions (some supportive, some celebratory, some conspiratorial), and instant spread of unverified claims stoked distrust.

Following his death, there were urgent calls in Congress and by state legislatures for more effective measures to protect public speakers, reform event security protocols, and penalize hate speech or extremist content. Some conservative-led states pushed back, arguing that such measures risked trampling on free speech or being used to censor dissent.

The comparisons started almost immediately. Journalists, clergy, and citizens drew parallels between Kirk's assassination and those of John F. Kennedy and Martin Luther King Jr.—both killed not only because of hatred or political violence, but because of what they represented: hope, change, moral challenge, and, in King's case, radical insistence on racial justice and inclusive love. Could Kirk occupy a similar place in memory?

Like Kennedy, Kirk appealed to younger Americans—students on campuses, social media audiences, and faith-based activists. His death reinforced for his supporters the idea that his vision of conservative renewal was unfinished, and opened space for a mythos around the "lost promise" of a leader taken too soon.

In Christian tradition, martyrdom carries special weight. Kirk's evangelical base interpreted his death as more than political—it was a spiritual testimony.

In Christian tradition, martyrdom carries special weight. Kirk's evangelical base interpreted his death as more than political—it was a spiritual testimony. Sermons likened him to biblical prophets. Christian media outlets began reframing his life and message with a prophetic tone: He had stood for moral truth, opposed secularization, and called the nation to repentance. These narratives would shape how generations remember him.

Though deeply an American figure, Kirk's death resonated abroad. His influence in conservative circles transcended U.S. borders, in part because many evangelical and conservative networks internationally follow U.S. culture, make connections with U.S. political movements, and share similar debates over culture, religion, and identity.

International conservative media, religious leaders, and politicians sent condolences. Countries with strong evangelical communities—Nigeria, Brazil, parts of Africa, the Philippines—saw their religious leaders invoke Kirk's death in sermons about persecution, Christian witness, and the global struggle for religious freedom.

As with JFK and MLK, the full impact of Kirk's life and death will only emerge in time. But certain trajectories seem likely:

- **Institutional Memorialization.** Plans for monuments, scholarships, and endowed institutions bearing his name are already faintly emerging. Turning Point USA, the evangelical churches he worked with, and political groups aligned with his values may establish Charlie Kirk fellowships or youth programs to continue his work. Schools, especially those he visited, may designate spaces or events in his honor.

- **Mobilization of Young Evangelicals.** On many campuses, interest in Christian political activism will grow after Kirk's death. Many young people who attended his events or followed him on social media now feel a personal stake. Where before some might have viewed him as a firebrand, his death turns him into a symbol of both what was lost and what must be defended.

- **A Reckoning**. On both sides of the political divide, there is likely to be a hardening. His supporters may invoke him to call out "cancel culture," claim persecution, and push for greater protections. Critics will likely hold that his style contributed to demonization, and will demand accountability for rhetoric—even by those on the same side as Kirk in broader politics but who worry about violent escalation.
- **Religious and Cultural Memory**. In Christian history, memory is powerful. Kirk may become part of a lineage of Christian public figures whose deaths are as much about their message as the manner of their departure. Christian books, sermons, and podcasts will revisit his teachings; memorial services will be annual events in certain communities; Christian colleges might treat his last speeches or debates as class material.

Conclusion: America at a Crossroads

Kirk's death is more than the end of a life; it is a mirror held up to a polarized nation's soul.

A nation is being radicalized by big media, social media activists, progressive advocates, anarchists, and secularists.

The grief, criticism, debates over rhetoric and responsibility—all signal that America is facing a turning point.

The question becomes not just how to remember him, but what happens next: whether the country will choose to heal, restrain the poisonous edges of political discourse, protect free speech without making it a free-for-all that enables violence, and ask whether faith, politics, and culture can coexist without annihilating the empathy that underpins democracy?

In death, as in life, Kirk may serve as both a warning and an inspiration.

His assassination should galvanize those who shared his vision.

But, ultimately, the measure will be whether America uses this moment to reaffirm its moral and civic foundations. As Kirk might have said, this is the moment for America to find God.

CHARLIE KIRK TIMELINE

BORN October 14, 1993
DIED September 10, 2025

October 14, 1993 — Charles James "Charlie" Kirk is born in Arlington Heights, Illinois, to Robert Kirk (an architect) and Kimberly Kirk (a mental health counselor), and grows up in Prospect Heights, Illinois, a Chicago suburb.

2008-2012 — Attends Wheeling High School. During this time, Kirk listens to Rush Limbaugh, is active in local and school political causes, volunteers for the U.S. Senate campaign of Illinois Republican Mark Kirk (no relation), authors an essay for Breitbart News on liberal bias in textbooks, and appears on Fox Business at age 17. After graduating high school, Kirk enrolls in Harper College in Palatine, Illinois; he does not complete a degree, dropping out to focus on political activism.

May 15, 2012 — At age 18, while delivering a speech at Benedictine University's Youth Government Day, Kirk meets Tea Party activist Bill Montgomery, and a month later, the day after Kirk graduates from high school, they co-found Turning Point USA as a nonprofit to identify, educate, train, and organize students to promote freedom, free market principles, limited government, and conservative values on college campuses.

July 18-21, 2016 — Kirk is a speaker at the Republican National Convention and meets donor Foster Friess, who provides early funding for TPUSA; Friess, Ginni Thomas, wife of Supreme Court Justice Clarence Thomas, and Barry Russell, CEO of the Independent Petroleum Association of America, serve on the organization's advisory council. Kirk also holds Turning Point USA rally and declares his beliefs: "Freedom. Be in control of your own life and your own destiny. I don't want Washington, D.C., to tell me how to live my life . . . I think states' rights matter, Washington, D.C., is full of corruption, bureaucrats, waste, inefficiency . . . and I think states created the federal government, the federal government did not create the states. And the beauty of individual liberty, if you decentralize the federal government, you can restore freedom back to the people, not have government rule our lives every day," and pledges: "I'll be voting for Donald Trump." Kirk later assists with Donald Trump Jr.'s media and travel arrangements during the Trump presidential campaign.

October 4, 2016 — Co-authors *Time for a Turning Point: Setting a Course Toward Free Markets and Limited Government for Future Generations.*

November 21, 2016 — Turning Point USA launches Professor Watchlist, whose mission is: "To expose and document college professors who discriminate against conservative students and advance leftist propaganda in the classroom."

November 14, 2017 — Named to Forbes' "30 Under 30" list in the Law & Policy category for his work with Turning Point USA.

2018 — Kirk launches Turning Point USA campus tours program: "To engage students in meaningful conversations about free markets, free speech, American exceptionalism, and the Constitution."

March 22, 2018 — Kirk attends "Generation Next" White House forum and moderates a Q&A with President Donald Trump on topics such as the economy, tax reform, and the opioid crisis.

April 13, 2018 — Kirk is told by Broward County Public Schools he will not be allowed to speak on gun rights — advocating for armed guards and gun detectors — on the campus of Marjory Stoneman Douglas High School in the wake of the Parkland shooting.

May 17, 2018 — Turning Point Endowment is launched to "support and benefit Turning Point USA's charitable purposes and long-term vitality."

October 9, 2018 — Authors *Campus Battlefield: How Conservatives Can WIN the Battle on*

Campus and Why It Matters, with a Foreword by Donald Trump Jr.

2019 — Turning Point USA moves to Phoenix, Arizona, and Turning Point UK officially launches.

July 1, 2019 — Kirk founds Turning Point Action as the political advocacy arm of TPUSA: "To promote social welfare through raising awareness about free markets and capitalism, initiating civic action amongst the younger generation, and educating youth in order to be a resource for free market thinkers to further advance their values to educate and empower the younger generation."

July 2, 2019 — Turning Point USA acquires Students for Trump and Kirk becomes CEO. Following the acquisition TPUSA places representatives in key battleground states for 2020 election, holding "Super Saturday" rallies and Get-Out-The-Vote initiatives across the United States to re-elect President Donald J. Trump.

July 7, 2019 — Kirk launches *The Charlie Kirk Show* podcast.

July 23, 2019 — Donald Trump speaks at Turning Point USA Teen Student Action-Summit in Washington, D.C.

October 22, 2019 — Kirk, Donald Trump Jr., and Kimberly Guilfoyle lead one of the year's Turning Point USA "Culture War" events at Colorado State University.

December 21, 2019 — Donald Trump speaks at Turning Point USA Student Action Summit in West Palm Beach, Florida.

March 3, 2020 — Authors *The MAGA Doctrine: The Only Ideas That Will Win the Future*; book serves as a manifesto for younger conservatives and becomes a *New York Times* bestseller.

July 28, 2020 — Turning Point USA cofounder Bill Montgomery dies at age 80. Kirk says: "I can't put into words how saddened I am by the death of my dear friend."

August 24, 2020 — Kirk is the opening speaker at 2020 Republican National Convention, where he says: "I run the largest pro-American student organization in the country, Turning Point USA, fighting for the future of our republic. Speaking to you in my personal capacity tonight as a 26-year-old, I see the angst of young people as well as the challenges facing new parents. I am here tonight to tell you, to warn you, that this election is a decision between preserving America as we know it and eliminating everything that we love . . . By reelecting Trump, we will ensure that our kids are raised to love our country and respect its Founding Fathers, not taught to hate or be ashamed of them." Kirk describes candidate Trump as the "bodyguard of Western civilization."

2021 — Turning Point USA expands to over 850 campus chapters; Kirk hosts major events like

AmericaFest, Student Action Summit, and Exposing Critical Racism tour, and founds Turning Point USA Faith as the Christian voters' advocacy arm of TPUSA and School Board Watchlist: "TPUSA Faith is dedicated to empowering Christians to put their faith into action. We engage, equip, and empower millions of grateful Americans who are prepared to defend our God-given rights, by giving them the tools to expose lies and articulate the connection between Faith and Freedom;" while School Board Watchlist "is the first in the conservative movement to actively identify school districts across the country that are abusing their power to push Leftist, racist, and anti-American propaganda."

April 18, 2021 — Kirk speaks at Turning Point USA's Young Latino Leadership Summit in Phoenix, Arizona.

May 8, 2021 — Charlie Kirk and Erika Lane Frantzve are married; Mrs. Kirk is a former Miss Arizona USA, basketball player, entrepreneur, and will eventually launch the Midweek Rise Up podcast and pursue a doctorate in Biblical studies at Liberty University.

May 27, 2021 — Kirk early adviser and Turning Point USA seed investor Friess dies at age 81. Turning Point USA eulogizes: "Foster Friess Was One Of The First To Believe In TPUSA. He Helped Change The Hearts And Minds of Young

Patriots All Over America Through His Steadfast Commitment And Inspiring Mentorship."

July 24, 2021 — Kirk introduces former President Trump at Turning Point Action's Rally to Protect Our Elections! in Phoenix, Arizona.

August 14, 2021 — Kirk speaks at Turning Point Action's Unite and Win Rally, encouraging pastors to become politically active.

September 1, 2021 — *The Charlie Kirk Show* is added to Salem Media Group's national radio syndication.

November 1, 2021 — Kirk speaks at Turning Point USA Exposing Critical Racism Tour in Clemson, South Carolina.

December 18, 2021 — Kirk leads Turning Point USA's AmericaFest in Phoenix, Arizona.

June 2, 2022 — Kirk hosts Turning Point USA Young Women's Leadership Summit and promotes biblical model for relationships and men as protectors.

June 8, 2022 — Turning Point USA launches Turning Point Academy to challenge "woke curriculum;" an "educational collaboration with Dream City Christian, the first in a growing network of schools that will launch across the country in the coming years. Dream City Christian, a Turning Point Academy, will be focused on raising a generation of well-educated, courageous, patriotic, and principled leaders ready to impact their communities, their country, and the culture at large."

July 26, 2022 — Authors *The College Scam: How America's Universities Are Bankrupting and Brainwashing Away the Future of America's Youth.*

August 23, 2022 — Birth of daughter.

December 20, 2022 — Steve Bannon speaks at Turning Point USA AmericaFest and tells the crowd they are an "awakened army" and asks attendees if they are prepared to "destroy the deep state".

March 13, 2023 — Turning Point USA announces a partnership with BLEXIT: "Turning Point USA is now OFFICIALLY powering the BLEXIT Foundation. BLEXIT empowers, awakens, and inspires Black Americans to embrace the American dream, pursue freedom without government dependence, and reject the victimhood mindset. Joining forces, we can expand our efforts and enlighten even more Americans to the truth: In America, we are all born FREE."

December 16, 2023 — Kirk leads Turning Point USA's AmericaFest in Pheonix, Arizona.

May 14, 2024 — Birth of son.

June 11, 2024 — Authors *Right Wing Revolution: How to Beat the Woke and Save the West.*

July 15, 2024 — Kirk speaks at the Republican National Convention in Milwaukee, where he says: "The American Dream has become a luxury item for the wealthy elites. Happy countries have children. Broken countries have addiction, depression, and suffering . . . Donald Trump is on a rescue mission to revive your birthright . . . This November, we are going to choose success. We are going to choose to put the future of Americans first. We are going to choose to no longer be spectators in this election. We together are going to do the work to save America." Kirk plays a key role in Trump's successful campaign, mobilizing young voters for the 2024 presidential election.

August 27, 2024 — Turning Point USA announces You're Being Brainwashed tour, featuring Charlie Kirk.

October 31, 2024 — Kirk speaks at Tucker Carlson Live Tour finale in Glendale, Arizona.

December 22, 2024 — Kirk Hosts AmericaFest in Phoenix with President-elect Trump, drawing tens of thousands.

January 19, 2025 — Kirk hosts Turning Point USA Inaugural Eve Ball in Washington, D.C., with Trump family and allies Vice President JD Vance and Donald Trump Jr.

January 20, 2025 — Kirk speaks at inauguration rally for President Donald Trump at Capital One Arena in Washington, D.C.

February 11, 2025 — Turning Point USA announces Kirk's American Comeback Tour. Kirk declares: "The American comeback is powerful and real, and it's sweeping the nation. However, one of the last strongholds of far-left, increasingly insane and out-of-touch ideologues is found inside the formerly hallowed halls of higher education. We have many of these purveyors of anti-American indoctrination on the run, but when they regroup, they will do so from inside the academy. So, we will take the fight to them. America's students are still only given one side of the story, the left-wing side, so we intend to continue balancing the scales and equipping local students to fight for their values. If you're a progressive, you get to come to the front of the line and make your best argument, and I'll make mine, as TPUSA celebrates the free exchange of ideas, open and honest debate, and the American comeback in our newest campus tour."

March 6, 2025 — Part of the American Comeback Tour, Kirk appears at California State University Northridge (CSUN), where students are encouraged to debate Kirk.

March 13, 2025 — Kirk debates students during his American Comeback Tour event at the University of Tennessee's campus in Knoxville.

May 19, 2025 — Kirk debates and participates in Q&A at the Cambridge Union, U.K. Among issues discussed: "Lockdowns were unnecessary," views about life beginning at conception, and criticisms of how universities handle diversity of thought.

May 20, 2025 — Kirk speaks at the Oxford Union, U.K. Topics covered include abortion, transgender rights, and "Red Pill" media. Sharing his views on conservatism, Kirk states "We oppose the woke stuff. We oppose mass migration. We oppose the importation of these insidious values into our country, into the West. What do we stand for? . . . We want to have the fertility rates reverse. We want to see church attendance go up. We want to see suicide rates take a 180-degree pivot in our country."

July 21, 2025 — Trinity Broadcast Network launches weekday talk show *Charlie Kirk Today*.

September 10, 2025 — Charlie Kirk is assassinated. He is shot while speaking during a "Change My Mind" debate at a TPUSA American Comeback Tour event at Utah Valley University in Orem, Utah. He dies at age 31, and the world mourns his passing. President Trump speaks to the nation: "Charlie was a patriot who devoted his life to the cause of open debate and the country that he loved so much, the United States of America. He fought for liberty, democracy, justice, and the American people. He's a martyr for truth and freedom. . . . Charlie Kirk traveled the nation joyfully engaging with everyone interested in good faith debate. His mission was to bring young people into the political process . . . to share his love of country and to spread the simple words of common sense . . . I ask all Americans to commit themselves to the American values for which Charlie Kirk lived and died. The values of free speech, citizenship, the rule of law, and the patriotic devotion and love of God. Charlie was the best of America, and the monster who attacked him was attacking our whole country."

September 11, 2025 — President Trump announces he will posthumously award Kirk the Presidential Medal of Freedom, calling him "a giant of his generation and a champion of liberty."

September 15, 2025 — Vice President Vance hosts *The Charlie Kirk Show* from the White House, and states: "I really do believe that we can come together in this country. I believe we must. But unity — real unity — can be found only after climbing the mountain of truth — and there are difficult truths we must confront . . . While our side of the aisle certainly has its crazies, it is a statistical fact that most of the lunatics in American politics today are proud members of the Far Left."

September 16, 2025 — Authors Foreword to *Pagan Threat: Confronting America's Godless Uprising* by Pastor Lucas Miles. Kirk writes: "A fearless warrior for Christ. Lucas is a man built to stand for the truth in a time of great apostasy. Don't just read Pagan Threat — internalize what it has to say. Then, share its message with your Christian friends, before they are seduced by Paganism themselves. We have a faith and a country to save."

September 18, 2025 — Kirk's widow, Erika, per her husband's stated wishes, assumes role of CEO and chair of Turning Point USA. After Kirk's murder, she states: "The evildoers responsible for my husband's assassination have no idea what they have done. They killed Charlie because he preached a message of patriotism, faith, and of God's merciful love. But they should all know this: If you thought that my husband's mission was powerful before, you have no idea . . . You have no idea what you have just unleashed across this entire country. In this world, you have no idea. You have no idea the fire that you have ignited within this wife. The cries of this widow will echo around the world like a battle cry."

September 19, 2025 — Congress overwhelmingly approves a resolution designating Charlie Kirk's birthday, October 14, as a National Day of Remembrance, which recognizes Kirk for his contributions to civic education and public service, and encourages schools, civic groups, and citizens to mark the day nationwide.

September 21, 2025 — The world pauses for Charlie Kirk's Memorial in Glendale, Arizona, with over 100,000 attending and millions more around the world watching and listening on TV, online, and the radio. In attendance with Kirk's family, President Trump, who eulogizes: "Our greatest evangelist for American liberty . . . He's a martyr now for American freedom." Also in attendance: Vice President Vance, Secretary of State Marco Rubio, House Speaker Mike Johnson, Senator Ted Cruz, Senator Rick Scott, Representative Celeste Maloy, Representative Lauren Boebert, War Secretary Pete Hegseth, Health Secretary Robert F. Kennedy Jr., Homeland Security Secretary Kristi Noem, Director of National Intelligence Tulsi Gabbard, Attorney General Pam Bondi, White House Chief of Staff Susie Wiles, White House Deputy Chief of Staff Stephen Miller, FBI Director Kash Patel, FBI Deputy Director Dan Bongino, Pastor Rob McCoy, Pastor Jeff Durbin, Tucker Carlson, Donald Trump Jr., Steve Bannon, Lee Greenwood, Ben Carson, Elon Musk, Laura Loomer, James O'Keefe, Matt Walsh, Benny Johnson, Dana White, Frank Turek, and many more political and religious leaders from across the nation and the world. Kirk's widow states: "God's love was revealed to me on the very day my husband was murdered . . .

God's mercy and God's love have been revealed to me . . . After Charlie's assassination, we didn't see violence, we didn't see rioting, we didn't see revolution. Instead, we saw what my husband always prayed he would see in this country. We saw revival. This past week, we saw people open a Bible for the first time in a decade. We saw people pray for the first time since they were children. We saw people go to a church service for the first time in their entire lives. My husband, Charlie, he wanted to save young men just like the one who took his life. That young man. That young man on the cross, our Savior said, 'Father, forgive them, for they know not what they do.' That man, that young man, I forgive him. I forgive him, because it was what Christ did, and is what Charlie would do. The answer to hate is not hate. The answer we know from the Gospel is love and always love. Love for our enemies and love for those who persecute us. The world needs Turning Point USA. It needs a group that will point young people away from the path of misery and sin. It needs something that will lead people away from hell in this world and in the next. It needs young people pointed in the direction of truth and beauty. And so, I promise you today, every part of our work will become greater."

September 22, 2025 — Fulfilling a pledge of Kirk's widow, Turning Point USA announces the American Comeback Tour will continue without Kirk, rebranded the Turning Point Tour in his honor, with speakers including: Erika Kirk, Tucker Carlson, Glenn Beck, Vivek Ramaswamy, Megyn Kelly, Michael Knowles, Frank Turek, Rob Schneider, Jason Chaffetz, Alex Clark, Allie Beth Stuckey, Savannah Chrisley, Senator Mike Lee, Representative Andy Biggs, Governors Glenn Youngkin, Spencer J. Cox, Jeff Landry, and Greg Gianforte, and other political and Christian leaders and conservative media personalities.

Just prior to Kirk's death, Turning Point USA reports over 900 official college chapters and 1,200 high school chapters, with a larger presence of over 3,500 college and high school campuses combined; includes more than 2,000 student groups and over 800 Christian chapters. Total student membership exceeds 250,000 and growing. And in the wake of Kirk's passing, TPUSA reports receiving over 50,000 inquiries to start new chapters, and many millions of dollars pour into the organization.

October 14, 2025 – President Trump awards the Presidential Medal of Freedom, the nation's highest civilian honor, posthumously to Charlie Kirk on what would have been his 32nd birthday, and eulogizes: "Charlie Kirk was a martyr for truth and for freedom. And from Socrates to Saint Peter, from Abraham Lincoln to Martin Luther King, those who change history the most, and he really did, have always risked their lives for causes they were put on Earth to defend." Erika Kirk accepts the award and says she will continue the work of her husband, and that Charlie's story tells the world: "to live free is the greatest gift but to die free is the greatest victory," and concludes "happy birthday, my Charlie, happy freedom day."

December 9, 2025 — *Stop, in the Name of God: Why Honoring the Sabbath Will Transform Your Life,* Kirk's final book written in his lifetime, publishes posthumously.

PHOTO CREDITS

Front Cover — Trump: Rebecca Noble/Stringer/Getty Images
Charlie Kirk/Alex Brandon/AP IMAGES
Flag/Dominic Gentilcore PhD/Shutterstock

Front Matter — Page I: Getty Images/Patrick T. Fallon/Contributor
Cross/Douglas Rissing©iStock
Page IX: Kirk/Getty Images/Joe Raedle/Staff

Introduction — Page XV: Getty Images/Mark Wilson/Staff

Chapter 1 — Page 1: Trent Nelson/The Salt Lake Tribune/Getty Images
Page 2: Candles/Maria Tolkacheva©iStock
Page 5: Cross/Joe Raedle/Getty Images
Page 9: Women/Megan Jelinger/AFP via Getty Images
Kirk Graphic/thecharliekirkshow.com

Chapter 2 — Page 13: AP Images
Page 14: Eagle/iStock/stocksnapper
Page 17: Getty Images/The Salt Lake Tribune/Contributor
Page 22: Nordin Catic/Getty Images for The Cambridge Union

Chapter 3 — Page 25: Getty Images/Nicholas Kamm/Contributor
Page 27: White House/stocksnapper©iStock
Page 29: Getty Images/Samuel Corum/Stringer
Page 30: Trump Jr./Joe Raedle/Getty Images/Staff
Page 34: Getty Images/Alex Wroblewski/Contributor

Chapter 4 — Page 37: Getty Images/SOPA Images/Contributor
Page 39: Megaphone/AVA Bitter/Shutterstock
Page 41: Kirk and Kelly/Newsmax TV
Page 42: Getty Images/Andri Tambunan/Contributor
Getty Images/Rebecca Noble/Stringer
Page 43: Getty Images/SOPA Images/Contributor
Getty Images/Alex Wroblewski/ Contributor

Chapter 5 — Page 49: Getty Images/Joe Raedle/Staff
Page 51: Jesus/picture©iStock
Page 53: Getty Images/Olivier Touron/Contributor

Chapter 6 — Page 61: Getty Images/Samuel Corum/Stringer
Page 63: Symbol/L Keskinen©iStock
Page 65: Photo courtesy of TPUSA Faith
Page 70: Hernandez/Craig Kohlruss/The Fresno Bee/Tribune News Service via Getty Images / Thomas/Rich von Biberstein/Icon Sportswire via Getty Images
Page 71: Signs/Kirby Lee/Getty Images

Chapter 7 — Page 75: From left to right, top to bottom: Jacek Boczarski/Anadolu via Getty Images / Charly Triballeau/AFP via Getty Images / David Ryder/Getty Images / AP Images / Michael Ciaglo/Getty Images / Phill Magakoe/AFP via Getty Images Eric Thayer/Getty Images / Jacek Boczarski/Anadolu via Getty Images / Official White House Photo/Daniel Torok / Bethany Baker/The Salt Lake Tribune/Getty Images
Page 77: Writing/powerofforever©iStock
Page 79: Nathan Posner/Anadolu via Getty Images
Page 85: Memorial/Getty Images/Joe Raedle/Staff

Timeline — Page 87: Andrew Harnik/Staff/Getty Images

Back Cover — Getty Images/Joe Raedle/Staff
Bottom: Phill Magakoe/Contributor via Getty Images

ABOUT THE AUTHOR

DICK MORRIS IS A NEWSMAX ANALYST, COLUMNIST, and contributor, and one of the most prominent political and presidential strategists in the U.S. and the world. Called "the most influential private citizen in America" by *TIME* magazine, Morris was instrumental in the winning campaigns of Bill Clinton in 1996, Donald Trump's surprise win in 2016 and reelection in 2024, and over 30 senators and governors nationally, as well as elected officials around the world. Morris continues to serve as an adviser to President Donald J. Trump. He is the author of over 10 New York Times bestsellers, including *Armageddon: How Trump Can Beat Hillary, The Return: Trump's Big 2024 Comeback,* and *Corrupt: The Inside Story of Biden's Dark Money.*

Visit the author at DickMorris.com.

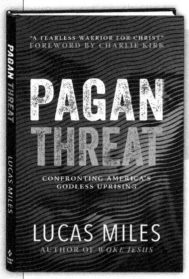

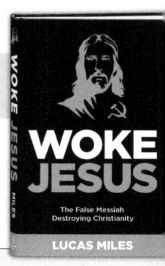

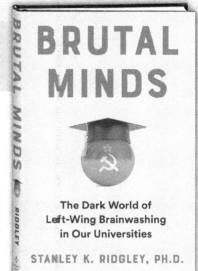

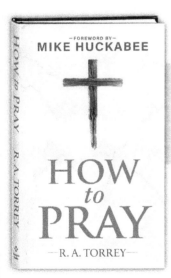

www.ingramcontent.com/pod-product-compliance
Lightning Source LLC
Chambersburg PA
CBHW061445221025
34291CB00003B/9

* 9 7 8 1 6 3 0 0 6 3 5 1 1 *

IN 60 SECONDS

JOHN ANKERBERG
DILLON BURROUGHS

HARVEST HOUSE PUBLISHERS
EUGENE, OREGON

Cover by Dugan Design Group, Bloomington, Minnesota

Cover photos © Michael Flippo / Fotolia; Lizard / Fotolia

GOD IN 60 SECONDS

Published by Harvest House Publishers
Eugene, Oregon 97402
www.harvesthousepublishers.com

ISBN 978-0-7369-2705-5

Printed in the United States of America

10 11 12 13 14 15 16 17 18 / BP-SK / 10 9 8 7 6 5 4 3 2 1

Contents

Spiritual Truth on the Go 5

Part One: Questions About God and Creation 7

Part Two: Questions About Jesus 15

Part Three: Questions About the Bible 33

Part Four: Questions About Salvation and Spiritual Growth 57

Part Five: Questions About the Afterlife 83

Part Six: Questions About Other Religions 91

Part Seven: Questions About Contemporary Issues . . . 103

How to Begin a Personal Relationship with God 131

Praying for Those Who Do Not Believe . . . 135

Spiritual Truth on the Go

Ask a person how they're doing today, and the number-one answer will likely be "keeping busy." Americans no longer work nine-to-five and sit down together for a nightly meal. Instead, we talk on mobile phones while driving, eating, working, and maybe even transporting kids—*all at the same time.* Americans average less sleep and more hours of work per week than ever before!

This frantic pace of life has left its mark on our Christian faith as well. Rather than making a practice of a daily devotion and church attendance multiple times per week, many people struggle to find time to read *anything* about God or the Bible from one Sunday to the next.

While there is no replacement for serious, extended study of the Scriptures, *God in 60 Seconds* is designed to help you grasp serious spiritual truth on the go. A bit of history: *The Ankerberg Minute* first began as a daily 60-second radio segment on a few stations. It has rapidly grown into a major portion of our work, broadcast or otherwise presented nearly 700 times per day nationwide in addition to receiving thousands of hits per day online. These sound bites of spiritual truth have found a receptive home with many listeners during commutes, workouts, office hours, and countless other activities.

We've now compiled and adapted many of these programs into the book you're holding. Our hope is that you'll become better equipped in your faith, yet also be challenged to take appropriate actions toward further spiritual growth through additional study and resources. Along the way, we encourage you to stop by our Web site, JohnAnkerberg.org, where you can find over 2,500 videos, audio downloads, and articles to help fuel your learning each step of the way.

Thanks for picking up *God in 60 Seconds* to assist you in your faith journey. May God use it to help you become more like Christ every second of your day as you strive to follow our risen Lord and King.

Part One:

Questions About God *and* Creation

1 What can I do when God feels far away?

Do you ever feel like God is distant when you pray? You're not alone. The psalmist wrote in Psalm 10, "Why, O Lord, do you stand far off?" God was not really far away, but the psalmist felt like he was. When you feel God is distant, don't stop praying. God promises that if we draw near to him, he will draw near to us. Our problem is not that God is distant, our problem is that we often give up before we hear his response to our situation. Don't quit—God is there. In Jeremiah 33:3 God says, "Call to me and I will answer you and tell you great and unsearchable things you do not know."

2 Does God care for us individually?

Does the Creator of the universe really care about each one of us individually? The answer from the Bible is *yes*. A brief glimpse at what God's Word says about who we are as believers reminds us of how much we matter to God. For instance, we are God's workmanship, God's temple; we are the salt and light of the earth; we can do all things through Christ who gives us strength. These are just a few examples of the hundreds of promises God makes to his children. If you're feeling a bit discouraged, take a moment to look once again at the love that God has revealed to us, especially in the life of his only Son, Jesus Christ. You won't be disappointed.

3 Where did everything come from?

Whether you're a scientist or a garbage collector, there are just three answers to the important question "Where did everything come from?" Francis Schaeffer has said the first view is that everything that exists came from absolutely nothing. Very few hold this view. The second view is that everything that exists came from an impersonal something, such as energy or matter. The impersonal is mixed with chance plus time, and out of that everything came to exist. But this view cannot explain why humans are of any more value than a tree or a drop of water. The third view is everything that exists came from a personal someone. The Bible says, "In the beginning God created the heavens and the earth" (Genesis 1:1). Only this third view explains why people are of great value and why there is meaning to our lives.

4 What is God like?

Do you know what God is like? We live in a culture where people want to pick and choose in constructing their view of God, like ordering from a restaurant menu. They make him up to suit their own desires.

The Bible is our most accurate source of information about God, and it tells us that he knows everything and knows all about us. He is everywhere in the universe at once. He is all-powerful. He is infinite love, and he is holy. These are just a few attributes that reveal the true nature of God.

If you want to learn more about what God is like, read his own words found in the Bible. Psalm 119:2 tells us that we are blessed when we seek him with all of our heart.

5 Does it really matter where we all came from?

Many have grown tired of the heated debates about the beginning of the universe and human life. More and more often, people ask, "Does it really matter where we all came from?"

The short answer is, yes, it does. Whatever we decide about the creation of the universe and the beginning of human life influences our beliefs on a whole array of other issues. *Who am I? What is my purpose in life? What happens when I die?* These basic questions rely on a biblical worldview for meaningful answers. If we believe we are simply the product of matter mixed with chance plus time, then we miss out on God's purpose and plan for our lives. It does matter where you and I came from. God is our Creator and worthy of our worship.

6 If God, why evil?

If God is real, why do we struggle with so much evil in our world today? Based on the problems we see on the Internet and the nightly news, this question is certainly a valid one. However, the existence of evil doesn't mean that God doesn't exist or doesn't care about what happens in our lives. According to Scripture, God will one day end all evil and correct all injustices. He will reward those who have trusted and lived for him and provide a new heaven and new earth for us to enjoy for eternity. The Bible tells us that each of us will continue to encounter problems in this life. Yet it also promises God will be there with us to help. Depend on him to help you with the struggles you face in your life.

7 Does God hear the prayers of unbelievers?

Do you think God hears the prayers of unbelievers? On one hand, as an all-knowing God he hears every word prayed to him. Nothing escapes his attention. But does God respond to the prayers of unbelievers?

In some cases, he certainly does. For instance, we know from the Bible that God responds to the prayers of those who truly search for God and choose to trust in Christ as their Savior. God may also provide answers to some prayers of unbelievers to show them he is real in the process of leading that person to faith in him. However, only those who know Christ by faith can truly call God "Abba, Father" and claim the many promises God offers in response to the prayers of his children. Have you talked to your heavenly Father today?

8 How can we respond to today's angry atheists?

Several bestselling books have recently argued

against God's existence. If you read these books, today's New Atheism is not just intellectual. It is often angry and antagonistic toward God and his followers. Some atheists have lumped all religions into one and then suggested that the world would be a better place without today's so-called "religious extremists."

But in many cases the anger is the result of the atheist's personal frustration with God or religious people. The only ways to see change among those who show such hostility are through our prayers, by living out our faith, and presenting our answers in kindness and love. God must work to change the heart, but our example can lead a person to be open to hearing the truth about Jesus and how to know him.

9 How can Christians respond to evolution?

How can Christians intelligently respond to the issue of evolution? First, evolutionary theory is just that—a theory. No one can scientifically prove evolution. The origination of the universe is a one-time event that cannot be duplicated in a laboratory setting.

Evolutionary theory is ultimately based on a

combination of science plus faith. When this is recognized, it should open the way to investigate other alternatives for which the universe came into existence. Science reveals tremendous complexity and design in the universe. Christians can highlight this wonderful creativity and complexity in the world around us to help point people to know our wonderful Creator and his Son, Jesus Christ.

10 Why do we feel close to God while in nature?

Why do we often feel close to God when surrounded by the beauty of nature? What causes these feelings? Psalm 65 tells us that God formed the mountains with his strength and cares for the land by watering it abundantly. When we experience the beauty of the natural world, we are seeing God's creative power at work. Throughout history, many have responded by worshipping aspects of the creation, such as the sun, moon, or stars. But God provided creation to point us to him. When you encounter the beauty of creation today, whether snowflakes or even a plant inside your home, take a moment to worship the Almighty God who made them. When you experience the beauty of creation, take that moment to express your love to its Creator.

11 What can we know about God?

Over 90 percent of Americans say they believe in God or some kind of higher power; they just don't agree on how to define this power.

The Bible, however, provides numerous insights into what God is like. For instance, we know he is sovereign, meaning he is in control of everything. He is holy, set apart from all created things. He is perfect, without sin and never changing. He is triune, consisting of Father, Son, and Spirit. He is also all-powerful, without equal. These are just five of his perfections that are found in Scripture.

When we're confused about what others say about God, or even have doubts of our own, the Bible provides the revelation we need to better define and understand who he really is.

Part Two:

Questions About Jesus

1 Did the disciples invent our version of Jesus?

How do we know that the first Christians after Jesus didn't invent a new Jesus? We know because only 50 days after Jesus' death and resurrection, the 12 apostles preached in Jerusalem at Pentecost to the very people who had seen Jesus die on the cross. In their message they testified to the facts about Jesus' life, death, and resurrection, and 3,000 Jews believed the apostles' testimony. Those 3,000 converts returned to 15 people groups across the Roman Empire, founding churches on the message they had heard. Think about it; the apostles didn't have time to invent a new Jesus in just 50 days. Today we can know for sure that we have the same message Jesus gave the apostles and that it has accurately been handed down to us.

2 What do the resurrection accounts claim about Jesus?

Some skeptics claim that the resurrection accounts of Jesus contradict one another. But is this true? The answer is no. In fact, if the accounts in the four Gospels were exactly the same, skeptics would argue that there had been some form of conspiracy. The four accounts provide individual perspectives on the events that took place surrounding Christ's resurrection. There may seem to be discrepancies, but there are no actual contradictions. No single account of the resurrection covers every detail. Some emphasize one aspect more than another. But their accounts each record the same events. Studied carefully, the four Gospels help us believe that Jesus is who he claimed to be—God's Son.

3 Why does the resurrection of Jesus matter?

Why does the resurrection of Jesus matter?

One of the most powerful reasons is the evidence of changed lives. Worldwide, the message of the resurrection has had a force for good that no other belief system in the world has ever had. Nations and cultures have been altered. For 2,000 years, countless families have been reunited, immoral people have become godly, and the proud have become humble. Historian Kenneth Scott LaTourette once noted, "Gauged by the consequences which have followed the birth, life, and resurrection of Jesus, these have been the most important events in this history of man."

Since he lives, he can also give those who believe in him the gift of eternal life.

4 Did the apostles really see Jesus alive after his death?

If you watched a car accident take place with your loved ones inside, wouldn't you be able to describe it in detail to a police officer a few minutes later? If someone died, we would definitely remember the events of that day the rest of our lives. Why? Because it's personal. Think about the 12 apostles. They spent three years with their friend Jesus, and then they witnessed his crucifixion and death. We can know that the four Gospels are true, simply because the events they describe were personal to the writers; they didn't forget.

Why should the four Gospels matter to us today? Because if Jesus' followers did see him alive, then he is God's Son and worthy of our full attention.

5 How can we discover the real Jesus?

Can you believe that recent television programs have claimed that Jesus had a wife and fathered children, and even that he was reburied by his friends in a different tomb? Has everything we've been told about Jesus really been false?

Well, keep in mind that the mainstream media does not strive to highlight the biblical, historical Jesus. The reason the media addresses a radical new Jesus is because it makes for flashy headlines and high ratings, even if it's not good history. If you desire to know the real Jesus and follow his teachings, remember that our true source for accurate news about Jesus is not television but the books of the New Testament. Why not pause for a moment and refresh yourself by discovering once again the amazing words of life that the real Jesus of history has spoken to guide you through your day?

6 Did Jesus fulfill the messianic prophecies?

Christians claim that Jesus fulfilled numerous Old Testament prophecies. Is this really true? Well, even the most liberal scholars will admit that the Old Testament was written at least 400 years before the life of Christ. Now, take one example from the book of the prophet Isaiah, a copy of which exists from more than a century before the life of Christ on earth. Isaiah wrote down 12 unique aspects of Christ's passion week that were all fulfilled exactly in Jesus. The odds against such accuracy in randomly predicting the future are beyond statistical measurement. Only God could make this many predictions with total accuracy, hundreds of years in advance. Don't take our word for it—open up your own Bible to Isaiah 53 and read it for yourself.

7 What evidence does the apostle Paul's life give for the resurrected Jesus?

Why does the apostle Paul's life, *before* he was a Christian, provide strong evidence for the fact that Jesus rose from the dead? It's because, when the 12 apostles first began to testify that Jesus rose from the dead, Paul was one of the strongest opponents of their message. He was so adamantly opposed to this movement that he requested permission to arrest Christians in neighboring towns; he even approved the stoning to death of Stephen.

So what caused him to change his mind? Paul himself tells us that the risen Jesus appeared to him on the road to Damascus. When you think of it, what other event could have caused Paul to believe that Jesus was the Son of God, the Messiah? And what about you? Have you placed your faith in the risen Jesus? If not, why not trust him today? If so, who are you telling about the love of Christ that has changed you?

8 What evidence exists for the resurrection?

The foundation of the Christian faith is based on the bodily, physical resurrection of Jesus. But what evidence do we have that he really returned to life? First, Jesus' tomb was found empty on the third day, a fact that no one has been able to account for, then or now.

Second, after Jesus rose from the dead, he made numerous physical appearances, during which he was seen and heard by as many as 500 people at one time. Sometimes people even touched Jesus or ate with him.

Third, there is the explosive growth of the early church and the willingness of its members to lay down their lives for this simple reason—they said they had seen the risen Christ and believed his promise that he would give them eternal life. There can only be one conclusion to properly account for this evidence—Jesus is alive!

9 What essential facts do we know about Jesus from the Bible?

In a culture that often blurs the line between fact and fiction, it's important to be reminded of the crucial facts about Jesus. Jesus is the Messiah, who was predicted hundreds of years in advance through very specific prophecies. Jesus was virgin-born and lived without committing a single sin. Jesus is deity, as he claimed, the only incarnation of God. Jesus is the only Savior, who died for our sins and offers eternal salvation as a free gift to anyone who will put their trust in him. Jesus rose from the dead as proof of his claim. Jesus is the Final Judge, who will return on the last day to judge every person.

The facts about Jesus are powerful, essential, and vital to our spiritual lives now and for eternity.

10 What does the Bible reveal about Jesus?

Did you know that Jesus Christ is referred to in all 66 books of the Bible, even though 39 of them were written before he ever came to earth? Christ is present in every book of the Bible because he is the central theme of the Bible. From the prediction made in Genesis that the promised seed of the woman would defeat Satan, to the declaration in Revelation that he is King of kings and Lord of lords, the entire Bible is filled with prophecies, descriptions, and declarations about the One who has saved us from sin and death. Jesus is at the center of the Scriptures because he alone is the most important person to ever live. Have you made him the center of your life today?

11 How is Jesus different from other religious leaders?

How is Jesus different from other religious leaders? First, he claimed to be God. In John 14:6 he taught that he alone is "the way and the truth and the life." Second, his claim to be deity and God's Messiah was verified by hundreds of Jewish prophecies that were made hundreds of years in advance of his birth. Third, he proved his claim of being God by his supernatural miracles, by casting out demons, and by his miraculous resurrection from the dead. Fourth, he lived a sinless life, something only God can do.

Faith in Jesus as God is not blind faith—it is

faith based on more evidence than we have for any other religious leader in history. How will you respond to the unique person and power of Christ in your life today?

12 Who moved the stone from Christ's tomb?

Early 1900s English journalist and skeptic Frank Morison believed that the story of Jesus returning from the dead was nothing more than a children's fable. To prove his theory he began to investigate the evidence for the historical Jesus in order to pick apart Christianity. He intended to later write a book exposing the church's deception.

But Morison was surprised to discover that the evidence was stronger than he had originally thought. His book *Who Moved the Stone?* was later released to wide acclaim. In the book he admitted that rather than finding a fable full of holes, he had discovered that the Christ of history had returned to life from the dead. The evidence is there for you to begin your own investigation today.

13 Why do Christians pray in Jesus' name?

After hearing a minister close his prayer in Jesus' name, a rabbi said, "For me, as a Jew, hearing the name of a first-century teacher isn't the worst thing in the world, but he's not my God." What does it mean to pray in Jesus' name?

The concept is taught in John 14:13-14, where Jesus said, "You may ask me for anything in my name, and I will do it." However, this does not mean there is some magic power in using the name of Jesus to conclude a prayer. Praying in Jesus' name points to the God who is addressed in our prayers. Rather than having a general, ambiguous object of prayer, we clearly note that he is God, the one who said in John 14:6, "I am the way and the truth and the life. No one comes to the Father except through me." Praying in Jesus' name marks our prayers as distinct from prayers to any other god from any other religion, focusing attention on the uniqueness of the Son of God, Jesus Christ.

14 Did Jesus physically rise from the dead?

Skeptics sometimes ask, "Was the resurrection of Jesus physical or merely spiritual?" In other words, did people see Jesus alive with a real body or see his ghost? According to the apostle Peter, Jesus physically returned to life. In his sermon in Acts 2 he said that God did not abandon Jesus' body to the grave, "nor did his body see decay. God has raised this Jesus to life, and we are all witnesses of the fact." In Acts 13, the apostle Paul taught that the physical body of Jesus did not decay but returned to life. These two leaders represented the consistent testimony of the early church that Jesus was resurrected physically, not just in ghostly form. Jesus is alive. He proved he is the risen King of kings and Lord of lords.

15 How do communion and baptism give evidence of the historical Jesus?

Do you know how communion and baptism provide evidence for the truth of Christianity? Communion, or the Lord's Supper, was celebrated every week in the early church from the very first time Christians met together for worship. In this ceremony that goes back to Christ himself, Christians are instructed to remember his death, burial, resurrection, and the forgiveness of sins.

Baptism is only performed once for each person, but with each new one who is baptized, the cleansing of sin and our new walk in Christ are taught over and over again.

Communion and baptism accurately present Jesus'

teachings. In the early church, if someone had tried to change the earliest message about Jesus, Christians would have rejected any such attempts, knowing that the facts about Christ were made evident in the original sacraments he designed for his followers.

16 Is Jesus just one among many spiritual leaders?

Increasingly in America today, Jesus is seen as just one of many other spiritual leaders. How is Jesus different? In contrast to Muhammad, Buddha, or other founders of religious movements, Jesus made the unique claim to be God in human form. Second, Jesus offered proof for his claim through miracles, authoritative teachings, and supernatural healings. Ultimately, the greatest proof Jesus gave was his resurrection from the dead.

Many skeptics have tried to deny these facts, but the testimony of numerous eyewitnesses and other evidence points to the conclusion that Jesus returned to life and did prove that he alone is God. His distinct claim to deity and the evidence to back it up make up the unique foundation of Christianity.

17 What does history say about Jesus?

If there were no Bible, do you think there would

be any other proof that Jesus really lived? One prominent scholar notes that over 129 facts from the life of Jesus and early Christianity can be found in the writings of ancient non-Christian authors. For example, the highly esteemed Roman historian Tacitus wrote just over 20 years after Jesus lived. He noted that Jesus was a teacher who was put to death by crucifixion under the Roman procurator Pontius Pilate, and afterward continued to have a growing number of followers who believed he was still alive. When someone tells you the New Testament accounts of Jesus' life are historically inaccurate, challenge them to check out their facts. Even ancient history outside of the Bible affirms the core message of a risen Jesus who changed history and continues to change lives today.

18 Was Jesus really born of a virgin?

Do you think the story of Jesus' virgin birth is similar to Greek and Roman mythologies told about Caesar Augustus, in which his mother was made pregnant by the Greek and Roman sun god Apollo? Or of Alexander the Great being conceived when his mother was a virgin?

Matthew and Luke both probably knew about

these pagan stories, and since they both wanted to talk about Jesus as the Messiah, the fulfillment of Judaism, which didn't have stories like the mystery religions, this was really kind of a dangerous thing for them to be getting into. A historian would ask, "Why would they do that?" The only reason Matthew and Luke included these stories in their Gospels is because they were convinced that these very strange events had actually happened when Jesus was born.

19 Can we really accept the miracle of the virgin birth?

Can we really accept the miracle of the virgin birth? We can't prove the virgin birth of Jesus the same way we can provide evidence for the resurrection. Without the resurrection, we can't explain the rise of early Christianity at all. But once we accept the resurrection, it forces us to hold our modern minds open and say, "If God was really in Christ, reconciling the world to himself, shouldn't we expect some other strange events as well?" Matthew probably wrestled with the accounts of Jesus' birth, and when he read the Old Testament and saw Isaiah 7:14, he said, "This is what Isaiah was talking about." Luke probably felt the same way. It's not the case that he had stories about angels and shepherds that he wanted to connect to Jesus. Rather, this is evidence he was given by those who experienced events that really happened.

20 Did Jesus perform miracles?

Did Jesus perform miracles or not? One reason we can believe that he did is because of multiple attestation, or multiple witnesses. In other words, not only does Matthew's Gospel mention miracles, but so do the three other Gospels and many other New Testament books. In addition, numerous accounts from other early authors outside of the Bible confirm Jesus did perform supernatural miracles. Most importantly, if he returned to life from the dead, by his own power, his other miracles are easy to believe in by comparison. Jesus' physical resurrection from the dead was his greatest miracle, proving he was God's Son. Have you placed your faith in the Jesus who was able to perform miracles?

21 Why *four* Gospels?

When the four Gospels present the details of

Jesus' resurrection, some people assume that the accounts contradict each other—therefore, the resurrection should not be accepted. But remember that the Gospel writers were independently recording these events. In a court of law, it's always true that four witnesses describing a traffic accident will supply some information that agrees and some information that differs. If the Gospel writers had recorded the exact same details, this would be considered collusion, not independent testimony. There's no reason for us to demand that they all report the exact same details. The accounts of Jesus' resurrection are solid, historical evidence for the person who really wants to know what happened to Jesus' body after his death.

22 Wasn't Jesus just a good teacher?

How many times have you heard that Jesus was a great spiritual teacher, but never claimed to be God's Son? First, consider that Jesus called himself "the way and the truth and the life" (John 14:6). In saying this, he claimed to be the exclusive means of access to God. Second, he used numerous names for himself that are clear references to deity, including Son of God, Son of Man, the I AM, and the

Messiah. Third, in John's Gospel, he claimed that he and the Father are one, a clear reference to his being equal with God.

It may be popular to claim that Jesus is only one way among many to God, but those who say this need to recognize they are in disagreement with the teaching of Jesus, who they claim was a good teacher.

23 Which Gospels should we trust?

Who would you believe—a person who claims to know secret and mystical facts about people in history, or someone who says, "I've researched the evidence from eyewitnesses, and here's what I've discovered"? The Gnostic, nonbiblical *Gospel of Thomas* claims, "These are the hidden sayings that the Lord Jesus spoke." Now compare this with Luke's Gospel, written over a hundred years earlier. He said the events of Jesus' life

> were handed down to us by those who from the first were eyewitnesses and servants of the word. Therefore since I myself have carefully investigated everything from the beginning, it seemed good also to me to write an orderly account for you (Luke 1:1-2).

Which is the better source: facts written on eyewitness testimony or mystical fiction written a hundred years later? You can be assured that the truth of Jesus' life is based on solid, historical testimony.

Part Three:

Questions About *the* Bible

1 How can we know the Bible is from God?

Have you ever thought, *I believe the Bible is true, but how can I really know for sure?* Well, rest assured that if you take the time to study about the Bible, you will discover that there are more than 25,000 manuscript copies with portions of the New Testament that have come down to us. Textual scholars have known since 1707 that no central doctrine of the Bible has been altered by any textual variant because they have determined the original wording in 99.9 percent of the text. In other words, what we have now is what the apostles and prophets wrote then.

Further, if we lost all 25,000 New Testament manuscript copies, we could reconstruct the entire New Testament (except for 11 verses) from the one million quotations of scriptures found in the writings of the Church Fathers. Remember, the evidence shows the Bible is accurate and complete, and can be trusted.

2 Why is the Bible called *God's* Word?

Have you ever wondered why the Bible is referred to as the "Word of God"? It's because it declares itself to be *God-breathed*. In other words, God inspired and used the human writers of the Bible to record the exact words he wanted to communicate to the world.

The result: Words both simple enough to be understood by the average person and complex enough to challenge even the greatest scholars. God then preserved those words through the centuries to provide us with a written, reliable copy from which we are able to learn his truth today. God has spoken to us through His Word, the Bible. It deserves our full and undivided attention.

3 Where did we get the Bible?

Where did the Bible come from? The Bible claims to come from God. Paul wrote of the Old Testament that all Scripture is God-breathed and useful for teaching (2 Timothy 3:16-17). Even the New Testament is called Scripture. Paul referred to Luke's Gospel as Scripture in 1 Timothy 5:18. Peter referred to Paul's writings as Scripture in 2 Peter 3:16.

Jesus himself gave the highest respect to Scripture. In Matthew 4, when tempted by Satan, he responded, "Man does not live on bread alone, but on every word that comes from the mouth of God." If Jesus thought the Bible was from God and worthy of our utmost attention, would you disagree with him?

4 When were the Gospels written?

When do you think that the New Testament Gospels were written? Recent evidence shows that their origin dates to a time right after Jesus lived. For example, even an increasing number of liberal scholars now suggest that the Gospel of Mark may have been written by the early 40s, only 10 years after the crucifixion and resurrection of Jesus, and the Gospel of Luke about AD 61. Scholars know that legend takes two or three generations to develop. But the Gospels were clearly written in the lifetimes of Jesus' closest followers, who knew what had happened and could correct inaccuracies. Take time today to check out the writings of the eyewitnesses for yourself and encounter the accounts of those who walked and talked with Jesus, the Son of God.

5 Are the Gospel accounts just legends?

Some people argue that the resurrection accounts in the Gospels are legends formed long after the events took place. Is there any truth to this claim?

New Testament books report that within 50 days of the event, Peter and the other apostles preached the resurrection to over 3,000 people, who quickly spread this message to 15 people groups across the Roman Empire. What was this message? That Jesus died, was buried, came to life, and appeared to them. In the book of Acts, Luke records Peter's sermons and numerous other events in early Christianity within 30 years of their occurrence.

There is no reason to believe these historical events were based on legend. The resurrection is the foundation of our faith and is based on solid, historical evidence.

6 Is it reasonable to believe the Bible is really perfect?

Why do you think it's reasonable to believe that

the Bible is without error? Three responses give a clear answer to this question. First, the Bible claims to come from God. If God is perfect, wouldn't it make sense that his words are perfect as well? Second, Jesus claims the Bible is perfect. Since he is the resurrected Messiah, we should take notice of his full support of the Scriptures as being without error. Third, skeptics have failed to prove a single error despite ample time and numerous investigations. Many experts who have set out to disprove the Bible have later become Christians as a result of their study.

The Bible is perfect. We can base our life on its message, but we must read and study it in order to know what God says.

7 Is the Bible corrupted?

Many argue that the Bible became corrupted during the history of the church. Others claim they have received a new revelation that completes the Bible.

But such views fail to honor the words of Jesus. Jesus said plainly in his prayer in John 17, "Your word is truth." Further, in John 16 Jesus taught that the Holy Spirit would guide the disciples into all truth. Clearly, Jesus did not believe that God the Holy Spirit would corrupt his own words.

As God's Son, Jesus was a perfect and reliable authority. As the only person in history to resurrect himself from the dead, his view of Scripture holds precedence over anyone else's. Take a fresh look at the Bible for yourself. You can trust that its words are faithful and true.

8 Does the evidence from archaeology support the accuracy of the Bible?

An Israeli archaeologist recently discovered what is believed to be the oldest existing Hebrew inscription. What does it reveal? In short, the five lines of faded characters, written 3,000 years ago, indicate that a powerful Israelite kingdom existed at the time of King David. This evidence, along with the surrounding ruins, is a further strengthening of the position that Old Testament history is completely accurate.

Archaeology does not prove that the Bible is true, but it has offered over 25,000 facts that have been confirmed—without one clear point of error. The Bible claims to have come from God, and it stands as the foundation for the Christian faith and for our study and application today.

9 Which Bible version is best?

Some argue that certain Bible translations are inaccurate or even wrong to use. Is this true? The truth is, today's English translations are all attempts to translate a perfect original message that was written in other languages. The Bible translations that take a more literal word-for-word approach provide the closest English equivalent to the ancient languages, offering translations that help us access God's Word today. Our goal is to understand the original message communicated. Comparing different translations can often help accomplish this desire.

Remember, no matter which translation you choose, you must read it in order to live out God's truth. The best translation, as someone has said, is the one you read and live out in your everyday life.

10 Why is the Bible important?

What do you think is the world's bestselling book? It's the Bible. God's Word has been published in more copies and more languages than any other book in human history. Why is the Bible so important? There are many reasons, but one major reason is because of its impact. It claims to be God's Word and reveals how we can know him personally through Jesus. Abraham Lincoln called it the best gift God has given to man. As the apostle John records, "Your word is truth" (John 17:17). If you really want to live a life of impact, invest time in the Bible. You'll have an eternal impact.

11 Is the Bible really without error?

Do the findings of modern archaeology support the claims of the Bible? Dr. Clifford Wilson, former director of the Australian Institute of Archaeology, wrote a 17-volume set of books addressing this very question. What was his verdict?

He wrote that over 25,000 specific details from the Bible have been confirmed, without a single error. Not one! This staggering observation points to the Bible's divine origin. Wilson's findings echo the words of Paul, who taught,

> Scripture is God-breathed and is useful for teaching, rebuking, correcting and training in righteousness, so that the man of God may be thoroughly equipped for every good work (2 Timothy 3:16).

The evidence from archaeology provides ample support that the writings of Scripture are rooted in accurate history and provide a trustworthy resource for our study.

12 Who wrote the New Testament?

Christians agree that the New Testament is important, but who wrote it? In total, there were nine people, who were either apostles or their associates. Matthew wrote one of the Gospels. John authored five books. Peter authored two letters and was the source of Mark's Gospel. Luke also based his Gospel on the eyewitness testimonies of the apostles. Paul penned 13 letters. James and Jude were brothers of Jesus. Many also believe Hebrews was authored by Paul or one of his associates.

All of the books of the New Testament were written during the lifetimes of Christ's first generation of followers for our guidance today. The Bible you hold in your hands includes the exact teachings given by Jesus himself. Take some time to reflect on it anew today.

13 How accurate are the Bible's prophecies?

Did you know that the evidence in the Bible clearly shows that Jesus fulfilled 456 specific prophecies that were given about him hundreds of years before he even came to earth? What are the odds that all of these prophecies would come true in one person in the future? A recent study showed that just one prophecy, such as the prediction of Jesus' birth in Bethlehem, has about a 1-in-300,000 chance of coming true randomly—just one prophecy! The chance of 456 prophecies coming true, for any single person, is beyond human comprehension. All of these prophecies were guaranteed to happen because they were made by God, who boldly claims they are proof that he exists and that Jesus is the One he sent.

14 Is Bible prophecy important to study?

Bible prophecy receives much attention in today's media, but does it really matter if we study it? The answer is yes. First, over 27 percent of the entire Bible contains prophetic material. Second, throughout the entire Bible, God encourages its study. The apostle Peter taught that we would do well to pay attention to it because biblical prophecy is not merely human words, but the very words of God (see 2 Peter 1:19). Third, Jesus personally encouraged the study of prophecy. Matthew 24 includes Jesus' discussion about the importance of understanding the end times.

Prophecy does matter. Don't avoid it—study it. Learn how God's teachings about the future can change your life today and for eternity.

15 Weren't the New Testament writers biased?

A growing number of scholars suggest that the New Testament writers cannot be trusted because of their personal bias as followers of Jesus. So, can we really trust Peter, Paul, and John? We certainly can. Just because you love your mother and are biased in your opinion about her doesn't mean you can't be trusted to tell anything truthful about her. Because you do love her, you are more likely to tell the truth about her.

If you have questions about the New Testament's accuracy, investigate it. The Bereans in Acts 17 were considered more noble because they checked out the teachings they heard. See for yourself what the Bible says. You may be pleasantly surprised.

16 What are some of the archaeological findings connected to the Bible?

Does archaeology confirm any of the historical

details found in the Bible? Many people are shocked to discover that over 25,000 different sites from the biblical world have been discovered and confirmed through archaeological research.

For instance, facts such as the census taken during the time of Christ's birth, Jacob's well from the book of Genesis, and even the pagan temple of Artemis mentioned in Acts 19 have all been discovered and confirmed as fitting the Bible's description. No other religion can claim such accuracy in its writings. The Bible is a uniquely accurate book, faithfully preserved through years of history. It tells us how God has interacted with people and nations and communicates his will for us today.

17 Does ancient history confirm the New Testament message?

The respected Roman historian Tacitus wrote about Emperor Nero's decision to blame Christians for the fire that destroyed Rome in the AD 60s. He wrote,

> Nero fastened the guilt on a class hated for their abominations, called Christians by the population. Christos, or Christ, from whom the name had its origin, suffered the extreme penalty

> during the reign of Tiberius at the hands of Pontius Pilate. And a most mischievous superstition [Tacitus speaks here of Jesus' resurrection], thus checked for the moment again broke out; not only in Judea, the first source of the evil, but even in Rome.

Tacitus confirms the New Testament account that Jesus died, that his followers claimed he was resurrected, and that Christianity had spread to Rome during the lifetimes of Christ's followers.

18 Why is Bible literacy important?

In a recent poll of teenagers on Bible literacy, 17 percent thought the road to Damascus was where Jesus was crucified; 68 percent couldn't identify who asked, "Am I my brother's keeper?"; 22 percent thought Moses was one of Jesus' apostles, a pharaoh, or an angel. Why is it important to understand what the Bible teaches?

Essentially, it is important to know the Bible if you intend to live out its message. You wouldn't expect to become a doctor overnight without serious study. Neither should you expect to become a mature Christian overnight without serious contemplation of the Scriptures. Take up the challenge to pursue God through his Word with utmost diligence. Experience how God changes your life and the lives of those around you.

19 What influence has the Bible had on America's history?

A recent survey of 39 English professors at America's top universities reveals that Bible knowledge is a deeply important part of education. One Northwestern professor stated, "The Bible is the most influential text in all of Western culture." If this is true of university students, it is certainly true in the education of all people. Why? Because the Bible has influenced more people throughout history than any other book.

More important, to read God's Word is to hear from God himself. If you desire to hear from him, start with the Bible. As Psalm 1 notes, the person who meditates on Scripture day and night is blessed.

20 What specific details prove the Bible is supernatural?

How can we know the Bible is God's Word? One scholar has chronicled 456 Old Testament prophecies fulfilled in the life of Christ. The probability of just 10 of these prophecies coming true randomly is astronomical. The fact that hundreds have been accurately fulfilled without error can only be explained by God's existence. How could prophets have known hundreds of years in advance that the Messiah would heal the blind, be betrayed for 30 pieces of silver, and in the end, suffer a painful death and be vindicated by a glorious resurrection? They could know only if God revealed it to them. The Bible was given by God to provide the information we need to confidently know God and his Son, Jesus, whom he sent.

21 How does Bible prophecy compare to the predictions of other prophets and psychics?

Does any other religious leader or prophet offer a record of fulfilled prophecy similar to that of Christianity? When one study researched the predictions of 25 top psychics, 95 percent of their predictions were proven wrong. The other 5 percent were questionable and could often be explained by chance or circumstances. In fact, the psychics' predictions were compared with those of people who just made random guesses about future events, and the statistics were found to reveal no significant difference.

Yet hundreds of prophecies have already been fulfilled in the life of Jesus Christ. To date, not one biblical prophecy has been disproved. No other religion can compare with the staggering number of fulfilled prophecies found in the Bible.

22 How much of the Bible is true?

How much of the Bible do you think is really true? Many people believe that only certain parts of the Bible, such as its moral teachings, can be considered accurate. Other parts such as science and history are considered inaccurate.

This idea is wrong for two reasons. First, nothing in Scripture even hints at the idea that only parts of it are true. In contrast, it tells us that the laws of the Lord are pure, making wise the simple. Second, faith is intimately tied to matters of science and history. The Bible is not a science textbook—however, history, science, and theology are linked in a way that cannot ultimately be separated. The entire Bible is true and worthy of our utmost attention.

23 Does it matter if the Bible contains errors?

People often ask, "Does it really matter if the Bible has errors?" It does matter. Both the Bible and Jesus himself claim that the Bible is without any error—inerrant. If both the Bible and Jesus were to falsely claim inerrancy, then why would we trust them on anything else they say?

Ultimately, this would make Jesus just another man and the Bible just another book. If the Bible contained inaccuracies in its original form, then we would have no solid basis upon which to discuss our faith. But by examining the evidence we have in the Bible, we can confidently believe it is God's perfect Word and Jesus is not just an ordinary man. They both speak the words of eternal life from God.

24 How do we know today's Bibles contain the original words of Scripture?

How do we know that the information from Jesus and the apostles has accurately been passed down to us? One way scholars have helped show the New Testament's accuracy is by the existence of numerous early manuscripts. Over 25,000 ancient copies exist of various portions, vastly outnumbering the known manuscripts for all other ancient writings combined! These manuscripts show an amazing level of consistency on all major teachings. Also,

99 percent of the New Testament's wording can confidently be determined. The remaining 1 percent primarily involves spelling errors, word order, and synonyms.

Christianity is a solid faith, built upon solid facts. If you have doubts about how we can know the Bible is accurate, check out the information for yourself. You'll discover its words are both accurate and true.

25 Is the Bible full of contradictions?

Have you ever heard someone claim, "Everybody knows that the Bible is full of contradictions!" Is this true?

The factual answer is *no.* There are some verses that seem to contradict others, but the context reveals the Bible is consistent. For example, one of the Gospels says, "Mary went to the tomb of Jesus," while another says, "The women traveled there." Which is correct? The answer is that both are correct. Mary was part of a number of women who had agreed to go to the tomb of Jesus at sunrise, but Mary was the first in the group to reach the tomb. This is not a contradiction, but an emphasis that one of the writers points out but another does not.

The Bible is a book of reliable information shared to transform our lives. Are you allowing it to change your life?

26 How can I improve my study of the Bible?

Christians claim that Bible study is important, but few read it regularly. How can we fit time to study God's Word into our crowded lives? One way is to listen to it; you can listen to the entire New Testament in only 20 hours of audio. That's less time than many of us spend driving each month.

A second way is to always keep a small Bible handy so you can read from it during short spaces, such as during a break at work. Some people even write down a verse and carry it throughout the day, frequently meditating on its words. You can even download your favorite version to your iPod! The most important part is to study something each day. God has already spoken to us. The question is, will we listen to the words he has already given?

27 Where did the Bible come from?

Have you ever wondered, *Where did the Bible come from?* That's a good question. First, we must understand that the Bible is not just one book. It's a collection of 66 books. It was written over a period of 1,400 years by over 40 authors on three continents—in three languages and in various moods and styles, ranging from poetry to history. Yet the information communicated through these authors, under the guidance of God, is one clear message: the good news that God loves you and has provided a way for you to know him personally.

Jesus said, "God did not send his Son into the world to condemn the world, but to save the world through him" (John 3:17). God has provided the way for you to know him and to live with him for all eternity. Have you taken him up on his offer?

28 What happens when there is more than one interpretation?

What happens when two people study the Bible and come to different conclusions?

The situation can usually be solved when we follow two important concepts. First, how does the controversy in question relate to the rest of the Bible? Often a difficult verse makes more sense when compared with what other verses teach on the same subject. Second, what does the context reveal? A look at the situation surrounding the verse in question will often reveal clues to proper understanding.

The Bible is not always easy to understand, but it is important to study. God calls it God-breathed (2 Timothy 3:16), and it was revealed for our learning today.

29 Is the Bible inconsistent?

Some claim that the Gospel writers contradict each other when they describe the events surrounding Christ's death, burial, and resurrection appearances because the writers describe situations in a different way. But is this true?

Think of three people witnessing a car accident. Each person will describe that accident from where they were standing. They will also tell the story differently, even though they are describing facts they saw at the same event. The same is true with the four Gospels. Often each author will describe what he witnessed and tell it a little bit differently, but they are describing the same event. There can be variation without contradiction.

The next time someone asks you about the contradictions in the Bible, help them discover the truth and accuracy of Scripture as it informs us about Jesus.

30 Can an intelligent person really believe the Bible is the Word of God?

Can an intelligent person really believe the Bible is the Word of God? Some of the most brilliant men and women throughout history have thought so. President Abraham Lincoln once said, "This great book is the best gift God has given to man." President Woodrow Wilson said, "The Bible is the one supreme source of revelation of the meaning of life, the nature of God and the spiritual nature and need of men." Benjamin Franklin told the Constitutional Convention on June 28, 1787, "We've been assured, sir, in the sacred writings, that except the Lord build the house they labor in vain to build it. I firmly believe this." If God has revealed his thoughts about man, life, and salvation in the Bible, what value do you place on this book?

31 How did Christians know what to believe before the New Testament was written?

How do you think that the early Christians

knew what to believe before the New Testament was written?

The 12 apostles and early Christian leaders made it a priority to communicate Jesus by their speaking, but soon wrote four Gospels and 23 other letters confirming Jesus' teachings. Yet even before the New Testament was written, some Christians knew the facts about Jesus from seeing him for themselves, or from listening to his living apostles, or from the theology in the first hymns they sang, or from the doctrinal teaching that freely circulated orally in the church, and finally, from the theology they learned during the celebration of the Lord's Supper and baptism.

Read the true message of Jesus for yourself in the Bible today.

Part Four:

Questions About Salvation *and* Spiritual Growth

1 How good do you have to be to enter heaven?

How good do you think you have to be to get into heaven? You may be surprised to learn that Jesus said, "Be perfect, therefore, as your heavenly Father is perfect" (Matthew 5:48). But if we must be perfect, how can *anyone* get into heaven? The wonderful answer is that God has provided the way and it doesn't depend on us. When we are willing to trust Christ to save us, at that moment Christ's atoning work on the cross covers our sins, and God credits Christ's righteous life to our account. God gives his complete forgiveness and the perfect righteousness we need to stand before him and be totally accepted. Right now, if you know you have a broken relationship with God, turn to Jesus for the answer to your point of need.

2 Is anyone too big of a sinner?

People often say, "I'm too big of a sinner to be a Christian. God would never forgive me." Is this true? The truth is that no one is too big of a sinner. The sacrifice of the Son of God on the cross was strong enough to cleanse the sins of the worst person. In fact, the apostle Paul claimed to be the chief of sinners. Why? He was so bad that he had tried to destroy the early Christian church, yet God forgave him and used him to change the lives of many.

Your sins can be forgiven by God. No one is good enough to make it on their own life's efforts. Only when we place our faith in Jesus' death on the cross for our sins as being all that God requires will we find God's forgiveness. God invites you to receive his free gift of forgiveness for your life.

3 Is it arrogant to claim Jesus is the only way?

Do you think it's arrogant to claim that Christianity is the only right religion? The quick answer is no. If something is true, it is accurate to say that it is right. For instance, it is not arrogant to say 2 + 2 is 4, because it's true. If Christianity is true, then it must be the *only* way, because it claims to be the only way.

In addition, all other religions contradict Christianity in ways that make it impossible to follow both Christianity and another religion at the same time. Of course, this means that the most important question is whether Christianity is true or not. The answer to this question is found in the person of Jesus Christ. This is why studying his life is the greatest pursuit a person can follow in life!

4 How can we end life well?

Many people start life well, but few finish well. What makes the difference? Acts 13:36 provides insight into the life of King David. It tells us, "When David had served God's purpose in his own generation, he fell asleep; he was buried with his fathers." David made many mistakes, but the difference in David's life was that when he got knocked down he got back up, resolving even more to serve God's purpose. That's why David was called "a man after God's own heart."

God has a purpose for your life as well. As you discover and live out that purpose you can find fulfillment and finish your life as God desires. Follow God and be a person who finishes well.

5 Why doesn't God always answer our prayers?

Why doesn't God always answer our prayers? Why do our prayers sometimes seem to remain unanswered?

James writes that we do not have because we do not ask God (see James 4:2-3). When we do get what we ask for, we sometimes use it for our own selfish desires. We've all been guilty of ignoring God or asking for things based on our own selfish motives. Instead, God desires for us to draw near to him. God always answers our prayers but he doesn't give us everything we want. Sometimes "no" is the best answer. Other times a period of waiting is God's best for us.

Regardless of your situation, as a child of God you can be confident that God is there and is listening to you when you call. Have you called out to him today?

6 How can we make the most of every opportunity?

God's Word says in Ephesians 6:5 that Christians are to be "making the most of every opportunity, because the days are evil." But how do we know if we are making the most of every moment?

It starts with our decision-making. Think back to the decisions you have made today. How did you decide yes or no? Was it based on what benefited you the most personally or what made the most difference for eternity? Making the most of every opportunity is ultimately about making decisions from an *eternal* perspective. As we look beyond our daily lives to examine life from an eternal viewpoint, each new decision takes on new meaning and allows each moment to make an eternal difference. Seize this day; make the most of every opportunity.

7 How should I respond when someone says, "That's good for you, but not for me"?

Are you tired of hearing people say, "Whatever you want to believe is good for you, but it's not for me?" Unfortunately, this is the response many people have toward Christ. How can we communicate the love of Jesus to those who don't seem interested?

God's Word provides two powerful insights. First, our lives must be consistent with the message we want to share. If you talk about the importance of your faith but your life is no different from other people, why would anyone want to know the

Jesus you talk about? Second, we must show others the love of Jesus through how we treat them. People notice how we act before we ever speak. The more we reveal our real love for others through our actions, the more effective we'll be in sharing the truth about how Jesus can make a difference in their life.

8 How can I know I'm accepted by God?

One of our basic human desires is for acceptance. We long to be accepted by parents, by a spouse, or by our friends. But how do we know we are accepted by God?

Those who trust in Christ by faith can confidently know that God has clearly accepted us in every way. In John's Gospel we are told that those who receive Jesus are called God's children. The same Gospel later calls those who believe Christ's friends. In other passages those who believe in Jesus are said to belong to God, to have been adopted by God, and to have been made complete in Christ. We are accepted by God because of Christ, not our own good works. If you have completely trusted Christ as your substitute for sin, you are already fully accepted by God as one of his own.

9 How can I share my faith in Christ with others?

As Christians, we are called to share Christ with anyone and everyone who will listen. However, each person has a choice. So when we attempt to take their choice away and force someone to believe the way we do, we are no longer sharing our faith the way God desires.

Another big problem is that we as Christians often fail to share our faith in Christ at all. This, too, is not God's desire. He longs for us to speak about Jesus whenever possible. Jesus himself commanded us to "go into all the world and preach the good news to all creation" (Mark 16:15). So don't force your religion on someone, but do share your faith in Jesus with someone today.

10 What should I do about my doubts?

As Christians, we claim to believe in the resurrection and the miracles of the Bible. But what happens when we have doubts?

The first thing to realize is that doubt is normal. Doubt is the result of unanswered questions about our faith or not trusting the promises God has made to us when we trust in Christ. Our doubts can lead us to seek answers that strengthen our learning and help us live with greater confidence in Jesus.

When you doubt, look to God and the promises and information in his Word. Don't hesitate to use numerous Bible study tools and consult pastors, teachers, and other resources to help you grow. Don't let doubt cripple you; let it *better* you. Take your questions to God and his Word.

11 Does prayer really work?

The book of James teaches that the prayer of a righteous person is powerful and effective. Elijah prayed for years that it would not rain in Israel, and it didn't. But later when he prayed for rain, it came that same day.

In our lives, we sometimes feel discouraged when we do not see immediate answers to our prayers. But this does not mean God is not listening. Some answers take years, and God sometimes says no for reasons we don't understand. God tells us he wants to hear from us. We can rest assured that when we pray, he hears. God promises he will answer according to his perfect ways in our times of need.

12 Is spiritual warfare real?

God, angels, Satan, demons—is spiritual warfare real? The Bible teaches that spiritual warfare is indeed very real. Ephesians 6:12 tells us that the Christian's battle is not against people, but really against spiritual forces of evil in the heavenly realms. The Bible also teaches that supernatural manifestations are not to be uncritically accepted, but rather tested by biblical principles. Satan's tactics include strong lies designed to deceive people eternally. We are called to be prepared for such deceptions as part of our spiritual fight. The good news is that Jesus said we have supernatural help and protection from the Holy Spirit if we are willing to obey and follow Jesus with all of our heart.

13 What is *apologetics*?

As Christian apologists, we're often asked, "What is apologetics?" The word *apologetics* originates from the Greek word *apologia,* which means to defend or to give an answer. The apostle Peter told Christians in 1 Peter 3:15,

> Always be prepared to give an answer to everyone who asks you to give the reason for the hope that you have.

Apologetics is not about apologizing. Apologetics is answering the tough questions people have about the Christian faith. This can include evidence for the resurrection of Jesus, for the fulfillment of Bible prophecy, or for creation of the universe. To some extent, every Christian is an apologist. God wants you to be prepared to answer those who ask you about your faith in Christ.

14 What power do our words have on others?

Recently a young man committed suicide in front of a live Web camera. Apparently those in the video chat room thought the suicide was a hoax. Many messages mocked the young man as a prankster rather than treating the situation as a real threat.

Such acts cause us to reflect on the issue of suicide in our culture. Statistically, it is likely you will run into someone this week who is at least considering the idea of ending his or her own life. The words you offer might be the difference between a person choosing life or death. Scripture says to let our conversations be seasoned as with salt (Colossians 4:6). Our talk should encourage others not only to life, but to the gift of eternal life through Jesus Christ.

15 How does the Bible teach us to respond to life's difficulties?

Economic crisis has increased home foreclosures and unemployment and has devastated the retirement accounts of many. In response, millions of concerned individuals are on the verge of panic. How does God encourage us to respond in these times of difficulty?

First, remember God is in control. He is not surprised by economic downturns. Second, God is there. He wants you to turn to him in your time of need, and he will answer according to his will. In your struggle, turn to the perfect power of God for hope and help. He can rescue you from any situation and provide help no other source can offer. As Scripture instructs, he is our strength in times of trouble (see Psalm 59:16).

16 How can I manage my time more effectively?

Every human shares one resource equally, and that's time. We each have 1,440 minutes per day—no more, no less. Psalm 90:12 asks God to teach us to number our days. In other words, our goal is to live each day to its fullest.

Try this exercise: Place a note card with the

numbers 1-4-4-0 in a place where you'll see them throughout the day. Each time you notice the numbers, ask, "Is what I'm doing right now making the most of the time that God has given me today?" As we reflect on the precious time God has given us, it will instill a renewed sense that every interaction of life is designed to honor our Creator.

17 How can a person pray without ceasing?

The Bible tells us to pray without ceasing. How does this work? Does this mean we cannot truly obey God unless we lead a life as a secluded monk—or is there a way that every person who follows Christ can practice this command?

Paul, the writer of these words, was certainly a person of action, yet he was also a person of prayer. His experience was to pray in every place and in every situation. It was about praying *along* the journey, not stopping his journey to only pray. If prayer is talking with God, you can do this anytime and in any place. Whether you're stuck in traffic or lying in bed at night, you can be aware of God's presence and communicate with him about your every need.

18 How can I develop deep and meaningful friendships?

We all crave deep relationship with others. However, many of us struggle to find even one true friend. What causes this relationship dilemma?

There are many possible reasons, but one critical concern is the issue of acceptance. We frequently fail to attempt a serious relationship because we fear rejection. Jesus modeled the perfect response to this modern dilemma: We love because he first loved us. When we realize that our acceptance is based on God's love, it instills hope for our other relationships. Broken relationships will still occur, but God provides a foundation of love that overcomes all heartache.

19 How can I choose the right friends?

Do the people we spend time with influence our behavior? According to Scripture, the answer is a resounding yes. In Psalm 1 we are warned, "Blessed is the man who does not walk in the counsel of the wicked or stand in the way of sinners...But his delight is in the law of the LORD."

We are to show love to all, but invest priority time in relationships with others who share our faith in Christ. More importantly, our character is shaped by God's truth. This same psalm shares that "on his law he meditates day and night." This is a clear call for us to be consumed daily with God's truth. God's people and God's Word are two solid ways to develop godly character that will improve our lives now and for eternity.

20 How do I choose my priorities in life?

If someone asked you what mattered most in your life, how would you respond? Most of us would answer that God, our spouse, children, family, or close friends would all be at the top of the list. However, when we look at how we invest our lives, can you say your actions properly align with these priorities? Other priorities including work or sports can redirect our attention to things that are secondary to the relationships God has given us.

Take a moment to look at the priorities in your life and recognize that what matters most is not what we say, but where we spend our time. As followers of Christ, we should understand that the time God has given us is sacred. Every interaction of life is designed to honor our Creator.

21 How can I reach my goals in life?

Did you know that 67 percent of Americans who make New Year's resolutions will make three or more? Unfortunately, the vast majority will fail to keep them. Instead of making a list of changes, choose just one. When we focus our energy on one significant change at a time, we find our ability to accomplish the goal much more reasonable.

Jesus said, "Suppose one of you wants to build a tower. Will he not first sit down and estimate the cost to see if he has enough money to complete it?" (Matthew 14:28). It is unwise to make a goal without a plan. Choose one thing that you most desire to change, create a plan, and ask God to help you move forward toward your God-honoring goal.

22 What goals should I choose?

When reflecting on their life, many people set new goals for their personal lives or business. What goals should we focus on as followers of Christ?

The apostle Paul wrote in 2 Corinthians 5:9, "We make it our goal to please him," speaking of Christ. Other goals, such as weight loss or financial changes, can be noble efforts, but God desires full devotion to him as our top goal. As you set your personal goals, where is he on your list? Don't make him *part* of your list; make him your top priority. Jesus said the greatest commandment is to "love the Lord your God with all your heart and with all your soul and with all your mind" (Matthew 22:37). This is the only goal that will change your life both now and for eternity.

23 What should be my top goal in life?

Have you ever seen someone include "more love" on their list of New Year's resolutions? Probably not. Most of our resolutions focus on personal goals like weight loss or to stop spending so much. However, the apostle Paul devotes an entire chapter of 1 Corinthians to explain what he calls the "most excellent way."

What is this excellent way? It's love. How do we implement more love in our lives? First, begin with your relationship with God; spend regular time with him. Second, make it a point to show love in your daily interactions. Opening a door, letting a car into your lane of traffic, or showing politeness to a waiter or waitress can go a long way to help others see the love of Christ in your life.

24 How can I become a better example in sharing my faith?

Someone once said, "You are the only Jesus many people will ever see." In fact, many people decide what Jesus is like based on how Christians act. The apostle Paul said, "Follow my example, as I follow the example of Christ" (1 Corinthians 11:1). Well, we too are to follow Christ's example so others will see who Jesus really is. As a result, others should want to live more like you. Then you'll have a wonderful opportunity to share with that person *why* you are different—because of Jesus living in you. When we live like Christ, we help those seeking him experience a little glimpse of what he is really like.

25 What does God call true religion?

As Christians, our ultimate goal and desire should be to live out our faith in a manner that pleases God. But how do we know how we are doing? James 1:27 teaches,

> Religion that God our Father accepts as pure and faultless is this: to look after orphans and widows in their distress and to keep oneself from being polluted by the world.

We intuitively understand that pure religion includes keeping our lives clean from sinful habits...but caring for orphans and widows? That often doesn't cross our minds when we think about growing spiritually. Yet the Bible is clear that our love for God is displayed by how we treat those in need. Widows and fatherless children are excellent opportunities to truly show your faith in a real and meaningful way.

26 What is the difference between faith and feelings?

When we choose to follow Christ we often expect a sense of overwhelming joy or other feelings. But is this really how faith in God works? Chronicles of Narnia author C.S. Lewis shared that when he came to faith in Jesus he expected a strong emotional experience, but that experience never came. It was not until later that he realized belief in Jesus as God's Son is not about the emotion of the initial act, but the changed belief and attitudes that take place from that point on.

If you are waiting for an emotional response to take place before deciding to obey God in an area of your life, stop. Make your decision based on God's Word in prayer, even when the emotions don't seem to follow.

27 How can I resist temptation?

Temptation happens to every one of us; it's how we respond to it that makes the difference. How can we resist the daily temptations we face? The best example of overcoming temptation is that set by Jesus. In Matthew 4 Jesus was tempted by Satan on three separate occasions. In each encounter, Jesus successfully resisted the temptation. What was his consistent response? He used specific Bible verses. It has been said that the Bible will keep you from sin, or sin will keep you from the Bible. Following and standing on God's promises is the one sure way to resist temptation and remain strong in your faith.

28 How can I be more faithful in reading the Bible?

Bible reading is part of how we grow spiritually. It can also be tough to do. How can we faithfully read it each day?

Here are a couple of suggestions. One great way to begin is by reading the Bible together with another person. Rather than studying, just meet and take turns reading verses. Talk about the verses that impress themselves on you. Another option is to listen to an audio version. If you commute 30 minutes or more each way to work, you can complete the entire New Testament in just four weeks.

Remember that the Bible is not just a book, it's God's Word. It might be tough to study it, but the spiritual transformation that takes place in your life will be worth the effort.

29 How can I improve my life's circumstances?

Do you ever wish you could do something to change the circumstances you are facing...start a new career, move to a new city? Everyone has an area of life where they desire to do something different. However, the apostle Paul's perspective on his circumstances included one additional word: *contentment*. He wrote in Philippians 4:12,

> I have learned to be content whatever the circumstances. I know what it is to be in need, and I know what it is to have plenty. I have learned the secret of being content in any and every situation.

He calls contentment a "secret." The way to live beyond the ordinary is not always to attempt something new. Rather, it's to live with an attitude of thankfulness to Jesus—being content with what we have while we experience life's journey.

30 What does God value?

If someone says they really tried to get to work on time but arrived late, how do you know if that person is being honest? God looks at our hearts and knows we cannot honestly say we've always tried to please him. That's why we will never gain entrance into his heaven by our own efforts. Jesus proclaimed the good news that heaven is not based on our efforts, even sincere ones. Our entry is based upon trusting him to do all the work necessary to get us into heaven. The Bible says, "God so loved the world that he gave his one and only Son, that whoever believes in him shall not perish but have eternal life." Eternal life is based on our relationship with the eternal Son of God, not our human efforts (Ephesians 2:8-9).

31 How can I share my faith?

Many would like to share their faith in Jesus, but

struggle with how to do it. How can we share our faith in a natural way? A great biblical example can be found in the life of the apostle Matthew. When he began to follow Christ, he invited his unbelieving friends to a meal where they could be around Jesus and other believers. As they heard stories of how Christ had changed the lives of those who were present, they were given their own opportunity to follow him.

Sounds like a great idea, doesn't it? Bring together both believers and unbelievers in an environment where people can experience how Jesus has changed lives. Try out a "Matthew Party" yourself. Perhaps God will use you to show a friend how to place their trust in Jesus as their Savior.

32 How do I find God's will for my life?

A news article told about a brother and sister in England who had spent 40 years trying to find each other, then recently discovered they lived only 300 yards apart. According to the brother, he had walked past her home several times, but never knew she lived there.

Many people seek God in a similar way. They search various alternatives, only to find God has been waiting right beside them the entire time. Jesus said in Matthew 7:7, "Ask and it will be given to you; seek and you will find; knock and the door will be opened to you." God is there. Read his book, the Bible. Let him reveal himself to you, right where you are today.

33 **"Why should I let you in?"**

One Christian man often asked his non-Christian friends, "If you were to stand before a perfect God someday and he asked you, 'Why should I let you into my heaven?' what would you say?" Those who do not understand the gospel message always respond with some kind of works: "I have always tried to do the right thing."

But entering heaven is not about earning your way; it's about understanding that because of your sins, you can never do enough to be accepted by God. Rather, you need him to rescue you and to save you. That's the biblical gospel. He sent Jesus to die on the cross to pay for your sins, and he invites you to trust Jesus to forgive and save you and to bring you to heaven. God promises to welcome all who will trust in Jesus into heaven when they die.

34 How can I share my faith with those in my family?

Over 70 percent of Americans mention family members as their most influential relationships. What can this finding mean to us when sharing our faith in Christ?

First, it reveals that our most effective sharing can be among the members of our own family. They are the most willing to thoughtfully listen to what we value. Second, this fact shows the vital significance of spiritual growth *within* the family. Church services and activities are important to our faith, but we often grow most in connection with those in our own households. In fact, God designed family as the *primary* place for spiritual influence for our lives. Remember, he can use you to change your entire family.

35 How good is good enough?

How good do you think you have to be to get into heaven? You may be surprised to learn that Jesus said, "Be perfect...as your heavenly Father is perfect" (Matthew 5:48). But if we must be perfect, how can *anyone* get into heaven?

The wonderful answer is that God has provided

the way, and it doesn't depend on us. When we are willing to trust Christ to save us, *at that moment* his atoning work on the cross covers our sins. God credits Christ's righteous life to our account. God gives us his complete forgiveness and the perfect righteousness we need to stand before him and be totally accepted.

Right now, if you have doubts about whether you are good enough for heaven, recognize that the answer to this question is not based on how good you are, but whether you know Christ, the perfect One who is the only way to know eternal life.

36 What did Jesus teach about becoming a better person?

Have you noticed that when we talk about becoming better people, we often focus on adding more activities to our lives? Yet most of us are already overworked. Isn't there a better solution?

While hard work is important, Jesus illustrated a better approach during a meal at the home of Mary and Martha. Mary stayed to listen to Jesus while Martha consumed herself with preparations for the meal. Finally, in frustration, Martha snapped at Jesus, "Tell Mary to help!" Jesus answered, "You are worried and upset about many things, but only one thing is needed. Mary has chosen what is better" (Luke 10:41-42).

In other words, the answer to becoming a better person is not always doing more, but doing the one thing that matters most—listening to Jesus.

Part Five:

Questions About *the* Afterlife

1 What happens when this life ends?

Tragic deaths, such as the 2007 shooting of Pro Bowl safety Sean Taylor of the Washington Redskins, cause us to consider the question, "What happens when this life is over?"

The Bible tells us this life is not all there is. All eternity is waiting once this life ends. This brings up the question, "Is it safe to die?"

The Bible tells us there is a real hell to shun and a real heaven to gain. But this life is all the time we have to choose. The Bible states that if you want to be sure you will spend all eternity with God in heaven, you must place your faith and trust in Jesus in *this* life. Acts 16:31 says, "Believe in the Lord Jesus, and you will be saved." Make certain you are ready for the life after this life.

2 What will heaven be like?

What do you think heaven will be like? Many misconceptions exist. What does the Bible say? In John 14:2-3, Jesus said,

> In my Father's house are many rooms…I am going there to prepare a place for you. And if I go and prepare a place for you, I will come again and take you to be with me that you also may be where I am.

In addition, the Bible says we will be reunited with believers of the past, including loved ones who have placed their faith in Christ. God will give each of us new bodies. In the end there will even be a new heaven and earth, where there will be no more tears or pain. Sin will no longer exist.

Heaven will be far better than just playing harps and floating on clouds. It will be the ultimate celebration for those who know Christ. Are you ready for heaven?

3 Will we recognize our loved ones in heaven?

A common question people ask about heaven is whether we will be able to recognize our loved ones. What does the Bible say? In 1 Corinthians 13,

Paul says we know in part, then we will know fully. While this statement does not answer every question about heaven, we can be certain of one thing. We will know more in heaven than we do on earth.

So will we recognize our loved ones in heaven? Yes! Even with new bodies we'll recognize in heaven those we knew on earth. We'll probably also recognize others who are there, like Noah, Daniel, and most importantly, Jesus. He's the most important figure in all eternity. Are you ready to meet him in heaven?

4 **Does hell exist?**

What can you say to a person who says there is no such place as hell? First, you can kindly point out that according to Jesus, hell is a real place. In fact, he spoke more about hell than heaven. In Matthew 10:28 he warned,

> Do not be afraid of those who kill the body but cannot kill the soul. Rather, be afraid of the One who can destroy both soul and body in hell.

In Matthew 13, Jesus described what would happen to those who rejected him. He said, as the weeds are pulled up and burned in the fire, so it would be at the end of the age. Hell is a real place. As Christians, we should be motivated by this reality to communicate the gospel of Jesus Christ, which can save people from going to the very real place the Bible calls hell.

5 Are angels real?

Did you know that three out of four Americans believe angels are real? What does the Bible say? First, Scripture is clear that angels are real. They are mentioned over 300 times in the Bible. Good angels are said to be messengers of God who serve him. Bad angels are identified as demons who participate in the spiritual battle going on in our world today mentioned in Ephesians 6:12. But second, angelic encounters are rare. When an angel appeared to people in the Bible, it was considered important, but astonishing.

Keep in mind that God does not tell us to pray to angels or to worship them. Rather, he tells us to believe in his Son, Jesus, who is the Savior of the world, who died for our sins to bring us to God.

6 Do guardian angels protect us?

Do guardian angels protect us in times of need? According to a 2009 survey in *Time* magazine, 55 percent of Americans answered *yes* to the statement, "I was protected from harm by a guardian angel." The Bible is clear that angels *do* exist and serve God's will.

Many today continue to believe their lives have been helped in some way by an angel. But why? Could God be allowing angels to intervene to point people toward Jesus? Hebrews 1:14 asks, "Are not all angels ministering spirits sent to serve those who will inherit salvation?" Angels serve not only to protect from harm, but to point us to Jesus. He is our ultimate rescuer. Are you looking to him for help today?

7 Can people really communicate with the dead?

In the 2008 movie *Ghost Town*, a dentist acquires the ability to see dead people after a routine surgery. What does the Bible teach about those who claim to see and communicate with the dead? First, it recognizes the existence of both good and evil spirits and tells us there is a spiritual battle going on in the unseen world. Therefore, second, those who claim to see and communicate with the dead are talking with either angels or demonic influences. In a culture that is fascinated with the supernatural,

Christians are called to embrace the truth of Jesus Christ. Our goal is to communicate with and follow only Jesus, the perfect Son of God.

8 What does the Bible teach about reincarnation?

An increasing number of Americans say they now believe in some form of reincarnation after death. What does the Bible say about what happens in the afterlife?

Jesus told the story of Lazarus and the rich man who both died, noting that only two options existed for their destinations—heaven or hell. Each person entered his destination immediately upon death, with no way to move from one location to the other. Those who go to hell experience eternity apart from God and eternal suffering.

Jesus' words should reawaken us to the importance of choosing him in *this* life, which will prepare us for eternity. According to him, there is no reincarnation or second chance in the afterlife. The decisions we make in this life determine our eternity.

9 Is reincarnation compatible with Christianity?

Do you think reincarnation is compatible with Christianity? Reincarnation is never once taught in the Bible. Rather, the Bible presents a completely different scenario about the afterlife. It teaches that all people will die only once, followed by eternity in one of two places, heaven or hell, after this one life on earth.

Further, it teaches that the choices we make in this life will determine our eternal destiny. This perspective forces us to move forward with a sense of urgency to accept God's only way of salvation—personal trust in Jesus: that he is our sin-bearer, the One who meets all that God requires for us to be fully accepted and be given the gift of eternal life.

Part Six:

Questions About Other Religions

1 Do we really pray to the same God?

Some think that those who believe in different religions all pray to the same God. Is this really true?

Christians pray to the one, infinite, unchanging personal God who is triune. Muslims deny the Christian God and pray to Allah. Mormons also deny the Christian God and believe in many gods, primarily worshiping a deity called Elohim that they call God the Father. Who is right? Does it make any difference as long as people are sincere?

Well, it does make a difference. As the Bible teaches, we are not to worship or pray to any other gods. If we are to worship God in spirit and in truth, as Jesus said, we must know and worship the one true God as he really is. Jesus commanded us to go and make disciples of all the nations, baptizing them in the one name of the Father and of the Son and of the Holy Spirit.

2 How often do people switch religions?

A recent survey has revealed that 28 percent of Americans have switched from the religion of their childhood to another. According to the study, our mobile culture has caused Americans to frequently change not only jobs, spouses, or homes, but also religious involvement. The focus is on what works *now*, rather than on the traditions of the past.

As Christians, our desire must be to help those who may be changing religions turn to Christ. As the apostle Paul wrote in Romans 1:16, "I am not ashamed of the gospel, because it is the power of God for the salvation of everyone who believes." Share your faith with someone today. Help others turn to the true life found in Christ.

3 Why do people change religions?

In my years of discussion with adherents of other religions, I (John) have been surprised to find that many originally came from Christian backgrounds. When I've asked, "What caused you to change religions?" many described a bad experience with other Christians, which caused them to look elsewhere.

Many of us can identify with a bad religious experience in the past, but does that mean Christianity is false and should be abandoned? The answer is no. I challenge people to, instead of abandoning the Christian faith, look at Christ and *re-evaluate* the faith for themselves. Christianity is a faith built on the life, death, and resurrection of Jesus from the dead. When the Son of God is the basis for faith, Christianity is true and can bring a life-changing relationship with him.

4 Do Muslims believe in Jesus?

Do Muslims believe in Jesus? Islam and Christianity both recognize Jesus as an important historical person, but quickly disagree after that. For instance, Islam rejects that Jesus claimed to be God's Son and rejects that he taught the concept of the Trinity. Christianity believes Jesus was telling us the truth when he claimed to be God in human form.

Further, the Qur'an denies that Jesus physically died on the cross and rose again. But the apostle Paul wrote in 1 Corinthians 15:14 that without the resurrection, the Christian faith is useless.

Regarding how we know God, the Bible teaches that salvation is only found when a person completely trusts in Jesus to be their Savior from sin. The Qur'an teaches that salvation can only be found in the Five Pillars of Islam.

Muslims believe in a make-believe Jesus, not the Jesus of history. Christians are called to spread the word about the resurrected Christ and communicate him to all who will listen.

5 Do all religions lead to the same place?

How can we respond to those who claim, "All religions are different paths to the same place"? First, if all religions are different paths to the same place, then why do different spiritual paths contradict each other? One or the other might be right, but they cannot all be right at the same time. Not all roads in your city take you to your house, do they?

Second, if a loving God exists, what would make more sense—for him to make many contradictory ways to find him, or for him to create only one way and mark it clearly? Christianity claims Jesus is the only way, and that the way to know him is by placing our faith in his sacrificial death on the cross for our sins. If you are trusting in anything else to get you to heaven, remember—you're in disagreement with Jesus.

6 Is it wrong to believe in astrology?

Is it wrong for a Christian to believe in astrology? An accurate definition of astrology is the divination of the supposed influences of stars and planets on human affairs. The Bible warns us about accepting such ideas. In Deuteronomy 18:10, it states, "Let no one be found among you...who practices divination."

To give a contemporary example, horoscopes may appear harmless, but because they are said to give spiritual information about life by discerning the position of the stars, this makes them out-of-bounds for those who follow Christ. Be like the people who became Christians in Ephesus, who abandoned their books on astrology and the occult as a sign that they would no longer follow such practices (Acts 19).

7 Is there more than one way to know God?

A recent survey has revealed that 70 percent of Americans who believe in God also believe that many religions can lead to eternal life. Is this consistent with what the Bible teaches?

Absolutely not! Jesus called himself *the* way. He taught that no one comes to the Father but through him (John 14:6). Jesus made it clear that he is the only way to eternal life, not one of many ways.

Then why do so many in our culture believe otherwise? The answer must be due in part to a severe lack of understanding of what Jesus taught. It is our job as Christ's followers to share the good news Jesus gave us to all who will listen.

8 How is the Bible viewed in other religions?

Did you know that the Qur'an teaches that the Bible has been corrupted? So does the Book of Mormon. Are these religious movements right?

Well, the answer is no. First, many Mormons and Muslims who argue that the Bible is corrupt do so to promote their own religious book. Second, the religious systems of both Islam nd Mormonism are more recent than Christianity, and their sacred books lack the historical credibility of the Christian Scriptures. When Muslims and Mormons point to what they call flaws in the Bible, boldly ask them whether they have really read it for themselves or if they're just repeating what they've heard from someone else. Then suggest they read the Gospels for themselves and allow God to show them the accuracy and the power of his Word.

9 What does Buddhism teach about Jesus?

Buddhism continues to grow throughout Western culture. What does it teach about Jesus? As a whole, Buddhism has little to say about Jesus directly. It acknowledges he was a great person but little else. In Buddhism there is no need to be saved from personal sin, so Jesus' role as Savior from sin is not seen as important. In fact, since Buddhists believe in reincarnation, there is no motivation to trust in Jesus for eternal life.

Now, either Buddha's teachings are right, or the teachings of Jesus are. They cannot both be true at the same time. And Jesus gave proof that his teachings are eternally true by physically rising from the dead. Buddha is still in his tomb. Ultimately, Christianity, not Buddhism, provides the eternal answers to life's questions through the person of Jesus Christ.

10 Is Mormonism the same as Christianity?

Mormons believe that the entire Christian church entered apostasy and lost the truth immediately after the death of Jesus' last apostle. But could this really be true?

Before leaving earth Jesus promised his followers, "Surely I am with you always, even to the very end of the age." In contrast with the Mormon church's teaching, Jesus has been with his people throughout history. Why? Because the end of the age has yet to come.

Mormons are very sincere in sharing their beliefs. However, this is only one of the many points that separate Mormonism from Christianity. Show love and respect to your Mormon friends, but be firm in sharing that only the Bible must be our basis for faith, not the Book of Mormon.

11 What is Wicca?

Wicca is today's most popular form of witchcraft. Rooted in the writings of British author Gerald Gardner from the late 1940s and 1950s, this movement soon spread to the United States, officially becoming a religion in 1986. Today on many Web sites, thousands of practitioners regularly discover Wiccan concepts, which are often linked to pagan religions of the past.

As Christians, we must help show a better

alternative than what is found in Wicca. First, pray for those involved in Wicca and other forms of witchcraft or earth-based spiritual paths. Second, familiarize yourself with crucial information about Wicca and Christianity. And third, show genuine friendship with those involved in Wicca in order to open up opportunities to share how Jesus changed your life and how he can change theirs.

12 What do Mormons believe about heaven?

Did you know that Mormons believe all people will end up in one of three "kingdoms of glory": the celestial, terrestrial, or telestial? The *celestial* kingdom is supposedly the highest glory. The *terrestrial* kingdom is for non-Mormons who live moral lives. The *telestial* kingdom is a lower level still, where they believe most people will go. This teaching is based on a distortion of Paul's words in 1 Corinthians 15:40. There he talks about only "heavenly" or celestial bodies and "earthly" or terrestrial bodies. He never even wrote the word *telestial*.

The Bible teaches that at death, all people go to either heaven or hell. The difference? It's not our faith plus works, but our faith alone in Jesus Christ.

13 Don't all religions teach the same thing?

We've all heard the question, "Don't all religions teach the same thing?" How would you respond? The truth is, each religion teaches very distinct things about God and issues of faith. Islam teaches that God's name is Allah. Jehovah's Witnesses teach that God's name is Jehovah. Shinto includes thousands of spirits and gods. Judaism has one God. Mormons have three destinations in the afterlife, while Buddhism believes in reincarnation. And these are just a *few* of the differences.

All religions definitely do not teach the same thing. That's why Jesus said, "I am the way and the truth and the life. No one comes to the Father except through me" (John 14:6).

14 What is karma?

Many today believe their good or bad "karma" will influence their future. Is this true?

In Eastern religions, *karma* usually refers to the debt a person accumulates because of good or bad actions in his or her life or past lives. If a person accumulates good karma, it means a better reincarnation. Bad karma results in a negative situation.

But the Bible never talks about multiple lives or reincarnation. It's our one life now and the decisions we make during it that will determine our eternity in the next life. Karma has no influence. The Bible teaches that sinful behavior will bring punishment, but that trust in Jesus as Savior and Forgiver will bring us eternal life.

15 What does the Mormon church teach about the Bible?

Did you know that the Mormon church teaches that the Bible is corrupted? In fact, Mormons have their own version of the Bible, called the "inspired version." Is there any truth to their claim?

The answer is no. There is *no* textual evidence that shows the Bible has been corrupted. There are 25,000 manuscripts or manuscript portions that have come down to us to compare, as well as over one million quotations from the Church Fathers. Taken together, all this provides overwhelming evidence that we have what the apostles and their companions wrote about Jesus.

If you have questions about the Bible's accuracy, check out its claims of itself and discover that it is inspired and inerrant, just as it claims.

16 Why should we care about other religions?

Why should we care about other religions? In a recent study featured in the bestselling book *Biblical Literacy*, it was observed that "even most American college students cannot correctly answer the most basic facts about world religions." However, as Christians we can greatly benefit from a better understanding of other faith systems. For example, if we know that a Hindu believes that his life is a series of reincarnations rather than one life followed by eternity in heaven or hell, we can interact more effectively in sharing Christ.

Remember that the apostle Peter commanded Christians to "always be ready to give an answer to everyone who asks you to give the reason for the hope that you have" (1 Peter 3:15).

Part Seven:

Questions About Contemporary Issues

1 What is the "secret law of attraction"?

Rhonda Burns's bestselling book, *The Secret*, has sold over 4 million copies. Why has it been such a success? Many attribute its popularity to the transforming power of its message, the "law of attraction." Thoughts become things. If you think hard enough about something it will take place. You are the one who creates your own circumstances.

The Secret calls upon us to use our own thoughts to gain our own selfish desires. The apostle Paul says just the opposite: "I urge you…in view of God's mercy, to offer your bodies as living sacrifices, holy and pleasing to God" (Romans 12:1). He asks us to follow Christ and live selflessly, not selfishly. You won't find the truth in following *The Secret*, but you will find it in following the teachings of Christ. The truth is no secret.

2 What is my purpose in life?

Have you ever asked yourself the question, "What is my purpose in life?" We all have. The Bible reveals that our *purpose* in life is to bring glory to God. Revelation 4:11 states, "You are worthy, our Lord and God, to receive glory and honor and power, for you created all things, and by your will they were created and have their being."

Second, God also has a *plan* for your life. Jeremiah 29:11 records,

> "I know the plans I have for you," declares the Lord, "plans to prosper you and not to harm you, plans to give you hope and a future."

God will reveal his exciting and fulfilling plans for you if you trust Christ as your Savior and Leader and live a devoted life to him.

3 How can I discern right from wrong?

Today's teenagers receive a lot of mixed messages about the issue of integrity. For example, reality TV portrays sex as a harmless pleasure. Drugs and alcohol are often portrayed as enjoyable pastimes.

How can parents help their children discern right from wrong? God provides two insights. First, parents are intended to be the primary influencers of their child's values and morals. Limiting time playing video games, setting TV viewing limits, and safeguarding Internet boundaries are the *parents'* responsibility. Second, parents can positively nourish their children with God's information about life, including reading the Bible together, listening to Christian music, and viewing videos and Web sites that promote biblical values. Mom and Dad can make the difference by both guarding and promoting God-honoring media choices for their children.

4 How can I decide what TV shows or movies to watch?

Do you struggle with what is okay to watch on television or at the movies? What guidelines can we find from the Bible to honor God with what we watch?

Philippians 4 shares that whatever is right or pure is what we should think about. A basic viewing principle is that we should watch only what helps us focus on right priorities. According to the Bible, Christians are called to be in the world but not of it. This means that occasionally watching a show or film to better understand our culture can be a helpful way to better communicate our faith. The key is to *think* through our choices rather than *consume* any show available. God desires the best for our lives in every area, including what we watch.

5 How should we respond to "cafeteria Christianity"?

Numerous people today choose to follow parts of Christianity without accepting all of it. How should we respond to this "cafeteria approach" to Christianity?

First, we must remember that Jesus didn't teach us to pick and choose what we believe. He simply told his followers to "follow me." When we choose to follow Christ, we choose to do what he wants whether the choices are easy or difficult. Second, cafeteria Christianity is not really Christianity at all. A Christian is a person who desires to be like Christ. This includes changing our lives to be more like him, not choosing what we like and don't like. So don't pick and choose with your faith; take the whole menu and follow Jesus the way he intended.

6 Can a person be spiritual but not religious?

Have you ever heard someone say, "I'm a

spiritual person, but I'm not into organized religion"? What's the difference?

Some people have decided their personal, spiritual beliefs and organized religion are two different things. In some ways this might be true, but the two are intimately connected. A person who believes Jesus is God's Son does so based on the same book that teaches Christians to regularly gather in church community for mutual encouragement and growth.

So when you run into someone who claims to be spiritual but not into religion, ask them what they really mean. Often they mean they are not into the religion they have experienced in the past. But if they encounter a group of genuine people following God, they just might change their mind.

7 What's the difference between the behaviors of Christians and non-Christians?

A recent book highlighted the fact that the lives of most Christians display no noticeable differences from those of unchurched Americans. How should we view this humbling observation?

The key question is whether our faith really matters. In our "whatever works" culture, how are Christians showing a faith that makes positive changes in their personal lives and communities? The place to start must be with our own lives. We need to ask ourselves, *Am I part of the problem or part of the solution?* When others see that Jesus makes a difference in our interactions at home and in the workplace, this will indicate that our faith really does matter. Only when people see that Jesus changes *you* will they desire for Jesus to change *them*.

8 Church—problem or opportunity?

Our culture quickly points the finger at the problem of hypocrisy in today's churches, often suggesting there is no reason for church involvement at all. But is this really the proper response?

The Bible calls the church the bride of Christ. This indicates that Jesus has a passionate love for those who gather together in his name. While churches often fail to live out God's desires, this does not mean that the alternative is to abandon it. The biblical word for church, *ekklesia*, means "called-out ones." We are called to make a difference through local churches, not to reject them when they mess up. What about you? What can you do to make your church better today?

9 Can devotion to celebrities be a form of worship?

Celebrities attract attention. Therefore, athletes sell shoes, actresses promote makeup, and musicians often speak out about the environment. But can celebrity worship actually hurt our spiritual lives?

Jesus, the apostles, and prophets all indicate that assigning any activity a higher priority than one's devotion to God is idolatry. You may not bow down to a statue, but when you buy clothing, a movie, or a CD, do celebrities influence your actions? Our true source for determining our values must be God. Jesus said the greatest thing we can do is to love the Lord with all of our heart, mind, and strength. Celebrities may try to influence you to live the way they do, but Christ is to be our eternal influence. He is the only one worthy of all our allegiance.

10 Do miracles really happen?

Do miracles really happen? Recent scientific evidence seems to increasingly indicate yes. For instance, in one double-blind experiment, medical experts evaluated the condition of patients who were prayed for versus those who were not. What happened? Those who were prayed for scored higher in 21 of the 26 evaluated categories. Yet none of the nearly 400 coronary patients knew they were the actual recipients of prayer.

This scientific study, while not an outright proof that miracles occur, is nonetheless evidence that the supernatural may exist and be involved. But always remember the strongest evidence for the greatest miracle is the resurrection of Jesus Christ from the dead.

11 Does absolute truth exist?

In today's postmodern culture, people ask, "Does absolute truth exist?" Some claim our beliefs and values are purely subjective, based on no absolute moral authority. But is this what the Bible communicates?

Certainly not! The Bible declares that God's words are absolutely true. The psalmist wrote that "the law of the LORD is perfect, reviving the soul." The apostle Paul noted that "all scripture is God-breathed and is useful for teaching, rebuking, correcting and training in righteousness." While today's skeptics may question whether truth exists, God has provided a clear response for those seeking a perfect standard on which to base their life. Allow God's perfect truth to refine your heart and life today.

12 Do moral absolutes exist?

When they are speeding or cheating on an exam, people will say that their morals are based on personal choice. But if they get cut off in traffic or cheated out of something, then they believe that someone else is violating their rights, and they suddenly believe in moral absolutes for everyone.

The Bible says,

> What may be known about God has been made plain to them...God's invisible qualities—his eternal power and divine nature—have been clearly seen, being understood from what has been made, so that men are without excuse (Romans 1:19-20).

In other words, all people realize inherently in their heart that there is a standard of right and wrong. It is God who has made us, who has put this knowledge in our hearts. Moral absolutes do exist, and what is found in our conscience matches what is found in God's Word.

13 How should Christians respond to pragmatism?

Today's Christians have become increasingly pragmatic in their lifestyles, choosing a "whatever works" mentality toward spiritual matters. Is this a healthy change? Not according to Scripture. In the book of Judges the nation of Israel repeatedly turned from God to do their own thing. The writer said of them, "Everyone did what was right in his own eyes."

Left to make our own decisions based on what we think is right at the moment, we will eventually turn toward our own selfish desires rather than God's ways. What's the proper alternative? Basing your whole life on Scripture, the source of God's truth. When decisions are based on what is right rather than what works, we can be certain that God will be pleased. His glory should be our highest goal.

14 Is there a spiritual significance in certain numbers?

Is there really any spiritual significance behind the use of certain numbers? From the TV show *Lost* to modern Kabbalah, spiritual phenomena have often been associated with various numeric combinations.

But the Bible is clear that God's truth is revealed in his words, not through some mystical interpretation of numbers. Such an emphasis on hidden meanings in numbers was common in the movement called Gnosticism, which focused on knowledge obtained by a privileged few rather than by any man or woman seeking God. This error is still found today. But remember, God promises he is available to everyone who will simply read the Bible. The truth is not a secret. It is available for all who search God's Word today.

15 Is it okay to be superstitious?

Fox News reported a jaw-dropping ritual in India in which infants are allowed to fall 50 feet from a tower onto a blanket to bring them good luck. Though Americans may not toss infants from buildings, many today trust in superstitions, whether it's reading their horoscope or simply wearing a lucky shirt.

But Jesus tells us not to trust in external traditions to know him. In John 1:12 he teaches that to all who receive him and believe in him, he personally gives the right to become God's children. It is only by placing your faith in Jesus, trusting that his death on the cross is the only payment for sin that God accepts, that we enter into an eternal, personal relationship with God.

16 What should Christians think about the "emergent church" movement?

The national media has recently reported on a current theological trend called the "emerging church." The driving force behind the ideas of this movement is that the world is radically changing and the church must change with it.

Yes, each culture requires Christians to understand its ideas, but the message of Christ must remain the same. The problem is, you will find that there is a spectrum of beliefs in this movement's theology. There's not one consistent creed. Beliefs vary from one church to another and even one member to another. For Christians, the underlying question is not how to respond to the emerging church, but how to communicate an unchanging Christ to an ever-changing world.

17 What is Gnosticism?

If you look in the religion section of any major bookstore you'll see an enormous number of titles on Gnosticism. What is Gnosticism? The Gnostics taught that a cosmic battle between good and evil was taking place and believed that all matter was evil. Only spirit was good. (The term for this kind of belief is *dualism*.) Therefore, they said, our evil physical bodies were to be seen as separate from our good spiritual souls. This led to the false belief that Gnostics could practice physical immorality and that it didn't affect any part of their spiritual life. It's also why the Gnostics denied the importance of Jesus' physical resurrection.

You can see why this kind of spirituality is popular. But Jesus denied spiritual dualism and taught he had come to redeem *all* of us—our body, mind, and soul. Jesus calls us to love him with all of our mind, soul, and strength.

18 How can churches navigate cultural change?

Our culture's rapid changes have also caused numerous changes within our local churches. How can we decide which changes are helpful and which changes are harmful for our local congregations?

First, churches must biblically define what must stay the same. This includes what the church believes, as well as why God wants a particular church to exist in its community. Second, while defining what beliefs must not change, a congregation should also discuss what areas need to be different so they can help believers grow and continue to reach new people. A healthy church will constantly evaluate where it stands biblically and where it must step next to make better disciples.

19 Is Jesus still relevant for life today?

Do you think Jesus is really relevant today? People unfamiliar with the facts about him assume he was no different than any other historical religious leader. And so they discredit his teachings as outdated and irrelevant to our postmodern culture. But the truth is, no one has come close to influencing humanity as much as Jesus has. He has been the reason for much of our world's greatest music, our hospitals, universities, and art.

Jesus also impacts people on a personal level. The claims he has made to be God and Savior show that each individual's present and future existence depends on a personal relationship with him. Jesus Christ is certainly relevant today. How is he making an impact on your life?

20 How can Christians respond about the dark spots of church history?

Some skeptics sincerely ask, "Why should I

follow a religion that was involved in the Inquisitions and witch trials?"

First, let's be clear. Those Christians disobeyed the teachings of Jesus, the founder of the Christian faith. They weren't following him well. He taught that we are to love our enemies and pray for those who persecute us. Second, we shouldn't deny that these events really happened. Though skeptics' allegations are at times distorted, even one death during the Crusades was one too many. These people dishonored Christ, and we must show concern for the tragedy they brought about. Third, we must live today in obedience to Christ. We can't change the past, but we can live out his life in our own day, in a manner that honors him and will attract those around us to his true message.

21 How can Christians respond to negative stereotypes of Christianity?

When Christians are portrayed negatively in today's news, how should those of us who believe respond? The easiest option is to become overwhelmed by the bad news and simply tune it out or turn it off.

However, Jesus taught that everyone would

know we are Christians by our love for each other. Instead of hiding from the negative images of Christianity presented in the media, we are commanded by our Lord to show everyday people how a follower of Christ really lives. The apostle Paul's words from Philippians 1:27 provide a remarkable example for us today. He said, whatever happens, conduct yourselves in a manner worthy of the gospel of Christ. If we do, we will find that our lives are impacting those around us.

22 What does the Bible teach about palm reading?

A recent study has shown that more than one-fourth of American teens have had their palm read or their fortune told. Is palm reading an activity acceptable for Christians?

The answer is clearly no. Palm reading originated in Hindu astrology, having the intent to determine a person's personality and predict his or her future. The interpretations, however, are guided by beliefs based on the worship of pagan gods. There is no scientific basis for the practice. It's offered as a psychic or spiritual service. Ultimately palm reading is based on the teachings of other gods rather than Christ. Thus, Christians should avoid this practice. Instead, we should base our future on God's Word and its perfect plan for our lives and the hope for our future.

23 What does the Bible say about talking with spirits?

Today, 10 percent of American teenagers claim to have communicated with the spirit of a dead person. What does the Bible say about talking with spirits?

Isaiah 8:19 says,

> When men tell you to consult mediums and spiritists, who whisper and mutter, should not a people inquire of their God? Why consult the dead on behalf of the living?

God condemns this kind of prying into the spirit world because there are spirits out there that are more intelligent than we are, and they want to deceive us. Instead, God challenges us to come to him for true information and real experiences. While paranormal experiences may seem exciting or stimulating, God is the only Source who provides truth for our lives.

24 Are Christians really under persecution today?

Did you know that it's illegal to share Christ in

51 countries around our world? What can we do to help those persecuted for their faith?

First, we must pray for those in places where physical suffering is a reality. While rare in America, prison, beatings, or even death await those who convert to Christianity in many countries of the world. Second, get involved in ministries already helping the persecuted church. Your local church is probably already helping in such efforts. Third, speak up for the persecuted. Start by living out your faith and then telling others the good news of Christ. If it has been awhile since you told someone how he has changed your life, do it today.

25 Why is prophecy important?

Someone once said that you'd better care about the future, because you're going to spend the rest of your life there. The prophecies of the Bible are an essential part of both the Bible and the Christian life. How?

First, realize that close to one-third of the Bible contains prophecy. Second, the eternal God gave prophecy not only to prove that he exists, but to call his followers to a deeper spiritual walk with him in the present. Billy Graham used to say, "I've read the last chapter of the book, and I know that in the end we win." The apostle Paul, after describing the glorious events of the rapture in 1 Thessalonians 4, told Christians, "Therefore encourage one another with these words." Prophecy is an important part of Scripture that is useful for our lives now.

26 What do Americans believe about how to obtain eternal life?

The Pew Forum on Religion in Public Life surveyed 35,000 Americans and found that 75 percent believe that many religions can lead to eternal life. Even more remarkable was the fact that 57 percent of evangelical Christians were willing to accept that faith in Jesus might not be the only path to salvation.

But Jesus clearly taught in John 14:6, "I am the way and the truth and the life. No one comes to the Father except through me." Christ loves people of all backgrounds, but presents only one way to spend eternity with him. If we believe his words, we must continue to share the message that *only* faith in Jesus Christ leads to eternal life.

27 Does church matter?

Some Christians have become disillusioned

with their church and have chosen to quit altogether, even though they say they still love Jesus. What does God think about this? Well, God sees the church as being the bride of Christ, illustrating its utmost importance to him. Wouldn't it be good for us to realize that there are many aspects of the Christian life that we cannot live out alone? Biblically, we are called to love one another, serve one another, and encourage one another. Each of these commands is impossible without interaction with other believers.

Of course, no church is perfect. But instead of quitting on church, choose to become part of the solution. Make it better by living out the commands of our Lord.

28 Why should I vote?

Why should I vote? Maybe you've heard a friend ask the question or have even wondered this yourself. Do our votes really make a difference? Well, as Americans, our vote is our voice. As Christians, we are called by God to voice our biblical values. Choosing not to vote is choosing to allow other voices to determine the future of our nation. We cannot afford to sit out in an election when critical

Christian issues hang in the balance: moral concerns including the family unit, the lives of the unborn, national security, and decisions regarding religious freedoms are all issues often at stake during national elections. As Christ's representatives, we are called to speak out on the issues that matter most. Be informed and vote your values. Be a voice and a force for good with your choice.

29 When does life begin?

How would you answer the question, "When does human life begin?" Is it at conception, upon exiting the womb, or at some point in between? Some argue these questions are religious issues. However, in 1971, two years before *Roe vs. Wade,* 220 medical experts submitted a brief to the U.S. Supreme Court testifying that the scientific and medical evidence showed life exists from the point of conception. One example they shared was that in the seventh week, the unborn child bears the familiar external features and all the internal organs of an adult. After the eighth week, everything is already present that will be found in the full-term baby. Life begins at conception according to both science and Scripture.

30 Redefining marriage—what does the Bible teach?

How should we respond to those who seek to redefine marriage in our culture? First, the family is the foundation of society. To change the family unit is to change society. This has been demonstrated through the weakening of the family unit through the epidemic of divorce. To further dismantle the traditional family through same-sex marriage poses a tremendous risk to our culture. Second, the Bible repeatedly calls homosexual activity sin. Christians must continue to embrace this often controversial truth. However, we are also called to communicate compassion toward all people.

Stand firm on the issue of family, using your life to show an example of how a person of God lives out faith in a culture where the definition of marriage is at stake.

31 What is "hate crime," and why does it matter?

One issue under discussion at the national level is hate crimes. What are hate crimes? They are defined as acts or words of discrimination toward other people. They can include racial slurs, gender discrimination, and even religious teachings. For instance, one Canadian pastor was arrested for preaching that homosexuality was a sin. Another was sentenced to community service for claiming Muslims would go to hell for not believing in Jesus.

Hate crime law is not designed to help end discrimination. It is a legal change that could be used to silence the religious convictions of Christians. Use your voice to show love rather than hate. Show that the Christ you follow desires to show his love to all who will place their trust in him.

32 Is the fairness doctrine fair?

The fairness doctrine has been the law in our country before. Though it was thrown out, it is now once again a topic of debate. What is the fairness doctrine? Simply put, the fairness doctrine would require all broadcasters to allow equal time on controversial topics. This would include radio talk shows, but could also apply to Christian ministries. For example, a Bible teaching program could be required by law to cut its time in half to allow a non-Christian to share why they disagree with everything just taught.

A fairness doctrine law would destroy virtually every Christian radio and television program on the air today. Pray that God would continue to keep it from being enacted. Pray, too, for those Christians who continue to communicate God's truth through media to effectively reach others with the message of Christ's perfect love.

33 Can legalizing same-sex marriage hurt the traditional family?

Could legalizing same-sex marriage truly hurt the traditional family? It definitely could. When a culture is taught that a healthy family can exist apart from the influence of both a father and a mother, it devalues the importance of fatherhood, motherhood, and the family unit. The Bible clearly mentions the infinite value of God's design for family. Ephesians 5 calls husbands and wives to serve one another in love, to care for their children in ways unique to both father and mother, and to honor God with their lives. Each of these values requires a traditional family.

Don't believe the lie that same-sex marriage will not affect your family. Continue to stand for the Bible's view of marriage whether others agree or not.

34 How would Jesus vote?

How do you think Jesus would vote today?

While we certainly don't have all of the answers on this, we can make some clear observations based on Scripture. First, he would vote according to biblical values. This would require knowing where candidates stand on moral issues. Second, he would look beyond the words of candidates. Politicians often shine in the spotlight, but God looks at the heart. Moral character is of utmost importance to him. Finally, he would pray for all candidates involved. In fact, 1 Timothy 2 calls us to pray for our leaders regardless of where they stand on the issues. Be like Jesus. Vote your values; pray for all candidates involved.

35 How should Christians handle Halloween?

Halloween has become a major holiday season in America, second only to Christmas in terms of how much Americans spend. But how should Christians deal with the dark spirituality surrounding it?

First, we cannot naively condone the practices of Halloween. It is a celebration of spirits and a holy day of those involved in witchcraft. As Christians, we must be distinctly different. But how can we celebrate Halloween in a way that honors God?

One option is to choose not to celebrate it at all. Also, as Christians, we can use this night to point people toward Jesus and share the good news of Jesus Christ, as do some believers who celebrate it as Reformation Day. Regardless, our emphasis must be to provide a distinct alternative to Halloween and shine as bright lights on a dark night.

36 How can I share my faith in the workplace?

When the discussion of God or faith comes up in your workplace, how do you respond? According to one survey, the vast majority of Americans feel underequipped to share their faith.

If you are one of them, then begin by determining that you will live out your faith so others can see it. Second, open your Bible and start to read it on a regular basis. You cannot share what you do not know. Then, third, become true friends of those in your workplace. The more others trust you, the more willing they'll be to listen to your perspective on the faith issues that arise. It's never easy, but talking about Christ is possible in the workplace. Ask God to teach you, use you, and give you the courage to share the hope that is within you (1 Peter 3:15-16).

37 How can we help people live according to their beliefs about the Bible?

A recent Barna survey revealed the amazing fact that 84 percent of Americans agree the Bible is a holy book. How can we help people move from agreeing that the Bible is a holy book to living its teachings? First, we must be changed by it ourselves. We naturally talk about what is most important to us. If the Bible is changing you, you'll be able to tell others about it more easily. Second, refer to it. In other words, mention the Bible when talking about issues with others. Say, "You know, the Bible talks about this too." This is a simple phrase anyone can use to insert what God shares on a topic. Remember, many believe the Bible is a sacred book, but they need to see you living it out.

38 Why attend church?

The Pew Forum on Religion in Public Life found that only 58 percent of evangelical Christians attend worship services on a weekly basis. Is the church no longer necessary? Are Christians fine without regularly gathering with other believers?

Not according to Hebrews 10:25. In that verse of the Bible, we read, "Let us not give up meeting together...but let us encourage one another—and all the more as you see the Day approaching [referring to the return of Christ]." Our goal and desire should be to gather with other believers for worship on a regular basis. According to God's plan, we are much better growing together than on our own. Attending church isn't always easy, but it *is* God's desire for his followers.

How *to* Begin *a* Personal Relationship *with* God

If you would like to begin a personal relationship with God that promises joy, forgiveness, and eternal life, you can do so right now:

1. Believe that God exists and that he sent his Son, Jesus Christ, in human form to Earth (John 3:16; Romans 10:9).
2. Accept God's free gift of new life which he offers you through the death and resurrection of his only Son, Jesus Christ (Ephesians 2:8-9).
3. Commit to following God's plan for your life (1 Peter 1:21-23; Ephesians 2:1-7).

4. Determine to make Jesus Christ the ultimate Leader and final authority of your life (Matthew 7:21-27; 1 John 4:15).

There is no magic formula or special prayer to begin your relationship with God. However, the following prayer is one that can be used to accept his free gift of salvation through Jesus Christ by faith:

> "Dear Lord Jesus, I admit I have sinned. I know I cannot save myself. Thank you for dying on the cross and taking my place. I believe your death was for me, and I receive your sacrifice on my behalf. I transfer all of my trust from myself and turn all of my desires over to you. I open the door of my life to you and by faith receive you as my Savior and Lord, making you the ultimate Leader of my life. Thank you for forgiving my sins and giving me eternal life. Amen."

If you have made this decision, congratulations! You have just made the greatest commitment of your life. As a new follower of Jesus, you will have many questions as you begin your new spiritual adventure. Here are some ways you can grow in your new relationship with God:

- Spend regular time in prayer and Bible reading.
- Find a Bible-teaching church where you can grow with other followers of Christ.
- Seek opportunities to tell others about Jesus through acts of service and everyday conversations.

For more information on growing in your relationship with God, please go to www.johnankerberg.org. You can also receive additional materials by contacting us at

The Ankerberg Theological Research Institute
PO Box 8977
Chattanooga, TN 37414
Phone: (423) 892-7722

PRAYING *for* THOSE WHO DO NOT BELIEVE

The Scriptures provide several ways for us to pray for those who do not know Jesus. However, it is often a daunting task to choose where to begin. The following outline of verses is designed to assist you in offering biblical prayers for those who do not believe.

1. Pray for God to draw the person to himself.

   "No one can come to me unless the Father who sent me draws him" (Jesus, in John 6:44).

2. Pray that the person would desire God.

   "In their distress they turned to the LORD, the God of Israel, and sought him, and he was found by them" (2 Chronicles 15:4).

   "God did this so that men would seek him and perhaps reach out for him and find him, though he is not far from each one of us" (Acts 17:27).

3. Pray for an understanding and acceptance of God's Word.

   "Faith comes from hearing the message, and the message is heard through the word of Christ" (Romans 10:17).

   "We also thank God continually because, when you received the word of God, which you heard from us, you accepted it not as the word of men, but as it actually is, the word of God, which is at work in you who believe" (1 Thessalonians 2:13).

4. Pray that Satan would not blind them.

   "When anyone hears the message about the kingdom and does not understand it, the evil one comes and snatches away what was sown in his heart" (Matthew 13:19).

   "The god of this age has blinded the minds of unbelievers, so that they cannot see the light of the gospel of the glory of Christ, who is the image of God" (2 Corinthians 4:4).

5. Pray that the Holy Spirit would convict them of sin.

   "When he comes, he will convict the world of guilt in regard to sin and righteousness and judgment" (John 16:8)

6. Pray for someone to share Christ with them.

   "Ask the Lord of the harvest...to send out workers into his harvest field" (Matthew 9:38).

7. Pray God provides his grace and repentance. (Repentance is a change of mind that leads to changed behavior.)

   "Repent...and turn to God, so that your sins may be wiped out, that times of refreshing may come from the Lord" (Acts 3:19).

   "It is by grace you have been saved, through faith—and this not from yourselves, it is the gift of God—not by works, so that no one can boast" (Ephesians 2:8-9).

8. Pray that they believe and entrust themselves to Jesus as Savior.

   "To all who received him, to those who believed in his name, he gave the right to become children of God" (John 1:12).

   "I tell you the truth, whoever hears my word and believes him who sent me has eternal life and will not be condemned; he has crossed over from death to life" (John 5:24).

9. Pray that they confess Jesus as Lord.

"If you confess with your mouth, 'Jesus is Lord,' and believe in your heart that God raised him from the dead, you will be saved. For it is with your heart that you believe and are justified, and it is with your mouth that you confess and are saved" (Romans 10:9-10).

10. Pray they continue to grow spiritually and learn how to surrender all to follow Jesus.

"Jesus said to his disciples, 'If anyone would come after me, he must deny himself and take up his cross and follow me'" (Matthew 16:24).

"Whatever was to my profit I now consider loss for the sake of Christ. What is more, I consider everything a loss compared to the surpassing greatness of knowing Christ Jesus my Lord, for whose sake I have lost all things. I consider them rubbish, that I may gain Christ" (Philippians 3:7-8).

"Just as you received Christ Jesus as Lord, continue to live in him, rooted and built up in him, strengthened in the faith as you were taught, and overflowing with thankfulness" (Colossians 2:6-7).

About the Ankerberg Theological Research Institute

Asking tough questions...Offering real answers

Mission Statement

The Ankerberg Theological Research Institute (ATRI) is a Christian media organization designed to investigate and answer today's critical questions concerning issues of spirituality, popular culture, and comparative religions.

> "But in your hearts set apart Christ as Lord. Always be prepared to give an answer to everyone who asks you to give the reason for the hope that you have. But do this with gentleness and respect, keeping a clear conscience, so that those who speak maliciously against your good behavior in Christ may be ashamed of their slander."
>
> —1 Peter 3:15-16

ATRI utilizes five strategies to accomplish this mission:

- *The John Ankerberg Show.* Our award-winning weekly TV program is broadcast into all 50 states and 200 countries worldwide via satellite. Our documentaries have also been featured as nationwide television specials.

- *ATRI Radio*. ATRI reaches thousands of people through its weekend one-hour program and one-minute daily radio commentary airing on nearly 700 outlets.
- *JohnAnkerberg.org*. ATRI's Web site reaches over 3.1 million unique visitors per year from 184 countries.
- *ATRI Resources*. In addition to nearly 100 combined published books and 3 million books sold by ATRI authors in 16 languages, its resources include over 2,500 free online articles, audio programs, and video programs.
- *ATRI Events*. Founder Dr. John Ankerberg has personally spoken to over 1 million people during his speaking and seminars in dozens of countries spanning five continents.

Due to ATRI's advanced research and long-standing work, founder and president Dr. John Ankerberg is regularly quoted by media including NBC, ABC, Daystar, and INSP. A board member for many Christian media organizations, Dr. Ankerberg also serves on the board of directors for the National Religious Broadcasters Association.

About the Authors

Dr. John Ankerberg is host of the award-winning *John Ankerberg Show*, which is on TV and radio in all 50 states and 200 countries. He has authored nearly 100 books, and his research is used by universities and experts worldwide on world religion and the evidence for Christianity. A graduate of Trinity Evangelical Divinity School and Luther Rice Seminary, he lives in Tennessee.

JohnAnkerberg.org

Dillon Burroughs is staff writer for *The John Ankerberg Show* and author or coauthor of 26 books, including *What Can Be Found in LOST?* and the revised Facts On series (with John Ankerberg and John Weldon—over 2 million sold). Dillon is a graduate of Dallas Theological Seminary and lives with his wife and children in Tennessee.

readdB.com

Other Resources from John Ankerberg and Dillon Burroughs

Taking a Stand for the Bible

Many so-called experts today are spreading inaccurate or biased information about the Bible. *Taking a Stand for the Bible* helps set the record straight, answering some of the most important questions both Christians and non-Christians are asking, including:

- How did we get the Bible?
- How accurate is the Bible?
- Is the Bible still relevant to us today?

You'll find helpful and well-documented answers backed by careful research. All of this together points to remarkable evidence that affirms the Bible's integrity and reliability.

What Can Be Found in *LOST*?

Insights on God and the Meaning of Life from the Popular TV Series

In one of the most popular TV series of all time, the characters struggle with issues of identity, conflict, relationships, and spirituality. The authors offer practical suggestions to make *Lost* a useful "point of reference" for talking effectively to others about spiritual themes such as the selfish bent of human nature and the darkness of evil; the hunger people have for acceptance and success; and the realization of our need for hope and for God.

What's the Big Deal About Other Religions?

Answering the Questions About Their Beliefs and Practices

With so many different religions, how can anyone know what to believe? The search for answers begins by going back to the basics—how these religions began, what they teach, and evaluating the validity of their claims. That's the goal of authors John Ankerberg and Dillon Burroughs as they share the core essentials about Christianity, Islam, Mormonism, Wicca, New Age religions, atheism, and many others.

Current research, comparative charts, and thoughtful analysis all work together to make this a valuable resource for those who desire clarity in their quest for truth.

To learn more about books from John Ankerberg,
Dillon Burroughs, and John Weldon
or to read sample chapters, go to our Web site:

www.harvesthousepublishers.com

The Supermarket Guide

Food Choices for You and Your Family

written for
The American Dietetic Association

by
Mary Abbott Hess, LHD, MS, RD, FADA

CHRONIMED PUBLISHING

Library of Congress Cataloging-in-Publication Data

The supermarket guide/ The American Dietetic Association

p. cm.

Includes index.

ISBN 1-56561-110-1: $5.95

Edited by: Jeff Braun
Cover Design: Terry Dugan Design
Text Design & Production: David Enyeart
Art/Production Manager: Claire Lewis

Printed in the United States of America

Published by
Chronimed Publishing
P.O. Box 59032
Minneapolis, MN 55459-9686

10 9 8 7 6 5 4 3 2 1

NOTICE:

CONSULT A HEALTH CARE PROFESSIONAL

Readers are advised to seek the guidance of a licensed physician, registered dietitian, or health care professional before making changes in health care regimens, since each individual case or need may vary. This book is intended for informational purposes only and is not for use as an alternative to appropriate medical care. While every effort has been made to ensure that the information is the most current available, new research findings and product reformulations may invalidate some information.

The American Dietetic Association is the largest group of food and nutrition professionals in the world. As the advocate of the profession, the ADA serves the public by promoting optimal nutrition, health, and well-being.

For expert answers to your nutrition questions, call the ADA/National Center for Nutrition and Dietetics Hot Line at 900/CALL-AN-RD (900/225-5267), and speak directly with a registered dietitian (RD). To listen to recorded messages, or obtain a referral to an RD in your area, call 800/366-1655.

Mary Abbott Hess, LHD, MS, RD, FADA
assisted by Jane Grant Tougas

The American Dietetic Association

Reviewers:

Heather Earls, RD
American Heart Association
Chicago, Illinois

Shari Steinback, MS, RD
Spartan Stores
Grand Rapids, Michigan

Susan Sundram, MS, RD
Shaw's Supermarket, Inc.
East Bridgewater, Massachusetts

Technical Editor:

Raeanne Sutz Sarazen, RD
The American Dietetic Association
Chicago, Illinois

Contents

Chapter 1—Healthy Foods, Healthy Eating.......1

Chapter 2—It's On the Label 9

Chapter 3—Stretching Your Food Dollar 25

Chapter 4—Up and Down the Aisles 41

Bread, Cereal, Rice, and Pasta 42

Breads and Bread Products

Baking Mixes

Cereal

Pasta, Rice, and Grains

Crackers

Cookies, Bars, and Snack Cakes

Packaged Snack Foods

Vegetables 63

Fresh

Frozen

Canned and Bottled

Fruits 81

Fresh

Frozen

Canned and Bottled

Dried

Milk, Yogurt, and Cheese 98

Milk and Milk Alternatives

Yogurt and Yogurt Products

Cheese and Cheese Products
Puddings and Custards
Meat, Poultry, Fish, Dry Beans, Eggs, and Nuts 113
Beef, Pork, Lamb, Veal, and Game Meats
Poultry and Game Birds
Fish and Seafood
Packaged Meats/Cold Cuts
Legumes
Eggs and Egg Substitutes
Nuts and Seeds/Nut Butters
Fats, Oils, and Sweets 143
Butter, Margarine, and Spreads
Cooking Fats
Vegetable Oils
Salad Dressings
Cream and Cream Substitutes
Frozen Desserts
Sugars, Syrups, Sweet Sauces, and Toppings
Jellies and Fruit Spreads
Combined Foods 164
Soups, Sauces, and Dips
Prepared Entrées
Baked Desserts
Deli Choices and Carry-Out Foods

Beverages..174
Coffee, Tea, and Cocoa
Soft Drinks, Sports Drinks, Water, and Flavored Waters
Wine, Beer, and Liquor
Seasonings and Condiments....................181
Baking Basics..184

Chapter 5—Keeping Food Safe 187

Index..195

Chapter 1

Healthy Foods, Healthy Eating

It's no secret that health and well-being are influenced by the choices we make in life. Even common, everyday choices have an impact. Take the food you eat, for instance. Over time, healthy eating habits can promote excellent health. They can also help you boost resistance to illness.

Making healthy food choices is what this book is all about. Use it as an aisle-by-aisle supermarket guide to making informed decisions about the food you buy for yourself and your family.

As you know, there's no shortage of choices to be made at the supermarket. Is corn on your shopping list? Should it be fresh, frozen, or canned? How about cereal? Should you go with a granola type or is presweetened OK?

And then there's the sometimes confusing nutrition and ingredient information on labels. What exactly does it mean and how should it influence your shopping decisions? Not to be forgotten is the important element of food prices. Is a whole chicken a better buy than pre-cut pieces even if you have to discard bones and other parts?

This handy book provides the answers to these and hundreds more questions.

You will start by learning how to quickly use the nutrition and ingredient labels as you shop, as well as evaluate health claims touted on packaging. To make shopping an even more rewarding experience, you'll receive tips on getting more for your food dollar.

Then, in Chapter 4, we'll take a close look at specific foods organized by food groups. Not only will you find out which foods give you the biggest nutrition bang for your buck—those that are nutrient-rich but moderate in calories, fat, sugar, and salt—but you'll probably find many new food options to look for and try. And the "Shoppers Should Know" sections will provide new and interesting facts to make you a more discerning shopper: how foods in each group compare to each other, current nutrition information, and food safety and storage tips.

Finally, in Chapter 5, you'll find even more food safety recommendations.

Nutrition Guidelines

The advice provided within this book follows the recommendations of the Dietary Guidelines for Americans. These seven guidelines, which are the basis for nutrition policy in the United States, promote a healthful diet for people 2 years of age and older.

The Dietary Guidelines for Americans

1. **Eat a variety of foods** to get the energy, protein, vitamins, minerals, and fiber you need for good health.
2. **Balance the food you eat with physical activity—maintain or improve your weight** to reduce your chances of developing a problem associated with being overweight, such as high blood pressure, heart disease, a stroke, certain cancers, and adult-onset diabetes.
3. **Choose a diet with plenty of grain products, vegetables, and fruits.** These foods provide needed vitamins, minerals, fiber, and complex

carbohydrates for good health and can help you lower your fat intake.

4. **Choose a diet low in fat, saturated fat, and cholesterol** to reduce your risk of heart disease and certain types of cancer. High levels of saturated fat and cholesterol in the diet are linked to increased blood cholesterol levels and obesity.
5. **Choose a diet moderate in sugars.** Some foods that contain a lot of sugar supply too many calories and too few nutrients for most people and can contribute to tooth decay.
6. **Choose a diet moderate in salt and sodium,** which may help reduce your risk of high blood pressure.
7. **If you drink alcoholic beverages, do so in moderation.** Alcoholic beverages supply calories but little or no nutrients. Drinking alcohol is also the cause of many health problems and accidents and can lead to addiction.

The challenge is to translate this advice into realistic food choices. For instance, nearly everyone buys some high-calorie, high-sugar, and high-sodium foods because they are their favorites or because the occasion is special.

Fortunately, there is room in a healthy diet for any favorite food—particularly if you eat moderate portions.

That necessary flexibility is reflected in the Food Guide Pyramid, which the federal government designed to ensure variety and the availability of nutrients essential to good health. The Pyramid (see page 7) graphically groups together foods that provide similar nutrients and suggests the number of daily servings to eat from each group.

Every healthy person, age 2 and older, should follow the Pyramid's guidelines and eat more servings of foods from the base of the Pyramid (grain products, vegetables, and fruits) and fewer servings of foods from the tip (sugars and fats). This will not only provide the nutrients that you and your family need but will help you to achieve or maintain a healthy weight.

Each food group contains a number of choices. Different foods within the same group provide varying amounts of fat, saturated fat, cholesterol, sugar, and sodium. For example, you can have your sandwich on a French bread roll that provides 1 gram of fat or on a croissant that provides 12 grams of fat. Both of these 2-ounce bread portions count as 2 servings from the grain group but have differing amounts of fat and calories.

Remember, all foods can fit into a healthy diet, but it takes knowledge and practice to learn which foods should be eaten most often and which foods should be chosen less frequently.

Eating should bring pleasure, comfort, and joy, and not create feelings of deprivation or guilt. But do yourself a favor. Try to balance your "indulge me" favorites with plenty of foods listed in Chapter 4's "Look For" sections. That way, your entire market basket will provide you and your family with a total diet that promotes wonderful eating and good health.

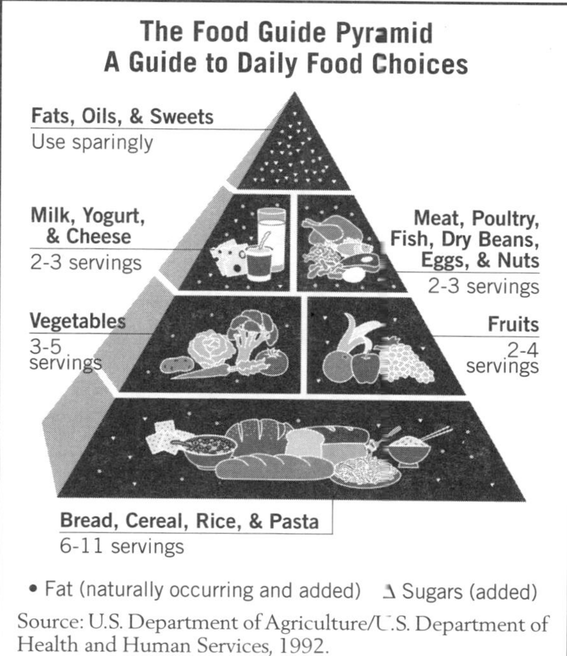

Source: U.S. Department of Agriculture/U.S. Department of Health and Human Services, 1992.

Chapter 2

It's On the Label

Smart shoppers take full advantage of the government-mandated labeling system that provides a wealth of nutrition information in a standard format. Everything from the Nutrition Facts panel to the ingredient list to the regulated descriptive terms on the front of the label will help you compare foods and make choices that better meet your health needs.

Although most foods sold in supermarkets provide nutrient and ingredient information right on the package, certain foods are exempt from labeling laws. These foods include fresh products, such as raw fruits, vegetables, seafood, poultry, and meat that would be difficult to label; products from very small manufacturers who may not be able to afford to label; and foods that provide little or no nutrients, such as coffee, tea, and water.

Although not required, many stores provide information on vegetables, fruits, meat, and seafood or on signs where the food is sold. And some manufacturers of bottled water, particularly fruit-flavored waters with no calories, choose to provide label information. Foods with small or unusual package sizes are permitted to use a modified label format. Foods for babies and children under 2 years of age use a different label format based on the nutrients young eaters need.

Manufacturers may list nutrients beyond the ones required and sometimes choose to do so, particularly if a food is an excellent source of a nutrient.

The Nutrition Facts Label

Using the Nutrition Facts food label is a key strategy for healthy eating. Directly under the label's "Nutrition Facts" title appears a serving size and the number of servings in the container. This information is important because the calories and nutrient data on the rest of the label relate to the specified portion size which may be as small as 1 teaspoon or as large as 1 cup.

Nutrition Facts

Serving Size 1 cup (248g)
Servings Per Container 4

Amount Per Serving

Calories 150 Calories from Fat 35

	% Daily Value*
Total Fat 4g	**6%**
Saturated Fat 2.5g	**12%**
Cholesterol 20mg	**7%**
Sodium 170mg	**7%**
Total Carbohydrate 17g	**6%**
Dietary Fiber 0g	**0%**
Sugars 17g	
Protein 13g	

Vitamin A 4% • Vitamin C 6%

Calcium 40% • Iron 0%

* Percent Daily Values are based on a 2,000 calorie diet. Your daily values may be higher or lower depending on your calorie needs:

	Calories:	2,000	2,500
Total Fat	Less than	65g	80g
Sat Fat	Less than	20g	25g
Cholesterol	Less than	300mg	300mg
Sodium	Less than	2,400mg	2,400mg
Total Carbohydrate		300g	375g
Dietary Fiber		25g	30g

Calories per gram:
Fat 9 • Carbohydrate 4 • Protein 4

When comparing food labels on similar items, first look to be sure that the portions are the same. For foods in single-serving containers, a portion is usually the whole container. For example, you may see 4-, 6-, and 8-ounce single-serving packages of yogurt as well as quart containers. However, if you compare labels for nutrients without realizing the differences in portion size, you will be misled. All the nonfat yogurts, for example, will probably have similar nutrient values for the same size portions.

It is also important to adjust the stated serving size to what you will actually eat. If the label says that a serving is 3 ounces of meat, and you will eat 6 ounces, expect to enjoy twice the calories and nutrients.

The next part of the label lists eight nutrients, their % Daily Values, and how much of each nutrient is in a serving. Total fat, cholesterol, sodium, total carbohydrate, dietary fiber, sugars, and protein are included.

Some nutrients listed on the label are probably more important to you than others, depending on your individual needs and health concerns. Most people are concerned about choosing a heart-healthy diet low in total fat and saturated fat. Unless your blood cholesterol is high, you may not need to pay much attention to the amount of cholesterol in the food you eat. Only about 10 percent of the general population experience elevated blood cholesterol levels from cholesterol found in food. Diets high in total fat, particularly saturated fats, are much more likely to raise your blood cholesterol level.

Sodium may be important to you if your blood pressure is elevated. People with diabetes must be aware of total carbohydrate intake, and vegetarians need to ensure adequate iron, calcium, and vitamin B_{12} intake. People with kidney problems usually need to restrict protein and sodium and monitor potassium intake.

The dietary fiber information appearing on the label is not used as often as it should be. Most Americans don't eat enough dietary fiber. Fiber helps you lower the risk of heart disease and certain cancers, and reduces constipation, while aiding in weight control. Most of us should be seeking more sources of dietary fiber from grains, vegetables, legumes, and whole fruits.

% Daily Value: What Does It Mean?

You can use the % Daily Value (DV) as a general guide to finding good sources of some nutrients, maintaining low intakes of others (such as fat and saturated fat), and comparing the nutrient levels of similar food. Selecting foods that are good or excellent sources of vitamins and minerals is wise unless you have a medical problem that benefits from restricting one of these nutrients.

Basically, 100 percent of the % Daily Value for each nutrient is an estimate of an appropriate daily amount of that nutrient to be obtained from a variety of foods in a 2,000-calorie daily diet. If a particular food provides 0 to 9 percent of the % Daily Value for a nutrient, it is not a good source of that nutrient. Good sources or nutrients fall between 10 and 19 percent of the Daily Value. But if it provides 20 percent or more of the % Daily Value, it is rich in that particular nutrient and an excellent source.

More is not always better, though. Try not to exceed the 100% Daily Value for fat, saturated fat, cholesterol, or sodium on most days. But try to seek greater percentages—at least 100 percent of the Daily Value—for fiber, vitamins, and minerals (except sodium) because these nutrients promote health and help prevent certain diseases.

The portion of the label listing vitamin A, vitamin C, calcium, and iron gives only percentages of the Daily Values and not the actual amount of these nutrients. Vitamins A and C build strong cell walls and promote resistance to infections; calcium and iron protect against osteoporosis and anemia, respectively.

Daily Value percentages on the Nutrition Facts food label are based on a 2,000-calorie daily intake, but you may need more or fewer calories to maintain a healthy weight. Adjusting daily calories will change percentages of some nutrients.

Few people, however, have the time or inclination to measure, record, and adjust food choices or amounts to ensure they reach 100 percent of the Daily Values. Even though specific percentages may not apply to your diet, you can still use % Daily Values to see which foods are sources of key nutrients. For example, if fat, cholesterol, or sodium is restricted in your diet, think twice about foods that provide more than 10 percent of the Daily Value of those substances in a single serving.

Label Battles

A few controversies about nutrition labels are still brewing. For example, the label breaks out saturated fat from the total fat numbers. At this time, manufacturers are not required to list amounts of other types of fat— monounsaturated or polyunsaturated fat—although manufacturers of some products high in monounsaturated fat voluntarily list this number.

Some advocates want the government to mandate including trans-fatty acids on the label and to count them as saturated fats. Recent data suggests that trans-fatty acids, a rearranged form of monounsaturated fat, may act like saturated fat in the body. But much research is still needed, and scientific consensus must be reached before this change is made. In the "Shoppers Should Know" sections of Chapter 4, foods with trans-fatty acids are identified for you.

You also may note that there is no % Daily Value listed for sugars, although grams of sugars are listed. Health authorities have not yet agreed on an appropriate Daily Value for sugars for the typical person. The grams of sugars listed on the label include a total of all sources of sugars—both naturally occurring and added. Fruits, some vegetables, and milk contain sugars as a natural part of their composition. Sucrose (table sugar), corn syrup (liquid sugar), or other forms of sugars may be added in food processing. As in homemade foods, manufacturers use various types and amounts of sugars in recipes to provide desired flavors and textures. Naturally occurring and added sugars are used exactly the same way in the body. Some people need to monitor total carbohydrate intake, which includes sugars, to control blood sugar fluctuations or weight.

The Ingredients of a Healthy Diet

Food manufacturers are required to list all ingredients by weight from the most to least. For example, if a canned soup has tomatoes as the first item on its ingredient list, that means the soup contains more tomatoes by weight than anything else. Ingredients found at the end of the list are present in the smallest amounts.

If you have food sensitivities or allergies you should carefully read the ingredient listing to avoid any ingredient that will result in a reaction. Specific questions about ingredients should be directed to the food manufacturer. Many manufacturers offer a toll-free number to answer questions about their products and ingredients.

Making Their Claims

It is hard to miss the food packages that tout special nutritional attributes, such as fat-free or sugar-free. These nutrient content claims, usually printed in big letters and bright colors, can help speed your shopping and expand your food horizons. Checking the front of the product label can help you find fat-free, light, low-fat, and low-calorie foods.

Remember that fresh fruits and vegetables, although not labeled with nutrient content claims, are naturally low in calories, cholesterol-free, and low-fat or fat-free. Some foods labeled low-fat or reduced-fat have other ingredients added that replace many of the calories from fat. For example, some reduced-calorie salad dressings have added sugar for flavor or carbohydrates as thickeners. So always check the Nutrition Facts panel for calories as well as fat.

Some common product label nutrient content claims and their meanings are:

Calorie-free: less than 5 calories per serving

Fat-free or sugar-free: less than 1/2 gram of fat or sugar per serving

Low-calorie: 40 calories or less per serving

Low-sodium: less than 140 milligrams of sodium per serving of most foods; and 140 milligrams or less sodium per 100 grams of complete meals such as frozen dinners

Low-cholesterol: 20 milligrams or less cholesterol and 2 grams or less saturated fat per serving

Reduced: altered to contain 25 percent less of the specified nutrient or calories than the usual product

Good source (of vitamins or minerals): provides 10 to 19 percent or more of Daily Value of that vitamin or mineral per serving

High in: provides 20 percent or more of the Daily Value of the specified nutrient per serving

High fiber: 5 or more grams of fiber per serving

Light foods are altered so that they contain 1/3 fewer calories or 1/2 of the fat of the usual food.

A light food that has most of its calories from fat must reduce fat by at least half.

Foods labeled **healthy** are low in fat and saturated fat and have limited sodium and cholesterol. And most healthy foods must provide at least 10% of the Daily Value of vitamin A, vitamin C, iron, protein, calcium, or fiber. By law, fresh fruits and vegetables all may be called healthy.

Lean meats, poultry, seafood, and game have less than 10 grams of fat, less than 4 1/2 grams of saturated fat and less than 95 milligrams of cholesterol per 3 1/2 ounce cooked serving.

Extra lean meats, poultry, seafood, and game have less than 5 grams of fat, less than 2 grams of saturated fat and less than 95 milligrams of cholesterol per 3 1/2 ounce cooked serving.

Claims About Health

To help you identify foods that fit into particular diets, the government strictly regulates the health claims that can appear on the front label of packaged foods. Eight areas in which health claims are currently allowed include:

1. A calcium-rich diet may help prevent osteoporosis (thin, fragile bones).

2. Limiting the amount of sodium you eat may help prevent hypertension (high blood pressure).
3. Limiting the amount of saturated fat and cholesterol you eat may help prevent heart disease.
4. Eating fruits, vegetables, and grain products that contain fiber may help prevent heart disease.
5. Limiting the amount of total fat you eat may help reduce your risk for some types of cancer.
6. Eating high-fiber grain products, fruits, and vegetables may help prevent some types of cancer.
7. Eating fruits and vegetables that are low in fat and good sources of dietary fiber, vitamin A, or vitamin C may help prevent some types of cancer.
8. Women eating adequate amounts of folate, a B vitamin, daily throughout their childbearing years may reduce their risk of having a child with a neural tube birth defect.

Other Label Information

Individuals who keep kosher look for one of several symbols on the label that indicate that the food has met particular content, sanitation, and processing standards of an authorized Jewish food inspector. This is entirely voluntary and done in addition to government safety inspection.

The kosher symbols, which appear on a variety of foods throughout the store, do not validate any nutritional qualities. Different certifying groups use these and other symbols.

A few foods carry health warnings for people with special health needs. Foods and beverages made with aspartame, a non-nutritive sweetener, carry warnings for people with phenylketonuria (PKU), a metabolic disease. Aspartame contains the essential amino acid phenylalanine, which can not be properly metabolized by people with PKU. Those with this disease must greatly restrict all protein-containing foods and have no need to use sugar substitutes anyway.

Some individuals are sensitive to sulfites, an additive used in food processing that preserves color and freshness. The words "contains sulfites" can be found on labels of some beer, wine, and dried fruits. Alcoholic beverages also carry warnings for pregnant women that drinking can result in birth defects.

The Truth, The Whole Truth

Remember that manufacturers frequently make changes in the foods they produce based on ingredient prices, preferred flavors, and sales data. By law, what is stated on the label (with small allowances for crop and seasonal differences), must be in the package. It's smart to check the labels on foods you buy frequently to be sure nothing has changed. The information in this book reflects food values of products on the market at press time.

Food manufacturers, especially major ones, are usually careful that the nutrient information on their labels is accurate. There are serious legal consequences for not meeting federal labeling requirements. Unfortunately, some manufacturers are not so careful and have been known to make unsubstantiated and untrue claims about their foods.

Deceptive labeling is not only unfair, it is dangerous for people with food allergies or those who must carefully monitor their intake of specific nutrients for medical reasons. Be especially cautious with foods sold in delis, bakeries, and health food stores, and keep in mind that if something tastes "too good to be true" the label information might be wrong.

If you are concerned about a specific food, talk to a dietitian about it or call the closest regional office of the Food and Drug Administration. FDA consumer affairs officers are excellent sources of information, and they are dedicated fraud-fighters.

Chapter 3

Stretching Your Food Dollar

Most shoppers fill their market baskets with about 75 percent of the same products almost every week. Pay particular attention to economical choices when it comes to the foods you buy repeatedly. A look at your register receipts will tell you which foods to look at closely in terms of price and value. Learn to compare prices and become aware of how much you are paying for value-added convenience items. You can save money by relying on these three tools: a well-planned shopping list, coupons and rebates, and in-store sales.

The Shopping List

Efficient shoppers almost always use a list. Organize your shopping list by food categories, preferably in the aisle-by-aisle layout of the store. Start your shopping list at the first aisle as you enter the store. Develop a standard form that includes foods you typically buy in each category along with space to write down other items you wish to add. Some supermarkets offer printed shopping lists that you can customize to reflect your special needs.

Keep your shopping list handy at home so you can jot down staples you are running out of and fresh foods you have used and want to replace. To finish your list, decide what recipes you will be making in the week to come and what foods you will need.

Plan to use produce that keeps longer in the refrigerator (like broccoli, cabbage, carrots, grapefruit, and tangerines) later in the week and more perishable items like fresh corn, ripe peaches, or Boston lettuce earlier in the week when it is at its peak flavor and texture. If you are buying fruit to eat today or tomorrow, buy it ripe. If you will use it later in the week, buy it less ripe. For example, most stores have bananas ripe and ready-to-eat as well as firmer ones that will be tastier in two or three days.

Use the Food Guide Pyramid to plan meals, and check the "Look For" lists in Chapter 4 for menu ideas and an expanded range of healthful choices.

Be flexible and plan to take advantage of seasonal items. For example, although you may write down zucchini on your list, you may actually choose crookneck or another summer squash variety because the quality is exceptional and the price is right.

In the United States, especially in large supermarkets, we can purchase almost any fruit and vegetable at any time of the year. The highest quality and lowest price for each variety is available during and at the end of its peak growing season. At that time you are likely to see larger quantities of that fruit or vegetable on display and often there will be advertised sales.

To promote variety and to find new flavors you and your family might enjoy, choose several varieties of a fresh fruit or vegetable that is in season. For example, rather than buying four plums or apples, buy one each of four different plums or four different apples and do a home taste comparison.

When making your list, check your refrigerator, freezer, and cupboard to make sure you are not duplicating items you already have. Plan to buy a few impulse items each week—new things to try, snacks that aren't part of your plan, or items that are a better value than what you planned to buy. But try to limit your impulse purchases overall. Impulse items usually come at a premium price—in money, calories, fat, or all three. Try to shop after you have eaten a meal. Impulse purchases are more tempting to hungry shoppers.

Coupons and Rebates

Clip coupons and rebate certificates for products you buy regularly. You'll find them in magazines, newspaper supplements, mailbox flyers, supermarket shelf dispensers, and register tapes.

At the store, compare similar products and package sizes to determine which is the most economical choice. Less-advertised brands, store brands, generic products, or sale items can be less expensive than the branded item with a cents-off coupon. Sometimes, you may prefer a particular brand for its flavor, texture, or some other quality. But when a coupon for another brand offers a significant price advantage, why not give it a try? After trying both products, you can make a more informed choice the next time.

Organize all coupons by product type (salad dressing, frozen pizza, etc.) and put them in order with highest values and those expiring soonest at the beginning of each category. Store coupons often are good only for a few days; manufacturers' coupons usually allow a longer time to buy the product. You may want to use a coupon organizer, paper clips, or envelopes.

Manufacturers and supermarkets issue coupons to build sales and brand loyalty. Some stores promote double or even triple coupons; others limit coupon use to one or two purchases per coupon. Regardless of your store's policies, don't waste time clipping or saving coupons for products that you will never use.

If possible, multiply your savings by using a coupon and mail-in proof of purchase for a rebate for the same product. Refunds and rebates may be in the form of cash, check, a coupon to be used on a future purchase, or a free product sample. Usually, you must mail in a coupon, register receipt, and/or a universal product code seal (bar code) or other packaging to get a rebate. Remember that you are paying postage and supplying an envelope, so obtaining the rebate costs you about 40 cents and it will take several weeks or months to receive. Make sure the rebate is worth your time and effort.

Look for rebate offers not only in newspapers and magazines but also on supermarket bulletin boards, at customer service counters, and on end-of-aisle displays. Some coupon books and value packs will come in the mail. Toll-free customer service lines may add you to their rebate mailing list.

In-Store Sales

Most stores have some foods on sale at special prices. Depending on store size and advertising budget, special prices may be promoted in circulars or newspapers. Many stores offer samples of new or selected products and offer a sale price on the item. Take advantage of the opportunities to taste-test new items before you buy them. When you see an item at a favorable price, consider substituting it for a similar food on your shopping list. Stock up and buy several cans or packages of frozen or canned foods during special sales—but only if you use that food regularly.

Over half of shoppers use frequent shopper programs or savings clubs weekly. Frequent shopper programs offer special prices to patrons who present a customer recognition card. This system gives stores an opportunity to track purchases and gives shoppers additional discounts for shopping regularly at a preferred store or chain. Often, the total amount saved appears on the register tape.

Some stores have "buy one–get one free," two-for-one specials, such as two 5-pound bags of potatoes for the price of one. Shop with a friend and divide the bounty and price, especially if you won't use 10 pounds of potatoes within a week or two. If you get a second item free, and don't expect to use it soon, try to prolong its value to you. For example, sauté and freeze a second package of mushrooms for use later.

Some shoppers go to several stores, selecting the discounted items at each. Consider the value of your time and the cost of mileage. Is an extra 30 or 40 minutes of shopping and transportation time worth more or less than the potential in savings?

Watch for discount value days or for senior discounts if you are eligible for them. Some stores have special days that benefit a worthy organization with a certain percentage of sales. You can support schools, community groups, or charities by doing your shopping on those days.

Working the Aisles

You've probably heard it before, but it's worth repeating: Eat first, then shop. Don't shop when you are hungry or rushed—those are the times you are more likely to indulge in expensive impulse purchases. If time is at a premium, shop when stores aren't crowded—early in the morning, late in the evening, or midweek rather than on weekends. Some stores are open around the clock; others have limited service hours.

Remember that store brands and generic food packages are usually less expensive than national brands, but they vary in quality. Some stores may have a regular brand and a premium one. Take a moment to check nutritional information, ingredients, and size of package. The only way to compare flavor and texture, though, is to try it. Some stores offer samples of new items or foods being promoted. This gives you a chance to taste before spending money on a new food or brand.

There are many foods that provide similar nutrients at widely varying cost levels. By making a decision to select the lowest-priced options, you can achieve substantial savings every time you shop.

To get the most for your food dollar, compare different forms of a food. For example, chicken breasts (typically $2.69 per pound) are far more costly than a whole chicken (typically 79 cents to $1.29 per pound). Expect to pay 10 to 20 cents more per pound for chicken that has been quartered or cut-up. A sharp knife or cleaver and about two minutes can save you more than 50 cents on a 3 1/2-pound chicken. Buy three or four whole chickens when the price is favorable and cut them up. Bag similar pieces in freezer bags in the amount you will cook in one meal or recipe.

Similarly, shredded cheese is more costly than solid cheese. Is the convenience worth the extra money? Can you easily slice or shred cheese at home to save $1.00 or more per pound? Pecan halves are usually more expensive than chopped or broken pecans. As a garnish, you may want halves; but broken or chopped nuts may be fine for cookies or in salads.

Also compare package sizes. Unit prices are usually higher for small packages. Some stores have shelf markers that tell you price per unit. The unit may be an ounce, a quart, or another measure. The best buy is the lowest price per unit. For example, a 22-ounce pizza at $4.79 (22 cents per ounce) is a better value than a popular brand of deluxe pizza in the 12-ounce size at $3.29 (27 cents per ounce). The store brand on sale for $2.50 for a 22-ounce pizza (11 cents per ounce) is the best choice in terms of price. For shelf stable foods, like rice or pasta, buying a larger size usually makes sense. But buy the economy or family packs only if you can use the whole amount before the food spoils or must be discarded. Buying economy packs of frequently used nonfood items like paper towels or cleaning supplies can save money and is a good strategy if you have space to store them.

Buy only the amount you will need—especially of fresh and perishable food. Purchasing deli foods by weight and purchasing cereal, dried fruit, or nuts from the bulk food section gives you control over amounts. Talk to the person at the meat counter or in the produce section if you want a smaller amount of prepackaged meat or produce. They should be willing to split and repackage a 4-pack of chops or split a bunch of parsley. Buy only as much dried spice and herbs as you will use in a few months; they lose flavor and pungency in prolonged storage. If you need just a little of a vegetable for a recipe, check out the salad bar. It costs more per pound, but you can buy 1/4- or 1/2-cup of sliced mushrooms or peppers for a stir-fry and have no waste.

At the checkout counter, pay attention to the price as the cashier scans each item. Be sure that you are getting the food at prices posted on in-store sales and on packages. Sometimes the price scanned is not the correct or current price. Remember to present coupons for items purchased before the checker begins checking your order. Buying groceries with some credit cards can earn frequent flyer miles. Earning frequent flyer miles makes sense only if you pay off your credit card balance each month, because interest charges will quickly erase any savings.

If your store doesn't carry something you want, ask for it. Many stores will make an effort to supply items or brands their patrons are seeking. The grocery business is very competitive. Consumers will be spending about half a trillion dollars in supermarkets by the year 2000.

Remember, you're the customer, and pleasing customers is what keeps stores in business.

The Price of Convenience

Many people are willing to pay more for the convenience of precut and prepared foods that save time and effort in the kitchen. Prepared foods to carry out or to heat and eat are one of the fastest growing supermarket categories. Although these "home meal replacement" products usually cost more, they save shopping and cooking time, have no waste, and minimize clean-up. If your goal is a quick, healthy meal with no mess, these "value-added" products offer great advantages. You'll find an ever-increasing array of value-added products in the fresh fruit and vegetable section of the store, such as bags of shredded carrots, fresh-squeezed juices, and cut, fresh pineapple. These alternatives are labor-free (for you) but command premium prices. For example, at one store, a pound of fresh carrots costs 59 cents; a bag of shredded carrots costs $1.89 for 8 ounces, or $3.78 per pound. Clearly if you have a few minutes to peel and shred plain carrots, you can save a lot of money.

Almost every store sells stalks of celery as well as bags of celery hearts. At one store, celery is 69 cents per pound, while celery hearts are $1.99. The economical choice is very clear. The large, outer stalks of celery can be used for chopping or for celery sticks.

Some premium-priced, value-added foods save only a few minutes of washing or preparation time. For example, a 3-ounce container of cinnamon sugar for making cinnamon toast costs 93 cents. Mixing ground cinnamon and sugar together takes less than a minute; you probably have both ingredients in your pantry. Three ounces of the homemade mix costs only about 9 cents.

Buying a few ounces or a single serving of mixed ingredients from a salad bar is more costly than buying, cleaning, and combining ingredients; however, there is no waste and your choice is packaged and ready-to-eat. But paying salad bar prices of $2.50 or $2.89 a pound for lettuce or spinach that is just washed and torn is generally a poor value. Bags of ready-to-eat mixed salad greens packaged with a gas that maintains their freshness can cost even more—$1.99 to $2.99

for an 8- to 10-ounce bag (about $4.44 per pound).

Buying frozen loose-packed fruit and vegetables in plastic bags is often an economical choice. (It's harder to use only part of a boxed fruit or vegetable that is in a frozen "brick.") You can pour out only what you need, reseal the bag, and return it to the freezer. Individually quick-frozen berries, peaches, and melon balls usually keep their shape and texture better if eaten while slightly frozen.

Single-serving packages of juices, cereals, yogurt, puddings, snacks, etc., are almost always more costly than the same food purchased in a larger container. Foods for single people and small families tend to carry premium prices. But additional packaging costs may be justified by a product's convenience and portability for lunch boxes and briefcases. Most of the time, however, pouring juice or scooping pudding from a larger container is the economical choice—as long as you can use the entire package while the food is of good quality.

Carbonated beverages are far more economical in 2-liter bottles than in 12-ounce cans or bottles. Once opened, however, they must be used fairly soon. Unless several glasses will be poured, single serving cans are usually a better choice because the quality and flavor remains intact in unopened cans.

Shopping from Home

Some stores have services that allow patrons to call or fax in orders and have the groceries delivered. A new option in some communities is on-line grocery-shopping services in partnership with local markets. This shop-at-home service can save time and is convenient especially if you have a computer and aren't one who feels the need to see, touch, and smell food before you buy it. For people who are homebound and for others who prefer their groceries to be delivered, on-line shopping is a plus. You should expect to pay additional fees for on-line time, delivery, and other electronic services, though. The service lists foods with prices so comparisons can be made and economical choices selected. Some programs will show you nutrition labels and ingredient lists to allow product comparisons. Some on-line services also offer weekly specials and coupons.

Recycling and Environmental Issues

The American Dietetic Association advocates personal and community-based activities to protect the environment and conserve natural resources. Many food and other products sold in the supermarket come in cans, bottles, bags, and other packages that can be recycled.

Do your part by recycling. Some plastic and foil containers and glass jars can be reused several times in your home kitchen or as storage containers. Choose products sold in containers that can be recycled and take advantage of recycling programs at your supermarket and in your community.

Chapter 4

Up and Down the Aisles

Whether it's a neighborhood grocery store or mega supermarket, there are plenty of choices to be made when you shop for food.

Here, in bite-sized pieces, we present information that will help you be an informed shopper. Organized in food groups based on the Food Guide Pyramid, you'll discover the key products or attributes to "Look For" as you make your way down the aisles. Then, we provide more general tips that "Shoppers Should Know"—advice that will help you become a savvy shopper. Through it all, you'll get the information you need to make the healthiest choices for you and your family.

Bread, Cereal, Rice, & Pasta in The Food Guide Pyramid

Bread, Cereal, Rice, & Pasta
6-11 servings

• Fat (naturally occurring and added) Δ Sugars (added)

Source: U.S. Department of Agriculture/U.S. Department of Health and Human Services, 1992.

Breads and Bread Products

Look For

- Whole-grain or multigrain breads and rolls with whole wheat, cracked wheat, spelt, oat, millet, or other whole grains as the first ingredient on the ingredient list.
- Enriched white breads and rolls.
- Breads, rolls, and muffins with 3 grams of fat or less per serving, including soft or crisp bread sticks, bagels, bialys, English muffins, lavosh, flatbreads, matzo, crumpets, pita bread, and soft corn or flour tortillas.
- Breads and muffins made with wheat bran, oat bran, or added pea fiber; bread products labeled "high in fiber" or "good source of fiber."
- Pita pockets, especially whole-grain ones. Fill them for sandwiches or toast them to make snack crackers for dips.
- Ready-made pizza crusts, including whole-wheat ones, for homemade pizza.
- Frozen or chilled pizza crust; Italian and French bread dough.
- Canned New England brown bread with molasses, whole-wheat, and raisins.

- Frozen low-fat waffles and pancakes, including whole-grain varieties.

Shoppers Should Know

The date on the label is a clue to freshness. Packaged bakery products usually have a longer shelf life than homemade items or ones baked in the in-store bakery.

Whole-wheat flour is made from the whole grain including the wheat germ and wheat bran. It is fuller-flavored, has more fiber and is more nutritious than all-purpose flour.

Wheat breads that don't specify whole wheat on the ingredient label are usually made from refined white flour. The first ingredient listed on the label is the primary grain. Some breads have added caramel (brown) color.

Rye and pumpernickel breads, although brown, contain primarily white flour. They are not whole-grain breads.

Enriched breads have the thiamin, niacin, riboflavin, and iron lost during the flour-refining process restored to them. They are more nutritious than unenriched white breads but lack most of the fiber, chromium, copper, folate, magnesium, zinc, vitamin B_6 and vitamin E of whole-grain breads. Folate added to enriched flour makes white breads a good source of folate.

Calcium propionate is an additive (with an excellent safety record) often used to keep bread products fresh longer. The additive provides some additional calcium.

Breads made with recipes that contain no fat (like traditional French or Italian breads) and those without preservatives become stale faster. Buy small loaves that can be used within a day or two. Store them at room temperature in a tightly closed bag. Cut stale bread into cubes and toast for croutons or to make bread crumbs.

Some breads labeled as light use refined cellulose (wood pulp) to provide added fiber. Because refined cellulose is not digested, it provides no calories. Refined cellulose does not carry with it several of the nutrients that accompany the fiber in whole grains.

Prepared garlic bread is usually quite high in fat and carries a premium price. Scrape off excess fat before heating it or make your own by brushing margarine or oil and garlic on French or Italian bread.

Challah and egg breads contain egg yolks and are sources of dietary cholesterol.

Bakery breads often don't have nutrition labeling. Look at the ingredient list to see what fats, flours, and sugars are used.

Some bread products are fortified with calcium. Check the label.

Most biscuits, croissants, scones, doughnuts, sweet rolls, cheese breads, and focaccias are high in fat.

"Giant" muffins, rolls, and biscuits can have four times the calories and fat as regular-sized ones. Look for small muffins, rolls, and biscuits or make your own with reduced-fat mixes or from recipes with little fat.

Flaky bread sticks that are layered twists of dough made with butter contain lots of fat to make and keep them flaky.

Frozen phyllo dough is fat-free. Most recipes call for brushing butter or margarine between layers. You can substitute butter-flavored spray.

Canned, chilled biscuit and roll doughs generally have 5 to 8 grams fat per biscuit or roll.

Lime-treated corn uses calcium chloride to help remove the tough outer hull of corn. This treatment, often used in making traditional corn tortillas, provides extra calcium and improves the protein quality. Most soft corn tortillas sold in supermarkets have little calcium. Check the Nutrition Facts panel.

Traditional fried corn tortilla, tostado, and taco shells are fried in lard. Soft flour and corn tortillas usually have little or no fat. Read ingredient panels to check the type of fat used and the Nutrition Facts panel to see the amount of fat. Choose baked, fat-free, or soft tortillas and similar products most of the time.

Folate, a B vitamin, helps cells divide normally and helps protect against birth defects. There is some medical evidence that increasing folate protects against heart disease. Folate added to enriched flour makes white bread and pasta good sources of folate.

Packaged plain bread crumbs have added salt, 185 to 225 milligrams per 1/4 cup. If sodium is a concern, make soft bread crumbs from leftover bread using a food processor or blender for immediate use. If you plan to keep breadcrumbs on the shelf, toast the bread before crushing it for crumbs.

Wheat-free breads for individuals sensitive to the gluten in wheat include corn tortillas, rice bread, and breads and rolls made with 100 percent rye or spelt flour. Carefully read labels because many breads contain several grains even though the main label may say rye or millet bread.

Baking Mixes

Look For

- Angel food cake mix.
- Light or reduced-fat mixes for cakes, brownies, cookies, and desserts.
- Whole-grain bread and muffin mixes.
- Low-fat quickbread and biscuit mixes.
- Pancake and waffle mixes that can be prepared without added fat, including buttermilk, buckwheat, Swedish, and blueberry varieties, or buy low-fat frozen waffles and pancakes.

- Pizza crust mixes and prepared pizza crusts that have 3 grams of fat or less per serving.

Shoppers Should Know

Most mixes have a two-column Nutrition Facts panel listing both mix alone and baked (prepared) values. The "as prepared" nutrient values are the important ones because they include the ingredients (usually fat, eggs, or milk) used in preparation.

Packaged stuffing mixes are usually low in fat, but the instructions say to add lots of margarine. Add half the recommended amount of margarine and some extra liquid or chopped vegetables for flavor and moistness. To boost calcium intake, replace half of the broth or water in stuffing mix recipes with skim or low-fat milk.

Two egg whites or 1/4 cup of egg substitute can be used to replace each egg called for in baking mixes. Mashed banana, applesauce, prune purée, or tofu can replace eggs in some products such as muffins. When replacing eggs or fat in a recipe, choose an ingredient that has a flavor compatible with the recipe and expect some difference in texture.

Packaged bread mixes for breadmakers command premium prices, often as much as bakery breads.

Cereal

Look For

- Whole-grain cooked and ready-to-eat cereals such as oatmeal and shredded wheat. They're economical and nutrient-rich.
- Cereals with at least 3 grams of fiber and 3 grams or less of fat per serving.
- Vitamin-and-mineral-fortified cereals. Most supply 25% Daily Value for key vitamins and minerals. Some provide 100% Daily Value making them comparable to a multivitamin and mineral supplement pill.
- Cereals with a grain as the first ingredient on the ingredient list.
- Low-fat, grain-based cereal and fruit bars. They make a portable, nutritious breakfast or snack.
- Grain-fruit-nut cereals with whole grains and dried fruits listed as the first three ingredients on the ingredient list.

- Toasted wheat germ, wheat bran, or oat bran to add fiber and nutrients to recipes.

Shoppers Should Know

The date on the box is a guide to shelf life.

Cereals aren't just for breakfast. They can be enjoyed as a light meal or snack, too.

Cereals that have sugar, honey, corn syrup, fructose, molasses, fruit juice sweetener, or malt syrup as the first ingredient contain more sugar than grain.

Eight grams of sugar per serving in a presweetened cereal is equivalent to one rounded spoonful of sugar, the amount many people add from the sugar bowl. If you would sweeten your cereal anyway, there is no reason to avoid presweetened varieties.

Wheat bran is only one of many beneficial fibers. Oats, oat bran, corn bran, and fruit and bean fibers offer heart-healthy benefits; wheat bran promotes regularity.

Wheat germ is rich in folate and other vitamins and minerals. Adding wheat germ to recipes adds a bit of crunch and boosts nutrients. Try it in meat loaves and casseroles, and mixed with bread crumbs whenever bread crumbs are used.

Granola-type cereals, muesli, and cereals with nuts or coconut usually have more fat than plain grain cereals. Reduced- and low-fat granola-type cereals are available.

Fortified cereals usually cost more than nonfortified ones. Because many of the vitamins and minerals in fortified cereals are sprayed on, be sure to drink all the milk left in the bottom of the bowl.

Oatmeal comes in many forms, each with different cooking times and different textures. Some refined types just require the addition of boiling water or 2 minutes of cooking. Steel-cut oats cook in 30 minutes.

Flavored hot cereals may contain added fat and sugar. Instant hot cereals are higher in sodium than regular cooked varieties. Read the labels.

Grits, cream of wheat, and cream of rice are refined grains and have little fiber.

Some cereals, including some brans and granolas, contain saturated fat or partially hydrogenated fat that can raise your blood cholesterol levels. Check the ingredient list and Nutrition Facts panel.

If artificial colors, flavors, sweeteners, or preservatives in cereal are of concern to you, look on the ingredient list to see if these additives are present. BHA, BHT, and TBHQ are added to some cereals as antioxidants and preservatives to maintain their freshness and crispness.

Pasta, Rice, and Grains

Look For

- All pasta, rice, and grain products.
- Pasta in all forms, including whole-wheat pasta.
- Grains including couscous, cornmeal, bulgur, buckwheat, barley, oatmeal, oat bran, quinoa, grits, kasha, cracked wheat, wheat germ, amaranth, kamut, millet, spelt, teff, triticale, wild rice, and brown rice for added nutrients and fiber.
- Lasagna, ravioli, tortellini, and manicotti filled with part-skim ricotta cheese.

Shoppers Should Know

Omitting salt from cooking water for pasta and rice reduces sodium intake.

Fresh pastas cook more quickly than dried pastas but are usually more expensive and should be used within two days of purchase.

Most dried pasta is egg free, with the exception of noodles. Egg noodles have 55 to 70 milligrams of cholesterol per serving. If cholesterol is a problem, choose yolk-free noodles. Fresh pasta is usually made with eggs.

To cut fat, serve pasta with tomato- and vegetable-based sauces instead of butter- and cream-based sauces. Try salsa to season pasta, rice, and grains.

Filled pasta entrées may contain cheese or meat fillings or sauces that are high in fat.

Frozen pasta entrées are often high in fat and sodium. Read labels and compare.

When pastas cook, they usually double in volume. When rice cooks, it usually triples in volume.

Pasta salad mixes often contain high-fat dressing. Check out those with light dressings.

Packaged macaroni and cheese mixes carry dual nutrition labeling—as packaged and as prepared. Look at the prepared values and the size of portion stated. Packaged macaroni and cheese is more economical than macaroni and cheese prepared from scratch. Most macaroni and cheese is high in sodium, whether from a mix, frozen, or prepared from scratch. Fat levels vary depending upon the cheese and other ingredients used.

Brown rice has almost three times the fiber of white rice.

Quick-cooking grains and seasoned grain mixes save time but are higher in sodium and usually carry premium prices.

Many grain and pasta mixes call for added margarine. Use only half the seasoning packet and half the amount of margarine. To save money and reduce fat, add herbs, vegetables, or low-sodium broths to season plain rice or pasta.

Gluten-free grains include amaranth, buckwheat, cornmeal, millet, quinoa, rice, teff, and wild rice.

Oriental bifun noodles are made with white rice flour and potato starch; saifun noodles with mung bean starch; soba noodles with buckwheat starch

Ramen noodles are sold in individual blocks with seasoning packets in many flavors, most with flavor-enhancing additives. To reduce sodium, use only half of the flavor packet. Check the Nutrition Facts panel for amounts of sodium and fat.

Crackers

Look For

- Crackers that are fat-free and low-fat (3 grams of fat or less per serving), such as rice, oat, or barley cakes; melba toast; saltines; lavosh; whole-grain flatbreads; matzo; wheat thins; pepper crackers; whole-grain wafers and imported wafer crackers; flavored crispbreads; and oyster crackers.
- Whole-grain crispbreads. They are low-fat or fat-free, cholesterol-free, and provide valuable fiber.
- Crackers you regularly choose in a reduced-fat or low-sodium version.
- Seeded crackers for a little extra fiber.

Shoppers Should Know

To check the Nutrition Facts panel for the number of crackers per serving and the calorie, fat, fiber, and sugars content.

The words "flaky," "rich" or "croissant" on the label usually mean the crackers are made with extra fat. Cheese crackers also tend to have additional fat.

Fat-free does not mean healthy or low-calorie. Calorie levels of fat-free crackers may be not much lower than in regular varieties.

Smaller servings of regular cracker varieties are fine if you prefer the taste over the low-fat, fat-free, or low-sodium varieties.

Many crackers are made with butter, coconut and palm oils, vegetable shortening, or hydrogenated oils. Check the ingredient list and the amount of saturated fat listed on the Nutrition Facts panel.

Cookies, Bars, and Snack Cakes

Look For

- Low-fat cookies with moderate amounts of sugar, such as graham crackers, animal crackers, arrowroot cookies, zwieback, gingersnaps, vanilla wafers, biscotti, and fruit-filled bars (such as fig bars).
- Small or single-serving cupcakes, doughnuts, and sweet rolls, instead of jumbo sizes.
- Granola bars, particularly low-fat ones and those without lots of peanut butter or chocolate, for a portable snack, dessert, or breakfast.
- Cookies, brownies, and bars that are reduced-fat, low-fat, or fat-free.
- Meringue cookies, baked meringue, dessert shells, and lady fingers. They are fat-free.

Shoppers Should Know

The Nutrition Facts panel on the label states the number of cookies per serving. All calorie and nutrient levels are based on that number of cookies.

When comparing cookies, it's important for you to check the label to see how many cookies are listed as a serving. About 1 ounce of cookies is a standard serving. Some manufacturers, however, label 1 cookie (0.6 oz.) as a serving, making it look like a lower calorie choice. Be sure to double the calorie value if you eat two of these very small cookies.

Fat-free does not mean healthy or low-calorie. Calorie levels may be similar to regular varieties because additional sugar may be added.

Smaller servings of regular cookie varieties are fine if you prefer the taste over that of low-fat or fat-free varieties.

Many cookies are made with butter, coconut, and palm oils, vegetable shortening, or partially hydrogenated oils. Check the ingredient list and amount of saturated fat listed on the Nutrition Facts panel.

Read the labels on frozen and refrigerated cookie doughs. Some brands have only 2 1/2 grams of fat per cookie while others have 12 grams of fat per cookie.

Toaster pastries are generally made from refined flour, fat, sugar, preserves, and artificial colors and flavors. This means they are not good sources of essential nutrients and fiber. There are reduced-fat pastries available.

Energy bars are used by athletes but many non-athletes eat them as snacks. Most energy bars contain at least 60 percent of calories from carbohydrates; most have 200 to 300 calories; many are vitamin- and mineral-fortified. If you are limiting your calorie and fat intake, choose a bar that contains less than 225 calories and less than 3 grams of fat per bar.

Packaged Snack Foods

Most packaged snacks are grain-based but some are from the fruit or vegetable food groups. Most are discussed here.

Look For

- Already-popped popcorn or unpopped popcorn without added fat for air poppers or microwave ovens. They have 3 grams of fat or less per 3-cup serving.
- Rice and popcorn cakes, which are available in many flavors.
- Fat-free, reduced-fat, or low-fat corn, tortilla, vegetable, or potato chips or crisps. Some are

baked, some made with less fat, and still others made with a type of fat that cannot be absorbed.

- Whole-grain, low-fat snack chips.
- Unsalted pretzels, which are also low in fat. Even salted pretzels are lower in fat and sodium than most other salty snacks.
- Fat-free or low-fat caramel corn, corn puffs, or cheese puffs.
- Small boxes or bags of raisins, trail mix, cereal mixes, and other fruit and nut combinations.

Shoppers Should Know

Many snack items are high in calories, fat, sodium, and/or sugar and have minimal nutritional value. Substitute fresh fruit or raw vegetables for fried or sweet snacks some of the time.

Fat-free potato chips made with olestra, a nonabsorbable fat, have half the calories of regular chips and taste like traditional potato chips. Some people report mild gastrointestinal symptoms after eating these snacks, especially in excess. If these, or any other foods, cause distress, either omit them from your diet or limit amounts eaten.

Individual (1-ounce) snack packs help to control portion size. Transferring snacks from larger packages to small plastic sandwich bags to make single servings reduces cost per serving—but may increase temptation to eat several "portions."

Candy, pastries, and chips in small, single-serving packages are good occasional treats. Eat them after you've met recommended servings from the various food groups.

Most brands of bagel and pita chips contain partially hydrogenated oils to retain crispness. A small (1-ounce) serving contains about 4 grams of fat. A fairly small (6-ounce) bag of bagel chips provides six servings.

One brand of apple chips has 4 grams of fat per ounce. Check the Nutrition Facts panel for the fat content of all fruit chips.

Doughnuts vary in size and all are fried. If you eat doughnuts, choose small doughnuts to keep fat in check.

Fat-free or low-fat dips, salad dressings, and salsas keep veggies and fat-free and low-fat chips low in fat.

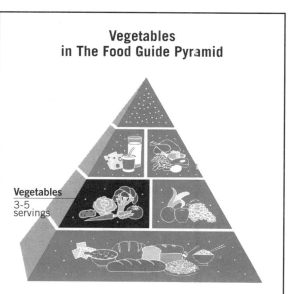

Vegetables in The Food Guide Pyramid

Vegetables
3-5 servings

• Fat (naturally occurring and added) Δ Sugars (added)

Source: U.S. Department of Agriculture/U.S. Department of Health and Human Services, 1992.

Fresh Vegetables

Look For

- Dark green, deep yellow, or orange-colored fresh vegetables (such as spinach or winter squash) and plan to eat at least one each day.
- Fresh vegetables that are in season. Many vegetables are available year-round, but quality and flavor are at their peak when vegetables are locally grown and abundant.
- Tomatoes in various sizes, shapes, and colors. Tomatoes should be firm, plump, smooth, and brightly colored with a clear skin. When ripe, tomatoes are firm but yield to gentle pressure.
- Small or medium-size colorful carrots that are crisp and smooth with pointy, firm tips. Fresh carrots have greens attached but carrot greens are inedible and must be discarded. Very large carrots are less sweet but good in soups or stock. Peeled and cut, baby and shredded carrots are convenient but carry premium prices.
- Any type of cabbage: red, green, Chinese, Napa, etc. All should be heavy and solid with unbruised, firm heads.

- Green, red, yellow, and other bell (sweet) peppers. They should be plump, glossy, and unblemished. All are very rich in vitamin C; red and yellow peppers have more beta-carotene than green peppers.
- Crisp stalks of broccoli and broccoli rabe that are firm, bright green with compact clusters of dark green buds and no yellow or dry patches.
- Mushrooms that are fairly clean with tightly closed caps and no dried-out, spongy, or pitted surfaces. Use mushrooms within two days.
- Ever-popular potatoes in all forms, which provide complex carbohydrate, vitamin C, and some minerals. Potatoes should be firm, unbruised, dry, and free of cuts. Avoid potatoes with a greenish cast, grey spots, or sprouts.
- Freshly picked ears of corn—they're the sweetest. Choose ones with plump, cool-to-touch kernels. Avoid corn with hard or shriveled kernels.
- Fresh herbs to flavor your food. Buy pots of herbs for your garden or windowsill.
- A variety of salad greens, including deep green leafy ones for salads and sandwiches. Lettuce should be crisp in texture with no brown or

soft spots and unblemished edges on the leaves. Iceberg lettuce should have a solid, crisp, tightly-packed head.

- Onions, garlic, and ginger—terrific flavor boosters with some health benefits. Onions, shallots, and garlic should be firm, dry, and well-shaped, free of sprouts or dark spots. Store them in a cool dry place but do not refrigerate. Gingerroot should be a fresh-looking firm root. A small root has a more delicate flavor than a large root. Break off a section that is the amount you wish to buy.
- Bags of sprouts such as bean sprouts, radish sprouts, and alfalfa sprouts to add crunch and nutrients to salads and sandwiches.
- Crisp celery in unscarred bunches with fresh-looking green leaves. Small stalks and celery hearts are more tender but much more expensive.
- Cucumbers that are firm, clear-skinned, and dark green. Choose slender ones, fairly thin in diameter, so there is more flesh and fewer seeds.
- Vegetables that are good sources of beta-carotene/vitamin A: dandelion; mustard,

turnip, and collard greens; spinach; broccoli; beets; bok choy; carrots; kale; red bell peppers; winter squash; sweet potatoes; Swiss chard; tomatoes; calabasa pumpkin; and sugar snap peas.

- Vegetables that are good sources of vitamin C: green, red and yellow bell peppers; tomatoes; Brussels sprouts; asparagus; broccoli; cabbage; cauliflower; spinach; kale; turnips; potatoes; mustard and collard greens; kohlrabi; snow peas; sugar snap peas; lotus root; potatoes; rutabagas; and sweet potatoes.
- Vegetables that are good sources of folate: asparagus, broccoli, okra, beets, artichokes, green peas, sugar snap peas, leeks, cauliflower, okra, parsnips, corn, lima beans, and all green leafy vegetables, such as spinach, cabbage, Brussels sprouts, romaine, leaf lettuce, chicory, escarole, beet greens, and turnip greens.
- Vegetables that are especially high in fiber: corn, artichokes, lima beans, baked beans, and other legumes, peas, winter squash, Brussels sprouts, and plantains.
- Vegetables that may help reduce the risk of cancer: cruciferous vegetables including

collard, mustard and turnip greens; Brussels sprouts; bok choy; broccoli and broccoli rabe; kohlrabi; cabbage; cauliflower; kale; and rutabaga.

- Vegetables that are good sources of vitamin E and calcium: deep green leafy vegetables such as spinach, kale, mustard greens, and turnip greens.

Shoppers Should Know

Although raw vegetables may not have nutrition labels, all are healthy choices. They are exempt from the requirement that all foods called healthy have a minimum of 10 percent of a key nutrient.

Beta-carotene is a substance that converts to an active form of vitamin A in the body. It is characteristically a yellow color and is present in yellow and orange vegetables and fruits, particularly carrots, winter squash, and sweet potatoes.

Buying fresh vegetables allows you to control the amount of added salt and fat used in preparation.

Store whole tomatoes at room temperature to maximize flavor; refrigerate cut tomatoes. Vine-ripened tomatoes are the most flavorful. Genetically engineered tomatoes have an extended shelf life when ripe.

Cabbage has many health benefits and is usually one of the least expensive vegetables.

Lettuces that are deep green have more vitamins than light green lettuces.

Eat corn as soon as possible after picking as it loses sweetness during storage.

Herb plants provide an ongoing supply at less cost than cut herbs by the ounce or bag. Fresh herbs are more flavorful, colorful, and aromatic than dried ones. Use herbs to add flavor to your cooking without adding fat or salt. Parsley, cilantro, and dill are the most economical herbs year-round. In the summer, enjoy bountiful basil, mint, rosemary, chives, and other varieties.

Washed, cut raw vegetables are a handy, low-calorie snack. Keep a jar or plastic bag of them in sight in your refrigerator. Reach for them often.

Most light-colored vegetables (iceberg lettuce, jicama, fennel, radishes, zucchini, celery, and cucumbers) have few nutrients but are good low-calorie fillers and munchies.

Precut vacuum-sealed salad greens are ready-to-use and convenient but command premium prices.

Organically grown fruits and vegetables meet varying criteria based on state regulations. Certification standards are based on the length of time the soil has been kept free from pesticides, herbicides, and contaminants from nonorganic fields. Organic foods are processed, transported, and stored without artificial preservatives, colorings, or irradiation. Earth-friendly food production may yield better tasting produce, but appearance and size of fruits and vegetables is less consistent, and the price of organic produce is often higher. Some supermarkets offer a wide variety of organic produce. Others offer a small selection at premium prices.

To enjoy their flavors and textures, vegetables should be prepared simply. Use minimal amounts of fats to enhance them.

Cut vegetables from the salad bar, ready-to-use spinach and mixed greens, and shredded carrots and cabbage reduce meal preparation time.

Some vegetables (broccoli, cabbage, kale, turnip greens, and collards) contain iron, but it is not absorbed as well as the iron in meats.

Buy only the amount of vegetables that you can use. When possible, split packs or bunches, especially when produce is priced by the pound rather than by the bunch.

Blended torn salad greens are convenient but usually more expensive than heads or bunches of salad greens.

Baking potatoes and sweet potatoes already cleaned and wrapped to prepare in the microwave are handy but command a premium price.

Pick up information about fresh vegetables on signs, brochures, and recipe cards in the produce section.

When a vegetable is not in season, a frozen or canned form is usually more economical and better quality.

Leftover cooked, chilled beets, carrots, beans, asparagus, and other vegetables make great salads and healthy snacks. Prepare extra vegetables at mealtimes for salads and snacks the next day.

"Breathable" storage bags, plastic bags with tiny holes, help to slow spoilage of fresh produce.

Eating potatoes and eggplant with skins left on boosts fiber intake. Zucchini and okra also add a fiber bonus.

Some vegetables and fruits, such as cucumbers and some apples, are coated with an edible wax to help prevent moisture loss and reduce shriveling. Peel skin from waxed produce.

Broccoli, cauliflower, cabbage, Brussels sprouts, and other cruciferous vegetables, whether fresh or frozen, contain substances that help protect cells of the lungs and breasts from potential carcinogens. Diets high in antioxidants including beta-carotene, vitamin C, vitamin E, and some phytochemicals (see below), protect cells from substances formed by inflammation and other disease processes.

The specific protective effects of many substances found in fruits and vegetables are a subject of current research. Phytochemicals are components in foods that are not nutrients, but may provide health benefits. It appears that phytochemicals present in many vegetables, prevent cell damage and neutralize potential cancer-causing agents. Identified phytochemicals include indoles, in cruciferous vegetables, that may reduce the risk of breast cancer; and allylic sulfides, in garlic, onions, leeks, and chives, that seem to stimulate cell enzymes that detoxify cancer-causing agents. Others include lycopene, present in red vegetables such as tomatoes and red peppers, which is a potent antioxidant with anti-cancer properties; terpenes, found in eggplant, also seem to produce enzymes that deactivate cancer-causing agents.

Science is identifying more and more protective phytochemicals in food. Because so many of them are found in vegetables, fruits, and grains, eating a wide variety of foods from these groups offers multiple, albeit not yet well-understood, health benefits.

Frozen Vegetables

Look For

- Plain frozen vegetables that are packed without sauces or breading.
- Frozen vegetables that are good sources of beta-carotene/vitamin A: dandelion, mustard, turnip and collard greens, spinach, broccoli,

carrots, kale, red bell peppers, winter squash, sweet potatoes, and Swiss chard.

- Frozen vegetables that are good sources of vitamin C: green, red, and yellow bell peppers; Brussels sprouts; asparagus; broccoli; cauliflower; spinach; kale; beet, mustard and collard greens; snow peas; sugar snap peas; potatoes; and sweet potatoes.
- Frozen vegetables that are good sources of folate: asparagus, broccoli, okra, beets, artichokes, green peas, cauliflower, sugar snap peas, asparagus, and all green leafy vegetables, such as spinach, and Brussels sprouts, and mixed blended.
- Vegetables that are especially high in fiber: corn, artichokes, lima beans, okra, peas, winter squash, and Brussels sprouts.
- Frozen vegetables rich in antioxidant vitamin E: deep green leafy vegetables such as spinach, kale, and turnip greens.
- Frozen cruciferous vegetables including collard, mustard and turnip greens, Brussels sprouts, broccoli, cauliflower, and kale, which may help reduce the risk of cancer.

Shoppers Should Know

Frozen vegetables are packed at their peak of freshness, so they are equal to fresh vegetables in nutrient content.

Plain (unseasoned) frozen vegetables allow you to control the amount of added salt and fat added in preparation.

Most frozen vegetables with sauces are high in sodium and/or fat. Look at the Nutrition Facts panel of vegetables with cream or butter sauces.

Bags of frozen chopped onions, green and red peppers, and chives kept in the freezer are handy when you need small amounts for recipes.

Some vegetables contain iron, but it is not absorbed as well as iron in meats.

Frozen vegetables in 1-pound bags are usually an economical choice and save preparation time. Remove as much of the vegetable as you will use; seal the bag with a twist tie and return it to the freezer.

Frozen baked potatoes, zucchini, okra, and eggplant with edible seeds and/or skins add a fiber bonus.

Breaded onion rings, hash browns, French fries, cheese-topped potatoes, twice-baked potatoes, batter-coated zucchini, spinach and corn soufflés, green beans with mushroom sauce, creamed spinach, and vegetables with cheese sauce are likely to be higher in fat than other veggies. If you choose these, eat moderate portions.

Canned and Bottled Vegetables

Look For

- Canned and bottled vegetables. They are quick and convenient sources of many vitamins and minerals as well as fiber.
- Canned tomatoes: peeled whole, puréed, crushed, sauced, stewed, diced and seasoned with herbs or vegetables. All are nutrient-rich and usually less expensive than fresh tomatoes for most cooking uses.
- Bottles of tomato-based sauces with a variety of flavors and textures. They are great to keep on the pantry shelf for a quick meal over pasta, polenta, or cooked vegetables.
- Canned legumes (peas, beans, and lentils), which are time-savers, economical, and excel-

lent sources of fiber, protein, and iron (see page 132).

- Ethnic prepared foods in cans or jars, such as eggplant capanota, olive blends, Giardiniera, roasted red peppers, and stuffed grape leaves.
- Jars of chopped, minced, or roasted garlic. They are real time-savers. They must be refrigerated after opening.
- Tomato, vegetable, and carrot juices. Choose low-sodium versions if sodium is restricted. Vegetable juices may be purchased freshly extracted, frozen, or bottled.
- Bottled beet borscht, unless sodium is restricted.
- Salsa as a dip, for seasoning other foods, or to top baked potatoes.
- Prepared salads in jars—corn relish, three-bean salad, pickled beets, and marinated artichokes.
- Good sources of beta-carotene, a form of vitamin A: canned greens, spinach, beets, carrots, asparagus, roasted red peppers, sweet potatoes, and tomatoes.

- Good sources of folate: creamed corn, canned greens, spinach, artichoke hearts, asparagus, lima beans, baked beans, refried beans, kidney beans, great Northern beans, and peas.

Shoppers Should Know

All canned vegetables carry a Nutrition Facts panel.

Canned vegetables are similar in nutrient value to freshly cooked vegetables.

Canned vegetables are precooked to retain texture and nutrients. To avoid overcooking, reheat with liquids from can just a few minutes until hot. Drained liquids from canned vegetables contain some nutrients and may be added to soup stock or sauces.

Many varieties of beans—baked beans, garbanzos (chickpeas), kidney, great Northern, red beans, butter beans, lima beans, and low-fat refried beans—come in cans. Drain and rinse beans before adding them to recipes if sodium is restricted. The liquid in the can contains salt to help keep beans firm.

Some canned vegetables can be combined to make easy salads or vegetarian entrées. Mix drained black beans with corn, and roasted red peppers with drained marinated artichokes.

Canned legumes such as baked beans, chickpeas, black-eyed peas, and black beans can be counted as servings from either the vegetable or the meat group in the Food Guide Pyramid.

If you need to restrict sodium, choose no-salt-added, low-sodium, or reduced-sodium canned vegetables.

Harvard or pickled beets and sweet and sour cabbage are generally low-fat or fat-free. Beets, especially pickled beets, are high in sodium.

Tomato juice, with just 40 calories per cup, is rich in vitamin C. Several recent studies have shown that tomato-rich diets are linked with lower incidence of stomach and breast cancers, although confirmation is needed. Tomatoes contain a variety of protective nutrients.

Carrot juice contains many vitamins, phytochemicals, and fiber. Try cooking couscous or other grains in carrot juice for an interesting flavor and added nutrient content.

Sauerkraut, marinated artichokes, sweet and sour cabbage, pickled vegetables, and some seasoned tomatoes have more salt than other canned vegetables.

If a can of vegetables is swollen or bulging or shows evidence of discolored metal inside, the can should be discarded.

Even canned foods don't last forever. There are some flavor changes and quality losses over time. From time to time, check your pantry shelves and use cans of food that have been there for several months. Tomatoes and high-acid vegetables and fruits should be used within 18 months for optimum quality. Other vegetables should be used within two years.

Fruits in The Food Guide Pyramid

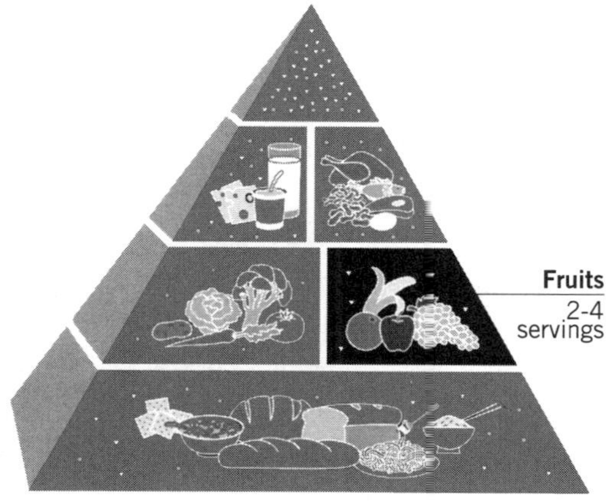

• Fat (naturally occurring and added) ∠ Sugars (added)

Source: U.S. Department of Agriculture/U.S. Department of Health and Human Services, 1992.

Fresh Fruit (including fresh juices/refrigerated fruits)

Look For

- Ripe, sweet fruit for use within a day or two; firm, less-ripe fruit to ripen at home for eating later in the week; bargain-priced, bruised, or overripe fruit to chop and use in baking or to make fruit preserves or chutneys.
- Nutrition information about fresh fruits on signs and flyers in the produce section of your grocery store.
- Locally grown fruit in season. It's likely to be at peak flavor and a good buy.
- New varieties of fruits you may not have tried before, such as fresh mangos and papayas. Expand the range of healthful fruit you enjoy.
- Oranges, grapefruit, lemons, limes, and other citrus that have thin unblemished but firm skins and feel heavy in relation to size. Use citrus zest and juice to season grains, vegetables, and meat.
- Bananas that have clear unbruised skin that is (ripe) yellow or (unripe) light green. They will continue to ripen at home at room

temperature. Never refrigerate bananas. Overripe bananas with black spots or dark skins are very sweet and can be used for baking.

- Red, green, and golden apples that are firm, bright-skinned and unbruised. Try different varieties of apples—many of the most tasty ones are not big, red, and shiny.
- Melons that are firm and unbruised. They continue to ripen at room temperature and then should be refrigerated. Cantaloupes and other small melons are ripe when they yield to gentle pressure at the stem end. Ask someone in the produce section to help you select a ripe melon until you can judge for yourself.
- Grapes that are firm, plump, and dry. They should adhere to stems and not be shriveled near the stem ends.
- Peaches that are firm, colorful, and unbruised. The shape, flavor, and size depend on the variety. Ripen at room temperature, then refrigerate. Ripe fruit yields to gentle pressure.
- Strawberries that are firm, dry, and uniformly dark red with fresh green caps. Size does not influence flavor. Avoid packages with any soggy berries or evidence of mold.

- Pineapples that are firm with a trace of orange color near the bottom. Pineapples do not ripen after picking. Hawaiian pineapples are generally the sweetest. Store at room temperature, since pineapple blackens if refrigerated. If cut, refrigerate and use within two days.
- Good sources of vitamin C: kiwi, mangos, cantaloupe, cherimoya, papayas, guavas, honeydew melons, tangerines, oranges, grapefruit, starfruit, strawberries, blackberries, raspberries, pineapple, and watermelon.
- Good sources of beta-carotene/vitamin A: apricots, cantaloupe, red and pink grapefruit and their juices, mangos, sapote, nectarines, loquats, persimmons, papayas, plantains, and prunes.
- Good sources of potassium: avocados, bananas, all melons, papayas, dried fruit, mangos, and oranges.
- Fruits that are especially high in fiber: berries, guavas, mangos, pears, plantains, pomegranates, rhubarb, and dried fruit.
- Good sources of vitamin E: mangos and avocados.

- Good sources of folate: watermelon, boysenberries, kiwi, oranges, plantains, strawberries, orange juice, grapefruit juice, and pineapple juice.

Shoppers Should Know

For peak sweetness and flavor fruits should be eaten when they're ripe.

Colorful fruits add eye appeal, texture, flavor, and nutrients to any meal.

Fruits offer big flavor with modest amounts of calories. Most contain no fat and very little sodium.

Be careful not to bruise ripe fruit in the shopping basket or shopping bag.

Beta-carotene converts into an active form of vitamin A in the body. Cantaloupes, mangos, red grapefruit, and papaya are particularly rich in beta-carotene.

Ruby-red grapefruit has far more beta-carotene than white grapefruit.

Avocados are a high-fat fruit but the fat is monounsaturated, a heart-healthy type. Try thin slices of ripe avocado on sandwiches instead of mayonnaise.

Whole fruits have more fiber than fruit juices and no added sugar.

Freshly extracted juices have optimal flavor and nutrient value but are usually more expensive than fresh frozen or other forms of juice.

Whole berries purchased economically in season can be frozen for year-round use.

Fresh fruit should be washed just before eating it. Store it covered but unwashed; it will keep longer.

Fresh fruit, packed in a plastic bag with a napkin, is an easy take-along sweet snack or part of a brown-bag lunch. Go beyond bananas, apples, and oranges; try grapes, cherries, and plums, for example.

Fruits and vegetables can provide all the vitamin C needed each day. In addition, when eaten together, vitamin C-rich foods triple the amount of iron absorbed from breads, grains, and cereals.

Citrus fruits include all varieties of oranges, grapefruits, tangerines, lemons, and limes.

Allow melons, apricots, plums, peaches, and pears to ripen at room temperature. Refrigerate ripe fruits, except for bananas, which should always be stored at room temperature.

When oranges and grapefruits are inexpensive or bags are on sale, squeezing fresh fruit for juice is more economical than buying juice.

Cantaloupes, honeydew, and other melons are easy to cube—and far less costly when purchased as whole or half melons than as cut fruit. The extra cost of cut, peeled fruit may be worthwhile for single servings or if you only need a little for a recipe.

Organically grown fruits and vegetables meet varying criteria based on state regulations. Certification standards are based on the length of time the soil has been kept free from pesticides, herbicides, and contaminants from nonorganic fields. Organic foods are processed, transported, and stored without artificial preservatives, colorings, or irradiation. Earth-friendly food production may yield better tasting fruit, but appearance and size of fruits and vegetables is less consistent and the price of organic fruit is often higher. Some supermarkets offer a wide variety of organic produce. Consumer demand and the philosophy of the store determines the amount, type, and pricing of organically grown produce.

Diets high in antioxidants (beta-carotene, vitamin E, vitamin C, and some phytochemicals) protect cells from damage. Diets high in antioxidants may reduce the incidence or severity of arthritis, coronary heart disease, cataracts, some neurological conditions, and cancers in some people.

Phytochemicals, food components that are not nutrients but provide health benefits, are present in many fruits. Several phytochemicals look promising based on limited studies. Ellegic acid, a phytochemical found in berries, may neutralize carcinogens before they can cause genetic changes in cells. Limonene, present in citrus fruit, may shrink tumors and prevent regrowth. It may also increase production of enzymes that may rid the body of carcinogens. Quercitin, found in grapes (and also wine from grapes), is a potent antioxidant that may protect cells from damage, aging and environmental effects such as pollution. Terpenes, in oranges, seem to produce enzymes that may deactivate cancer-causing agents. Much research needs to be done before scientists agree on specific health benefits for specific phytochemicals. Most experts now agree that eating more fruits and vegetables promotes health and that most Americans should boost the intake of both fruits and vegetables.

Irradiated fruits carry a flower-like irradiation logo. Fruits and imported spices may be irradiated to destroy bacteria, and they stay fresh longer. Some strawberries and other fruits are irradiated.

Frozen Fruit

Look For

- Frozen fruits packed without added sugar.
- Frozen 100 percent juice concentrate—single fruits or blends.
- Frozen fruit bars made with 100 percent fruit juice; chocolate-coated frozen bananas.
- Excellent sources of vitamin C: frozen strawberries and raspberries, and orange, tangerine and grapefruit juices.
- Frozen cantaloupe balls which contain beta-carotene/vitamin A.

- Frozen strawberries, blackberries, boysenberries, and raspberries for fiber.
- Good sources of folate: frozen blackberries and strawberries and orange, pineapple, and grapefruit juices.

Shoppers Should Know

Frozen 100 percent fruit juice concentrates are often the least expensive form of real 100 percent juice.

Frozen fruit-flavored juice beverage concentrates, punches, and ades usually contain only 10 to 15 percent juice.

Frozen berries are usually less expensive than fresh. When thawed, they are somewhat mushy, but are fine for sauces or baking.

Frozen 100 percent lemon juice is similar to fresh-squeezed lemon juice in flavor.

"Homestyle" orange juices have some bits of fruit pulp, which makes them taste a bit more like fresh-squeezed juice but adds no useful amount of fiber.

Reduced-acid frozen orange juice is available for those who can not tolerate fresh or regular frozen orange juice.

Washed blueberries or stemmed seedless grapes can be frozen on a baking sheet. Once frozen, transfer them to a freezer bag or airtight plastic container and use within a month. Keep them on hand for a refreshing snack that kids and adults enjoy, especially in warm weather.

Canned and Bottled Fruits and Juices

Look For

- Canned fruits packed in juice or light syrup.
- Juices and juice blends that are 100 percent juice.
- Jars of chilled orange segments, grapefruit segments, mango slices, papaya slices, pineapple chunks, and mixed fruit salads.
- Calcium-fortified juices—an excellent option, especially if intake of dairy products is limited.
- Sparkling apple cider or sparkling grape juice for festive occasions.
- Canned pumpkin and jars of stewed prunes. They are loaded with fiber, vitamins, and minerals.

- Applesauce, including varieties made with Granny Smith, McIntosh, and other apple varieties. Some are unsweetened.
- Reduced-sugar fruit pie fillings.
- Excellent sources of vitamin C: mandarin oranges, orange and grapefruit segments; orange, grapefruit, and tomato juices; cranberry juice cocktail and other vitamin C-fortified juices; and fortified fruit drinks.
- Good sources of beta-carotene/vitamin A: mandarin orange segments, sour cherries, apricots, apricot nectar, and tangerine juice.
- Juices that contain potassium: orange, grapefruit, tangerine, pineapple, and prune juices and tropical fruit blends.
- Pineapple juice is an excellent source of folate.

Shoppers Should Know

Fruit juices offer far more nutrition for the money than soft drinks.

Canned and bottled fruits are nutritious and convenient alternatives to fresh fruits, especially when a fruit is not in season.

When the label says 100 percent juice, it means the drink contains an unmodified pure juice with some fruit pulp. Fruit juices that are not 100 percent juice usually have color, taste, aroma, or other properties altered by additives or processing.

Single-serve juice boxes filled with 100 percent fruit juice and fruit cups are convenient and portable, but they are more expensive per serving than larger packages of juice and fruits.

Fruit packed in heavy syrup has more sugar than juice-packed fruits or fruits packed in light syrup. If fruit packed in heavy syrup is preferred, drain off the syrup to reduce calories from sugar.

A product labeled no added sweeteners has no added sugar, corn syrup, or artificial sweetener.

Bottled, canned, and frozen pure or blended juices made from concentrate, labeled 100 percent fruit juice, are nutritionally equivalent to fresh pressed juices but are less expensive.

A cup of orange juice made from frozen concentrate contains two times the daily requirement for vitamin C.

Fortified juices contain vitamins or minerals added to boost the nutritional value. If you don't drink milk, juices with added calcium are a good choice.

Fruit drinks, punches, and juice beverages are sweetened water with a small amount of juice added. They don't count as a serving from the Fruit Group and fall within the Fats, Oils, and Sweets Group in the Food Guide Pyramid.

Full-strength cranberry juice is too acidic and concentrated to drink alone, so water and sweetener are added to make cranberry cocktails and cranberry-fruit blended drinks. Cranberry juice contains a substance that may prevent bladder infections in some people, so it might be helpful for those who are prone to urinary tract problems.

Apple and grape juices, apple cider, and pear and apricot nectars generally have less vitamin C than other fruit juices. Some have vitamins added; check the label.

Dry fruit-flavored drink mixes are available sweetened, unsweetened, or artificially sweetened. All are mixes of artificial flavor, colors, and additives, often with some vitamin C added.

Fruit-flavored sports drinks are mixes of water, artificial color, flavor, and additives with sugar, sodium and, sometimes, vitamins and minerals added.

Regular canned tomato and tomato-vegetable juice blends contain salt. Low-sodium tomato and vegetable juices are available for those on sodium-restricted diets.

Dried Fruits

Look For

- Dried prunes, including those flavored with orange or lemon essence. They are good sources of dietary fiber and vitamin A and are one of the least expensive dried fruits.
- Dried raisins, apricots, figs, peaches, pears, nectarines, bananas, cherries, currants, blueberries, sweetened cranberries (that look like raisins), and mango strips. All dried fruits are excellent sources of fiber and many provide potassium.
- Bags of chopped dried fruit to add to cereals, rice, and grains.
- Excellent sources of beta-carotene/vitamin A: dried apricots, mangos, nectarines, peaches, papayas, and prunes.

- Apricots and some other dried fruits, which absorb iron if they are dried on iron racks. Check the Nutrition Facts panel for iron levels of packaged dried fruits.

Shoppers Should Know

Dried fruits are shelf-stable and convenient. Look for them in the produce or baking supply sections of the store. Packaged dried fruits are labeled with a "use by" date.

Because water is extracted in drying fruits, all are concentrated sources of sugar and fiber. Small portions provide many key nutrients. Only 1 1/3 ounces (40 grams by weight) of a dried fruit is a standard serving. This is about 4 to 5 prunes or 2 tablespoons of raisins.

Some dried fruits are treated with sulfur dioxide to retain bright colors and moist texture. If sulfite is added, the label will say so. Individuals who are sensitive to sulfites should read labels carefully to avoid reactions which can be severe.

Some dried fruits, including most bananas, cranberries, and diced dates have sugar added.

Banana chips are deep fried, often in tropical oil like coconut oil, and have sugar added. One ounce of dried banana chips has about 150 calories and nearly 10 grams of fat.

The yogurt coating on raisins is primarily sugar and hydrogenated palm kernel oil—about 135 calories and 6 grams of fat. Don't think of them as a source of low-fat, calcium-rich yogurt.

Dried shredded coconut is high in saturated fat but fine to use in small amounts for flavor and texture and as a garnish.

Only pitted prunes and dates should be given to young children. They can choke on prune or date pits.

Milk, Yogurt, & Cheese in The Food Guide Pyramid

• Fat (naturally occurring and added) Δ Sugars (added)

Source: U.S. Department of Agriculture/U.S. Department of Health and Human Services, 1992.

Milk and Milk Alternatives

Look For

- Skim and low-fat milks including skim milk, 1% fat milk, evaporated skimmed milk, nonfat dry milk, and nonfat or low-fat buttermilk for everyone over the age of 2.
- 2% fat milk and 2%t fat buttermilk, with fat content midway between skim and whole milk. They are good choices for young children, those who do not like skim milk, and individuals seeking to maintain weight.
- Whole milk for those who do not like low-fat milk or need to gain weight and for babies and toddlers who need some fat in milk for normal development.
- Nonfat or low-fat flavored milks such as chocolate milk.
- Fat-free or low-fat pasteurized eggnog.
- Low-fat sweetened condensed milk and canned, dry buttermilk for baking.
- Pasteurized goats milk for those intolerant of cows milk.

- Nonfat, 1% 2% lactose-reduced, or lactase-treated milk for those who can not properly digest the lactose in milk.
- Sweet acidophilus milk for people with digestive problems.
- Hot cocoa mixes made with skim milk.

Shoppers Should Know

Milk and dairy products are the primary dietary sources of bone-building calcium. Milk also provides protein and minerals; almost all milk is fortified with vitamins A and D. Different milk and dairy products provide various amounts of fat, saturated fat, cholesterol, and calories.

One cup of milk equals 1 serving from the Milk Group in the Food Guide Pyramid. Two to three daily servings of low-fat dairy products are suggested—3 servings a day for pregnant women, teens, and young adults; and 4 servings daily for lactating women.

Milk is always labeled with a "sell by" date. The sell by date is the last date a food should be sold to allow several days of freshness for home use. Check date at the store and put milk in the refrigerator as soon as possible. Discard milk that has changed flavor, turned sour, or is curdled.

Milk can be stored in the freezer for up to 1 month. An "emergency quart" is a good idea especially if there are children or a pregnant woman in the household.

Nonfat dry milk and dry buttermilk are economical, nutritious choices to drink or use in cooking. They are shelf-stable; keep some on hand. Add dry milk powder to dishes to add calcium and other nutrients from milk.

Milk made from nonfat dry milk tastes better if it is chilled several hours before drinking or is mixed with a small amount of 2% milk.

Most milk sold in the United States is pasteurized, which means the micro-organisms that cause diseases (such as salmonella) and spoilage have been destroyed by heating, then quick-cooling.

Ultrapasteurization (also called ultra-high temperature [UHT] processing) uses high heat (280°F for 2 to 4 seconds) and sterilized containers to destroy almost all bacteria in milk and cream. UHT dairy products can be stored unopened for up to 3 months without refrigeration. The heat processing significantly alters the flavor of the milk and/or cream.

Acidophilus milk has added "friendly bacteria" which can reintroduce helpful bacteria to the colon after diarrhea or antibiotic use.

Switching to a lower fat milk should be done gradually. Switch from whole milk (about 3.5% milkfat) to 2% (2% milkfat), then to 1% (1% milkfat) or skim (0% milkfat). Let your palate adjust.

Buttermilk is made by culturing milk with helpful bacteria. Despite the name, it contains no butter. Salt is added for more flavor. When you want a creamy, thick texture and tangy taste, try low-fat or nonfat buttermilk. It is an excellent base for salad dressings and sauces, in cream soups, and in mashed potatoes. Buttermilk is higher in sodium than other milk.

Eggnog, sold around some holidays, is a blend of milk, eggs, sugar, cream, spices, and vanilla. Look for low-fat pasteurized eggnog.

Equal portions of 1% milk and evaporated skimmed milk can replace light cream (half-and-half) in recipes.

Use evaporated skimmed milk or nonfat dry milk as a coffee creamer with a calcium bonus. Evaporated milk is concentrated milk fortified with vitamins A and D. Once opened, it needs refrigeration.

For coffee drinkers, a latte made with skim milk is an excellent choice. Each cup of latte contains about 1/2 cup of skim milk and about 150 milligrams of calcium.

Goats milk is easy to digest. It has slightly more fat than whole milk.

Chocolate milk made from low-fat and whole milk is available. Low-fat chocolate milk is made with skim milk, cocoa, thickening gums, artificial flavors, and sugar or sugar substitute. Chocolate milk made from whole milk usually contains similar ingredients plus sugar syrup. It is not a good choice for individuals with diabetes. Chocolate milk contains as much protein, calcium, and other nutrients as the milk it is made from. Check the label for calories and carbohydrate content.

Pasteurized chocolate drink contains some whey but no real milk. It provides only a bit of protein and calcium. It is sometimes found in the dairy case; bottled and canned chocolate drinks also can be found with the carbonated beverages.

Nondairy milk alternatives made from soy, almonds, or rice are usually low in fat and always cholesterol-free. Unless fortified, they do not provide the calcium and key nutrients of milk.

Skim milk, soy milk, and rice beverages should not replace infant formula or milk for children under the age of 2. The fat and other nutrients in formula, whole, or 2% milk are necessary for brain and nerve development in infants and young children.

Bovine Somatotropin (BST) is an engineered hormone developed to increase milk production in cows. The milk from BST-treated cows can not be differentiated from milk from non-BST-treated cows according to the Food and Drug Administration.

Organic dairy products meet the requirements of the federal organic certification program. Livestock must be fed organically produced feed, raised in a humane manner, and not be fed growth promoters, hormones, antibiotics, or other medications (other than vaccinations) on a regular basis. Organic dairy products must be processed separate from regular (non-organic) dairy products.

Yogurt and Yogurt Products

Look For

- Low-fat and nonfat (fat-free) yogurt and frozen yogurt with or without fruit flavoring, fruit topping, granola, or crunchy topping.
- Yogurts with active cultures. Most carry a label stating they meet National Yogurt Association criteria for live and active culture yogurt.
- Kefir and other low-fat yogurt drinks, with or without fruit flavor.
- Dairy-free fruited yogurt substitute for vegetarians.

Shoppers Should Know

One cup of yogurt is considered 1 serving from the Milk Group in the Food Guide Pyramid.

Eight ounces of plain yogurt has between 1 and 7 grams of fat depending on the type of milk used in making it. Low-fat varieties have less than 3 grams of fat. Nonfat yogurts are fat-free.

Yogurt is often thickened with milk solids and is an even better source of calcium than milk.

Yogurts with active cultures help keep your digestive system populated with helpful bacteria. After use of antibiotics, which destroy bacteria in the digestive tract, many are advised to eat yogurts with active cultures to restore good bacteria and normal elimination.

Some yogurts come in 8-ounce cartons, others come in 4- or 6-ounce containers. The nutrient values listed on the Nutrition Facts panel are for the full single-serving carton.

Yogurt should be stored in the refrigerator. If unopened, it should stay fresh up to 10 days after the "sell by" date.

Nonfat or low-fat yogurt is a good mayonnaise or sour cream replacement in some chilled foods. Mix some nonfat yogurt with mayonnaise or sour cream to create reduced-fat versions of homemade dips and spreads.

Custard-style yogurts are thicker but do not necessarily have more fat. Check the Nutrition Facts panel for fat content.

Most fruited and flavored yogurts are highly sweetened. Light yogurts contain sugar substitutes and are low-fat or fat-free. Reach for light yogurts if you're watching calories.

Chocolate-coated frozen yogurt bars have twice as many calories as uncoated bars and about 7 grams of fat instead of 1.

See additional comments on frozen yogurt in the Frozen Desserts section, page 156.

Cheese and Cheese Products

Look For

- Low-fat or part-skim cheeses including ricotta, part-skim mozzarella, scamorze, goat, string, feta, light cream cheese, Neufchâtel, and cottage cheese.
- Fat-free and low-fat cheese products containing 3 grams of fat or less per serving such as nonfat or low-fat cottage cheese, ricotta cheese, fromage blanc, and fat-free cream cheese.
- Any cheeses containing 5 grams of fat or less per serving including reduced-fat versions of your favorite cheeses.
- Light (reduced-fat), soft spreadable cheeses.

- Cheeses lower in sodium, or sodium-reduced cheeses if sodium is restricted, including some mozzarellas, ricotta, Jarlsberg, Neufchâtel, Swiss, Muenster, and cheddars. Check the Nutrition Facts panel.

Shoppers Should Know

One and a half ounces of natural cheese (such as cheddar), 2 ounces of processed cheese (such as American), or 1 1/2 cups of cottage cheese is considered a milk serving from the Food Guide Pyramid and provides similar amounts of calcium. These serving sizes are not the same as the amounts stated on the Nutrition Facts panel. Nutrients on the Nutrition Facts label are based on 1 ounce of most cheeses and 1/2 cup of cottage cheese.

Cheese should be stored in the refrigerator and sealed in the original packaging or well-wrapped in foil or plastic wrap to keep it from drying out or absorbing odors from other foods. Packaged cheeses often have a "sell by" date; most cheese stays fresh at least one week after that date.

Cheese usually does not freeze well and changes texture if it is frozen.

Traditional cheeses, particularly high-fat ones, are major contributors to total fat and saturated fat in the diet. Many manufacturers have met consumer demand for reduced-fat and fat-free cheeses, but these products vary greatly in taste, texture, and cooking properties. Try some to find those you enjoy.

Fat-free sliced, shredded, and grated cheeses have a different texture and taste than cheese with fat. Use them when appropriate.

Use only small amounts of cheeses with 8 or more grams of fat per ounce (processed American, blue, brick, cheddar, Colby, fontina, Gruyère, and Havarti).

One pound (16 ounces) of hard or semi-firm cheese yields 4 to 5 cups of grated or shredded cheese.

Save money and fat calories and boost flavor by using small amounts of strong-flavored cheeses, such as Parmesan cheese, rather than large amounts of mild cheeses. Grated Parmesan has less than 2 grams of fat per tablespoon.

Creamed cottage cheese doesn't have as much cream (fat) as its name suggests. 1/2 cup of 1% fat creamed cottage cheese has 1 gram; 2% fat creamed cottage cheese has 2.5 grams; 4% creamed cottage cheese has 4.5 grams. Dry curd cottage cheese has 0.5 grams of fat.

Some brands of cottage cheese have extra calcium added, which is useful for those who don't drink milk.

Whole milk ricotta has 8 grams of fat in only 1/4 cup; part-skim ricotta has 5 to 6 grams. A fat-free version with no fat is available.

Unlike other cheeses that are rich in calcium and protein, cream cheese is primarily fat and contains little calcium and protein. Light and fat-free cream cheeses are available.

Processed cheeses are blends of different cheeses that are pasteurized to lengthen shelf life and treated with gelatin thickeners to give a smooth texture. They melt well.

Cheese spreads and cold pack cheese foods contain 3 to 9 grams of fat per serving and often a lot of sodium. Check the Nutrition Facts panel. Some brands are available in light forms. Only 2 tablespoons of cheese spread is a serving.

Breaded frozen cheese nuggets have 290 to 420 calories and 15 to 20 grams of fat per 3-ounce serving.

Puddings and Custards

Look For

- Rice, tapioca, and bread puddings, which have more grain and less sugar than butterscotch or chocolate puddings.
- Low-fat or fat-free prepared puddings, pudding mixes, and pudding pops.
- Low-fat or fat-free prepared custards or flans, or mixes.
- Pudding pops. They contain 70 to 80 calories without chocolate coating and 125 to 130 calories if coated.
- Chocolate mousse mixes that can be prepared with skim milk.
- Sugar-free mixes, if limiting calories or sugar.

Shoppers Should Know

A half cup is a standard serving of pudding or custard. Add raisins or other dried fruits to rice, bread, or tapioca pudding to boost fiber and nutrients. Prepare with skim or 1% milk.

Sugar-free puddings, prepared from a mix with skim milk, contain 70 to 100 calories per 1/2-

cup serving. Single-serve fat-free prepared pudding snacks have 100 calories per snack.

Single-serving fruit-flavored, chocolate, and vanilla snack puddings are made with skim milk but contain partially hydrogenated cottonseed oil. Some have artificial flavors and colors. Each 1/2-cup container provides 160 to 170 calories and 5 to 7 grams of fat including 2 grams of saturated fat.

Meat, Poultry, Fish, Dry Beans, Eggs, & Nuts in The Food Guide Pyramid

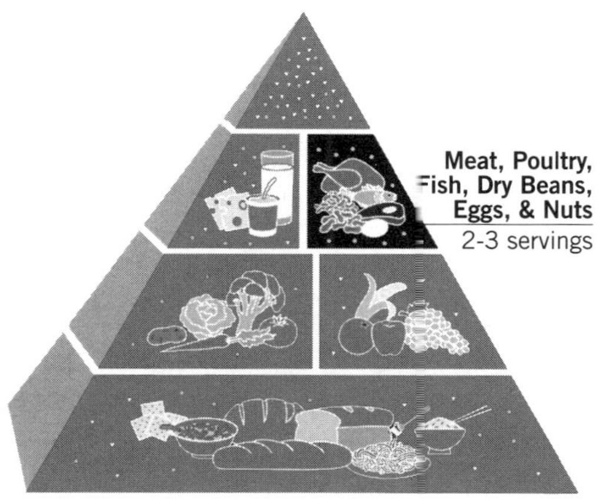

• Fat (naturally occurring and added) ∠ Sugars (added)

Source: U.S. Department of Agriculture/U.S. Department of Health and Human Services, 1992.

Beef, Pork, Lamb, Veal, and Game Meats

Look For

- Meats labeled extra-lean. They have less than 5 grams of fat, less than 2 grams of saturated fat, and less than 95 milligrams of cholesterol per 3 1/2-ounce cooked serving. All are excellent choices.
- Meats labeled lean. They have less than 10 grams of fat, less than 4 1/2 grams of saturated fat, and less than 95 milligrams of cholesterol per 3 1/2-ounce cooked serving.
- Meat graded USDA Select or Choice.
- The leanest cuts of well-trimmed beef including flank, sirloin, and tenderloin; round, ribeye, T-bone, porterhouse, and cubed steaks; and eye of round roast, rib, chuck, and rump roasts.
- The leanest cuts of well-trimmed pork including fresh, canned, cured, and boiled ham; Canadian bacon; and pork tenderloin, loin chops, rib chops, and roasts.
- Lean, well-trimmed cuts of lamb and veal including lamb roast, chops, and leg; and veal chops, arm steaks, blade steaks, "scallopini" cuts, cutlets, and roasts.

- Game that is lean including venison, antelope, beaver, rabbit, beefalo, bison, buffalo, caribou, elk, and goat.
- Lean or extra-lean ground beef, pork, lamb, and veal (at least 90percent lean). Check the "sell-by" date; ground meats are especially perishable.

Shoppers Should Know

Meats are good sources of protein, highly absorbable iron and zinc, vitamin B_{12}, niacin, potassium, phosphorus, and other minerals. Meat also provides fat, saturated fat, and cholesterol—substances best limited to moderate amounts.

The Food Guide Pyramid recommends 5 to 7 ounces of meat or its equivalent from the Meat Group each day.

One serving of meat from the Food Guide Pyramid is only 2 to 3 ounces of cooked lean meat, poultry, or fish. Three ounces of cooked meat is about the size of a deck of cards, an audio-cassette, or the size of the palm of a woman's hand.

One pound of boneless lean meat should yield about 4 (3-ounce) servings when cooked.

If you cook whole steaks, limit portion size by thinly slicing the cooked meat and fanning it out. A moderate serving will look like a more generous portion.

If you want to serve a meat portion larger than 3 ounces, plan on 2 standard servings (6 ounces cooked) and don't eat servings from the meat group at other meals that day.

Always check the "sell-by" date on fresh meats. Cook whole and cut fresh meats within 3 to 5 days of purchase (or the "sell-by" date) and ground meat within 1 to 2 days or wrap and freeze it for later use.

Refrigerate or freeze fresh meat immediately. Store it in the coldest part of the refrigerator. To maintain quality longer, wrap it in freezer paper, freezer bags, or plastic film before freezing it. Mark the wrapper with contents and date frozen.

Trimming visible fat from meat can cut the fat content considerably.

Barbecuing, broiling, grilling, and roasting are cooking methods that drain fat.

For ground beef, ground round is usually the leanest followed by ground sirloin, ground chuck, and then regular ground beef. If you don't see ground round, the meat cutter can usually grind it from round steak. Ground sirloin is usually more expensive than ground round but many prefer the flavor of ground sirloin for burgers. A less expensive ground beef, cooked and drained, will taste about the same when cooked in sauce or combined with highly flavored ingredients.

Ground meats should be cooked to at least medium doneness (at least 160°F) for food safety. Never serve ground meat raw or rare. Steak tartare and rare burgers are risky.

When cooking ground meats, drain fat well before combining cooked ground meat with other ingredients.

Meat graded Select has less fat but is less tender and flavorful than meat graded Choice. Prime grade meats contain the most marbling (internal fat), are most costly and tender, and are primarily sold to fine restaurants.

The color of a meat indicates freshness. Beef should be bright red with no grayish areas. Both young veal and pork are pale grayish pink. Older veal and pork are darker pink. Lamb varies in color depending on what it was fed.

Higher-fat meats include pork spareribs, beef ribs, short ribs, tongue, ground pork, most sausages, and bacon.

Organ meats, such as beef liver, kidney, and heart, are very high in iron and many vitamins but also high in cholesterol.

Veal is lower in total fat than most other red meats but is higher in cholesterol—usually 90 to 130 milligrams of cholesterol and 130 to 170 calories per 3-ounces of veal in comparison to 70 to 85 milligrams cholesterol and 150 to 250 calories per 3-ounce serving of beef.

Some high-fat meats, such as corned beef brisket, are available in low-fat forms from processors that choose the leanest cuts and trim them very well. These meats are usually branded and say "lean" or "extra lean" on the front label. Check the label for sodium content if sodium is a concern.

When pork is cured to make ham, salt is added. Although most ham is now lean, it is usually high in sodium.

Preseasoned and precooked roasts, ribs, and other meats save time but cost considerably more than fresh, raw meats. Check the sodium level.

Beef certified by USDA as natural has been grown without hormones, antibiotics, or preservatives. It carries a premium price.

Cured meats are processed with salt, sugar, and often nitrites to preserve them and add flavor. Ham, bacon, some sausages, and lunch meats are cured. USDA regulates the amount of nitrite used in curing meats and requires the addition of vitamin C, sodium ascorbate, or sodium erythorbate to bind the added nitrites because nitrites have been associated with increased risk of cancer in some studies.

Canned hams are fully cooked. Fresh ham labeled "smoked" or "aged" does not mean that the meat has been cooked. Unless the label says "fully cooked," cook ham like fresh pork.

Avoid buying meat in a package that is not tightly sealed, contains excessive juices or is not cold. Do not buy meat having any brownish or grayish patches.

Always defrost and marinate meat in the refrigerator. Do not use the marinade as a sauce unless it is first brought to a rolling boil.

Poultry and Game Birds

Look For

- All types of poultry, including chicken, turkey, Cornish game hens, duck, pheasant, squab, and quail.
- Plenty of chicken and turkey. Watch for sales and stock up when prices are low.
- Table-ready rotisserie or roasted chicken, turkey breast, and breast tenderloin.
- Lean or extra-lean ground turkey and chicken. Check the label for fat content.
- Game birds that are extra-lean including guinea fowl, pheasant, quail, emu, and ostrich.
- Game birds that are lean such as squab and skinless duckling.
- Canned chicken packed in broth or water.

Shoppers Should Know

White meat of poultry (the breast) has less fat than dark meat (thighs or legs).

Half of the calories in chicken are in the skin. Buy skinless parts or remove the skin of cooked poultry before eating it. Skinless chicken has the same fat content whether it is cooked with or without skin, and cooking chicken with skin on retains moisture.

Skinless, boneless chicken breasts usually command premium prices. Watch for sales or buy chicken breasts with bone in. Remove skin before eating.

Chicken and turkey wings have a high percentage of skin and are higher in fat than other parts of the birds.

Whole or split broiler-fryer chickens (3 to 4 pounds) are usually less expensive than chicken parts. Save money by cutting up whole chickens and packing similar parts in freezer wrap or bags for use in different meals.

Ground poultry is very perishable. Cook it within 1 or 2 days or freeze it.

Ground turkey breast or chicken breast is generally lower in fat than regular ground turkey or chicken (or nuggets or rolls), which usually contains skin and dark meat.

Chicken livers are very rich in vitamins and minerals but high in cholesterol. Check the "sell-by" date and cook chicken livers within 2 days of purchase.

Frozen turkey and rock Cornish hens are often less expensive than fresh.

Turkey parts, often thighs, are economical and healthy choices. Roast the thigh and serve it sliced or diced in salads. Barbecue turkey legs or use them to make soup.

Seasoned, marinated, or precooked chicken and turkey breasts or parts save time but command premium prices.

Self-basting turkeys are injected with fat and are higher in fat than fresh turkeys. They also may be seasoned with salt making them higher in sodium.

Rotisserie chicken tends to be high in sodium. Removing the skin of rotisserie chicken before eating it removes much of the sodium and fat.

Use fresh poultry within 2 days of purchase or freeze it. Frozen poultry should thaw in the refrigerator, never at room temperature. A frozen turkey can take up to 4 days to thaw.

For food safety, poultry should be rinsed under cold water and cooked thoroughly. Use a separate cutting board for raw poultry. Wash the board and utensils with hot, soapy water and rinse with a chlorine bleach solution (2 teaspoons chlorine bleach mixed with 1 quart of water) after each contact with raw poultry. Do not cut vegetables or other foods you will eat without cooking on the same board that has been used for raw poultry.

Cook prestuffed chickens within 1 day after purchase. They are very perishable and do not freeze well.

Organically raised poultry is raised in accordance with federal standards for the organic production of farm animals and is fed organically produced feed and raised in a humane manner. Growth-promoting hormones and antibiotics (given in the absence of illness) are prohibited.

Free-range chickens are no more nutritious than traditional chickens and are more likely to carry bacteria because their feed does not contain additives that control bacterial growth. Some people believe free-range chickens have more flavor.

Duck is leaner than it used to be. Cooking it so the skin is very crisp or removing the skin makes duck a good choice. Duck and pheasant, well-drained and eaten without skin, are similar in fat content to chicken and turkey.

Fish and Seafood

Look For

- A seafood department with a fresh, mildly sea-weedy, but not strong, fishy smell.
- Seafood that has been kept well-iced or frozen. Cooked fish products should be separated from raw seafood.
- Ways to eat at least 2 servings a week of fish and seafood.
- Fresh finfish that is moist and firm with bright eyes, red gills, firm, moist flesh, scales that cling tightly to the skin, and no fishy smell. There

should be no browning or drying around the edges of filleted fish.

- Fresh shrimp with firm meat, mild odor, and natural pale gray color that are not slippery or slimy. They should have no black or dry spots. Cooked shrimp should have reddish shells, firm pale pink meat, and a pleasant odor. Check the seafood and deli departments, salad bar, frozen food case, and canned fish aisle for seafood choices.
- Lobster, crab, and crayfish, sold live unless they are frozen, canned, or cooked. Shucked (with shells removed) oysters and scallops should have a mild, fresh scent and somewhat clear (not milky or slimy) liquid.
- Surimi—imitation crab, scallops, lobster, and shrimp.
- Canned fish with soft edible bones, such as sardines and salmon, for calcium. Both are also high in omega-3 fatty acids.
- Fresh fish, frozen fish without breading, and canned fish packed in water or broth, which are lower in fat and calories than breaded or oil-packed fish.

- Fresh and salt-free canned fish, if on sodium-restricted diets.
- Frozen, farm-raised, or locally caught fish, which are usually less expensive than fresh fish that has been flown in.
- Easy-to-prepare, cleaned shrimp, scallops, mussels, octopus, calamari, or mixed seafoods in the frozen foods case.
- Reputable shellfish dealers who buy from harvesters licensed with the National Shellfish Sanitation Program (NSSP).

Shoppers Should Know

Two and a half to 3 ounces of cooked fish or other seafood equals 1 serving from the Meat Group in the Food Guide Pyramid. (Weight includes edible seafood without shells, skin, bones, etc.) Plan on buying 3/4 pound per serving of whole fish; 1/2 pound per serving of dressed fish or fish with bones; 1/4 to 1/3 pound per person of fish fillets, scallops, peeled shrimp, cooked shelled lobster, or crabmeat.

Salmon, tuna, mackerel, rainbow trout, sea trout, bluefish, herring, bonito, pompano, sardines, and anchovies, which are good sources of heart-healthy omega-3 fatty acids.

Omega-3 fatty acids, found especially in higher-fat fish, have been shown to protect against heart disease by thinning the blood, lowering blood fats, and decreasing the tendency toward plaque formation, which narrows arteries.

All fish and shellfish (crustaceans, mollusks, and cephalopods) are good sources of protein, vitamins, and minerals. They are low in saturated fat and lower in total fat and calories than most other sources of protein.

Crustaceans, including shrimp, crayfish, and lobster, are higher in cholesterol than other seafood but very low in saturated fat and total fat. Scallops and mussels are low in fat, saturated fat, and cholesterol. Prepare and serve them in ways that do not add a lot of fat.

Oysters, clams, scallops, and mussels are mollusks.

Octopus and squid are cephalopods, a shellfish that carries its shell inside. Cleaned and dressed octopus and squid are available fresh or frozen and are particularly popular in Greek, Italian, Asian, and Portuguese cooking.

Whole fish and dressed fish (with head, tail, and fins removed) cost less than steaks and fillets but you need to buy more because there is some waste.

Aquaculture is the cultivation of farm-raised seafoods in ponds, cages, tanks, or pens attached to natural bodies of water. This method allows control of the water supply and increases seafood yield usually reducing fishing costs and prices to consumers. Farm-raised catfish and salmon are less expensive than fish from natural lakes and streams but are not as flavorful.

Whole salmon and salmon steaks are usually less costly than salmon fillets. Canned pink salmon is less expensive than red sockeye salmon.

Surimi is imitation shellfish made from processing and molding mild-flavored fish and adding color and flavor so that it looks like crab, scallops, lobster or shrimp. It is lower in price and cholesterol, but higher in sodium than fresh seafood.

Drain oil from canned tuna and sardines or buy water-packed tuna. Canned chunk light tuna costs less than solid white tuna and is equally healthful.

Shrimp is sold in many sizes. Larger sizes are more expensive. Per pound there are fewer than 15 colossal shrimp; 31 to 35 large shrimp; and over 70 tiny shrimp.

Fresh fish and shellfish should be kept tightly wrapped in the coldest part of the refrigerator. Use it within 1 to 2 days of purchase. Rinse all seafood with cold water before cooking it.

Thaw frozen fish in the refrigerator and use thawed fish within 24 hours.

For food safety reasons, eating raw shellfish, mollusks, and fish (sushi and sashimi) should be avoided.

Seviche is raw fish or shellfish marinated in lime juice or other acid. Although the fish turns firm and opaque, it carries the same health risks as other raw seafood.

Breading and frying seafood (or any food) raises fat, calorie, and sodium levels. Frozen batter-dipped or breaded fish, shrimp, and scallops are high in fat.

Smoked salmon (lox) and other smoked fish may be low in fat but are high in sodium.

Cocktail sauce is a fat-free condiment for seafood. Tartar sauce, however, is usually high in fat.

Packaged Meats/Cold Cuts

Look For

- Lean sliced meats, such as plain or seasoned lean roast beef, turkey, and lean ham.
- Processed luncheon meats and sausages labeled fat-free or low-fat.
- Canadian-style bacon, turkey salami, and turkey ham. Most brands are low-fat—check the Nutrition Facts panel.
- Fat-free or reduced-fat hot dogs, sausages, cold cuts, and breakfast meats.
- Freshness dates on packages—usually a "sell-by" date. Packaged meats stay fresh longer than most other meats, at least 1 week after the "sell-by" date, if tightly sealed.
- Plain roast beef, turkey, or chicken breast or reduced-sodium varieties of cold cuts and sausages if sodium is restricted.

Shoppers Should Know

It's smart to compare the Nutrition Facts panel on packaged luncheon meats.

Most regular sausage products, including hot dogs and cold cuts, are high in sodium and fat.

Processed meats, sausages, and luncheon meats can contain large quantities of hidden fat, saturated fat and sodium. Many reduced-fat varieties are now available. Lean deli meats are convenient and add variety and flavor without a lot of fat.

Turkey and chicken franks do not always have less fat or calories than beef or beef and pork franks. Check the Nutrition Facts panel.

Canadian bacon is much lower in fat than regular bacon. Turkey bacon varies in fat content. Check the Nutrition Facts panel.

Liverwurst and other sausages containing liver and specialty sausages containing organ meats are high in cholesterol and fat but rich in iron, vitamins, and minerals. Eat them only occasionally.

Legumes

Legumes can be counted as servings from either the Meat Group or the Vegetable Group on the Food Guide Pyramid, but not both.

Look For

- Split peas, black-eyed peas, kidney beans, navy beans, black beans, adzuki beans, great Northern beans, lentils, garbanzos (chickpeas), lima beans, pinto beans, and varieties of heirloom beans. Look for dried beans with smooth surfaces and bright colors, with no holes or discolorations in bags that aren't torn. All are excellent sources of protein, fiber, iron, folate, and zinc.
- Tofu (soybean curd), which is a high-protein, cholesterol-free meat substitute. It is usually found in the produce section. Check the freshness date on the wrapper. Buy tofu that has been processed with calcium to boost your calcium intake.
- Soy products such as tofu, tempeh, miso, soy burgers (veggie burgers), and vegetarian sausages.
- Canned legumes including reduced-fat or fat-free vegetarian baked and refried beans.

- Hummus, a spread made from garbanzo beans (chickpeas).

Shoppers Should Know

Legumes are plants that produce pods with edible seeds—beans, peas, and lentils.

A half cup of cooked peas, lentils, or beans or 3 ounces of tofu is equal in portion size to 1 ounce of meat.

Peas, lentils, and beans add protein, minerals, and variety to meatless meals. They add thickness and heartiness to soups, chilis, stews, and casseroles.

Dry split peas and lentils, an inexpensive meat substitute, join eggs as the least expensive source of protein. One pound, about 2 1/2 cups of dry beans or lentils, swells to 5 to 6 cups when cooked. Most dried beans take about 1 1/2 hours to cook; lentils cook in 30 to 45 minutes.

Canned and frozen beans save time. Most canned beans have added salt. Rinse canned beans under cold running water if sodium is restricted.

Organically grown beans are certified to be produced in accordance with federal organic certification using methods to enhance soil fertility, biologic cycles, and diversity. No prohibited fertilizers or other chemicals have been applied to the soil for at least 3 years prior to marketing as organic.

Blended bean mixes and gourmet packs of beans are usually at least three times as expensive as plain legumes.

The fiber found in lentils and beans may help lower blood cholesterol and reduce the risk of some types of cancer.

Peanuts are actually legumes—not nuts. Since most people would look for information about peanuts in the section on nuts, we describe peanut products on page 139.

Dried beans and peas can produce gas and bloating in the digestive tract, especially if they aren't eaten often. Legumes that are usually easier to digest include adzuki beans, anasazi beans, black-eyed peas, lentils, mung beans, tofu, and tempeh.

Soy promotes estrogen production in women and may help protect against heart disease. Soy products contain several phytochemicals including genestein and flavenoids that have been shown to keep cancer-causing agents from attaching to cells and prevent growth of tumors.

Miso, a fermented soybean paste, can be used to season foods and in salad dressings.

Soybeans are high in iron but contain several inhibitors that block some iron absorption. Traditional methods used to produce fermentation in soy foods (tempeh, miso, soy sauce, tofu) increase the availability of iron by breaking down these inhibitors, making fermented soy foods a useful source of iron.

Soft, "silken" tofu is lighter and more delicate than regular tofu. It can be blended with fruit into beverages or seasoned and used as a dip or spread. Add sliced, firm tofu to soups, stirfrys, and vegetables.

Textured vegetable protein (TVP) is made by removing 90 percent of the carbohydrate from defatted soy flour. The result is a concentrated protein sold as granules or chunks to be used as a meat replacement that contains no fat or cholesterol.

Products that contain soy may list "textured vegetable protein," "hydrolyzed vegetable protein," "soy protein," or "soy concentrate" on the ingredient panel.

Meat substitutes made from soy such as burgers, hot dogs, or breakfast sausages strive for a meaty flavor and texture. Some brands fare better than others in taste tests.

Some legume and soy-based convenience foods have a lot of fat. Meatless does not necessarily equal low-fat. Check the Nutrition Facts panel.

Eggs and Egg Substitutes

Look For

- Fresh, uncracked clean eggs kept in a refrigerated case. Open the container to check.
- The USDA inspection shield on grade AA and A eggs. Inspection ensures proper quality and dating, and that eggs have been kept refrigerated before and after packing.
- Egg substitutes, if you are restricting cholesterol or want to use raw eggs in a recipe (such as Caesar salad). Because they are pasteurized, they are safe to eat even if uncooked.
- Tiny quail eggs to use as garnishes and in gourmet cooking.

Shoppers Should Know

If there is a price difference of 7 cents or less per dozen between two sizes of eggs, the larger eggs are a better buy. Eggs come in six sizes—jumbo, extra-large, large, medium, small, and pee-wee. Most stores offer three sizes.

One egg is equal in protein to 1 ounce of meat.

Eggs are an economical, excellent source of protein and contain almost all essential vitamins and minerals. They are quick to fix and versatile.

One large egg contains 6 grams of protein, 5 grams of fat (3 grams of unsaturated fat, 2 grams of saturated fat), 210 milligrams of cholesterol, and 70 calories.

All of the cholesterol and fat is in the yolk of the egg. The American Heart Association advises no more than 4 egg yolks per week per person. Use egg substitutes or egg whites in place of more eggs.

Some branded eggs come from chickens fed special feed. These eggs are rich in vitamin E (25 percent of the Daily Value per egg) and some research suggests that they do not raise serum cholesterol levels.

To reduce cholesterol and fat, 2 egg whites can replace 1 whole egg in many recipes; 2 egg whites plus 1 egg can replace 2 eggs. Most baking recipes use large eggs.

Brown eggs, fertile eggs, and nest eggs are equal in nutrient value to white eggs.

Eggs will keep up to 4 weeks in the refrigerator at 40°F or below.

Egg substitutes vary in ingredients. Some have fat and others do not. Most are sold frozen in small cartons. Generally 1/4 cup egg substitute equals 1 fresh egg. Egg substitutes cost about twice as much as fresh eggs.

For food safety reasons (potential salmonella), soft-cooked or raw eggs in beverages, uncooked meringues, homemade ice creams, and salad dressings should be avoided.

Canned, dried, pasteurized egg whites are sometimes available in the baking supply aisle of the store.

The egg industry is testing ways to pasteurize eggs in the shell to reduce risk of salmonella. Pasteurized whole eggs (removed from shells) are available to food service operators but are now becoming available in supermarkets. Watch for both forms of pasteurized eggs.

Commercial vegetarian egg substitutes are made from potato starch, tapioca flour, leavening agents, and a vegetable-derived gum.

When storing eggs, keep them in the original carton to maintain freshness.

Nuts and Seeds/Nut Butters

Look For

- Unsalted nuts in the baking supply aisle; salted nuts with snack foods; whole nuts in shells with produce.
- Nuts that are firm, with smooth surfaces and uniform color.
- Nut butters, especially reduced-fat varieties.
- Reduced-fat and regular peanut butter. Two tablespoons of either contain 120 to 150 milligrams of sodium, which is not excessive unless sodium is restricted. If sodium is a concern, choose unsalted peanut butter.
- Chestnuts, the only low-fat nut.

- Oil-on-top or "natural" nut butters for less saturated fat.
- Tahini, sesame butter, and whole sesame seeds, almonds, and almond butter—all of which contain some calcium.

Shoppers Should Know

Two tablespoons of peanut butter is a standard serving equal to 1 ounce of meat. But this much peanut butter provides about 190 calories, the caloric equivalent of about 3 ounces of lean meat.

Smooth, chunky, and crunchy-style peanut butters are nutritionally equal—some are just ground more finely.

Regular peanut butter contains about 17 grams of fat per 2 tablespoon serving and 190 calories; reduced-fat peanut butter contains 12 grams of fat per 2 tablespoon serving and 180 to 200 calories. Reduced-fat peanut butter usually has added sugar.

Seeds, nuts, and seed and nut butters provide protein, fiber, and antioxidant vitamin E but are high in fat and calories. Seeds and nuts contain unsaturated fats which are more heart-healthy than fats found in meat and dairy products.

The fat in most nuts—almonds, cashews, chestnuts, filberts, pistachios, macadamia, peanuts, and pecans—is primarily monounsaturated, like that found in olive oil.

The fat in walnuts, Brazil nuts, pine nuts, and sesame, sunflower, and pumpkin seeds is primarily polyunsaturated, like that found in corn oil.

One ounce of shelled nuts contains 160 to 195 calories and 13 to 22 grams of fat.

Macadamia nuts have the most fat (21 grams per ounce) followed by filberts (hazelnuts), Brazil nuts, pecans, and walnuts.

Dry-roasted nuts have about the same calories and fat as oil-roasted nuts.

Coconut is a source of saturated fat, but a few shreds of coconut as a garnish contribute flavor and texture and little total or saturated fat.

Cashews, peanuts, and almonds have a bit less fat than walnuts and pecans. Almonds provide some calcium.

One ounce of shelled nuts contains as much fiber as two slices of whole-wheat bread.

Sesame butter is a peanut butter-like spread made from whole ground sesame seeds. Tahini is a thinner, milder version made from hulled sesame seeds.

Hydrogenating some of the oil in peanut butter keeps the oil from separating but increases the saturated fat content a bit.

Sometimes sugar is added to peanut butter to balance and improve the flavor, especially in reduced-fat peanut butter. There is no real advantage to sugar-free peanut butter.

Once opened, large containers of peanut butter should be refrigerated. Keep a small amount at room temperature. You'll use less if it's easy to spread.

Nuts should be refrigerated or stored frozen in an airtight container unless they are vacuum-packed. Unopened vacuum-packed nuts can be stored at room temperature in your pantry.

Toasting nuts a few minutes intensifies their flavor. You can then use fewer nuts in recipes or toppings.

Flaxseed, which can be used in breads or sprinkled on salads, is rich in omega-3 fatty acids.

The Food Guide Pyramid
A Guide to Daily Food Choices

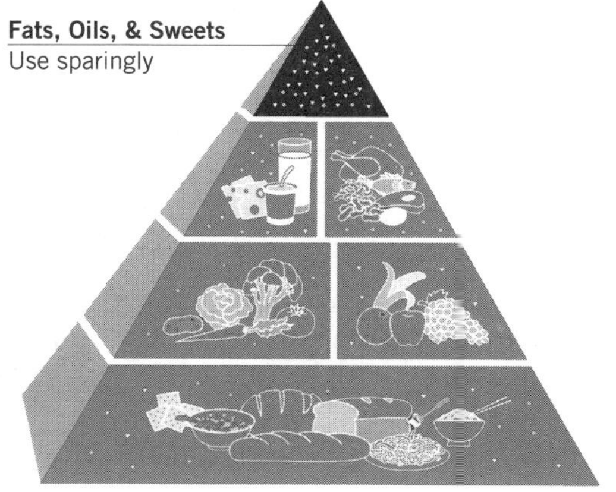

• Fat (naturally occurring and added) Δ Sugars (added)

Source: U.S. Department of Agriculture/U.S. Department of Health and Human Services, 1992.

Butter, Margarine, and Spreads

Look For

- Soft tub margarines or spreads or squeezable bottles or sprays. The first ingredient on the label should be liquid vegetable oil or water.
- Low-fat, light, reduced-calorie, or diet margarines and spreads.
- Butter substitutes (sprinkles or sprays) for seasoning vegetables and popcorn. They are fat- and cholesterol-free.
- Fat-free spreads in sticks or tubs. See if they pass your taste test.
- Margarines with added buttermilk or yogurt solids, or margarine-butter blends. They offer some of the health benefits of margarine with more of the flavor of butter.
- Butter, to be used in moderation.
- Unsalted butter or margarine, if sodium is restricted.

Shoppers Should Know

Regular butter and margarine have 100 to 110 calories per tablespoon; spreadables have about

80 calories; whipped varieties have about 70 calories; light varieties have 50 to 60 calories.

Both butter and margarine are at least 80 percent fat and have 12 grams of fat per tablespoon.

Butter provides 11 milligrams of cholesterol per tablespoon; margarine has none.

Salted butter keeps longer; unsalted (sweet) butter has a more delicate flavor. Keep one stick in the refrigerator, the rest in the freezer.

Unsalted (sweet) butter contains less than 20 milligrams of sodium per tablespoon; regular salted butter has about 110 to 120 milligrams of sodium per tablespoon.

Many people find that butter melts better, works better in baked goods, and tastes better than margarine.

Margarines are mixtures of water or milk and hydrogenated vegetable oil.

Trans-fatty acids in hydrogenated and partially hydrogenated fats (such as stick margarine) have been shown to increase levels of LDL "bad" cholesterol in the blood and may decrease levels of HDL "good" cholesterol.

Soft, spreadable margarines are more heart-healthy than stick margarines or butter. They are less hydrogenated.

Whipped butter has air whipped in. It has fewer calories and less fat than stick butter and spreads well.

Light or whipped butter and margarines are not recommended for baking or frying. Their added water causes spattering and poor baking results.

Light butter with 6 grams of fat and 50 calories per tablespoon is made from butter and skim milk with added ingredients. Nondairy additives add color and flavor.

Granulated butter substitutes work best on hot, moist foods such as vegetables. They add flavor without fat. Flavored butter granules are also available.

Butter-flavored sprays can be used liberally because they are fat-free. Try butter-flavored spray between layers of phyllo dough or for other cooking uses to replace melted butter.

Cooking Fats

Look For

- Butter and margarine to use in moderation and for selected uses. See page 144.
- No-stick cooking sprays, including olive oil, garlic, and butter-flavored varieties.

Shoppers Should Know

Use the Nutrition Facts panel to help you choose cooking fats lower in total fat, saturated fat, and cholesterol. See page 149 for information on vegetable oils.

All fats should be used sparingly in cooking and at the table.

Many recipes work perfectly well using less butter or other fat than specified. Reduce cooking fat to the lowest level that still yields tasty results.

Applesauce, prune purée, or mashed ripe bananas can be substituted for up to half the fat in many recipes for cakes, muffins, and quick breads.

Using no-stick cooking sprays reduces the need for oil to keep food from sticking to skillets and pans. Nonaerosol pump sprays are environmentally friendly.

Chicken fat contains primarily heart-healthy monounsaturated fat (the type found in olive oil) and only 10 milligrams of cholesterol per tablespoon. Each tablespoon has 13 grams of fat including 4 grams of saturated fat and 120 calories.

Lard and butter are primarily saturated fat. Use them in moderation and substitute heart-healthy fats whenever possible.

The most popular all-vegetable shortening has 12 grams of fat and 110 calories per tablespoon. Although the label indicates 4 grams of monounsaturated fat (and 50 percent less saturated fat than butter), the first ingredient listed is partially hydrogenated oil. It may be a monounsaturated fat but it acts more like saturated fat in the body because it is partially hydrogenated.

Hot oil or shortening shouldn't be poured into shortening containers unless the container is metal. Most brands now come in paper "cans."

Vegetable Oils

Look For

- Olive, almond, canola, rapeseed, avocado, and peanut oils. All contain primarily monounsaturated fat.
- Safflower, sunflower, corn, flaxseed, walnut, sesame, and soybean oils. All contain primarily polyunsaturated fat.
- Small bottles of sesame, avocado, and nut oils.
- Infused oils flavored with garlic, herbs, lemon, or other seasonings.
- Cold-pressed, unrefined oils.

Shoppers Should Know

All oils and fats are high in calories (about 120 calories per tablespoon) and fat and should be used in moderation.

Most liquid oils are less saturated and, therefore, more heart-healthy than solid fats.

Polyunsaturated oils (corn, sunflower, and safflower), labeled "cold-pressed" are unrefined oils. More sensitive to heat and light, they should be refrigerated. They carry more protective antioxidant vitamin E and essential fatty acids than the same oils that are regularly processed. Cold-pressed oils usually carry a premium price. Some studies suggest that cold-pressed oils contain other protective substances but more research is needed to validate that benefit.

Small amounts of flavored and nut oils—sesame, walnut, almond, chili, garlic, mushroom, etc.—add great flavor to foods. Keep them refrigerated; they are more perishable than other bottled oils.

Some oils are lighter in color and milder in flavor than similar oils. They may say "light" on the label but usually do not contain less calories or fat than regular oils. This use of the word "light" describes a color or characteristic and is the exception to the reduced-fat and calorie regulation.

Extra-virgin olive oil comes from the first pressing of the olives. It is more expensive and flavorful than other grades of olive oil and it changes flavor when heated to high temperatures. Use it in dishes in which you can appreciate its flavor. If a dish calls for high heat, lots of spices, or strong flavors, virgin olive oil—or a lesser grade—is adequate.

Coconut, palm, and palm kernel oils (sometimes called tropical oils) are very high in saturated fat. Most people don't cook with coconut oil (except ethnic dishes), but tropical oils are used in processed foods, so watch for them on ingredient lists.

Salad Dressings

Look For

- Fat-free or low-fat salad dressings.
- Light or reduced-fat salad dressings.
- Reduced-fat, light, or fat-free mayonnaise and sandwich spreads.

Shoppers Should Know

Two tablespoons is a standard serving of salad dressing, but many people use more, especially on large salads.

Regular dressings contain 10 to 20 grams of fat in a 2-tablespoon serving; reduced-fat and light dressings have 1 to 7 grams of fat; low-fat dressings have 3 grams or less of fat per 2-tablespoon serving; fat-free dressings have 0.5 grams of fat or less per 2-tablespoon serving and 5 to

20 calories per tablespoon. Check the Nutrition Facts Panel.

Vegetable oil in salad dressing doesn't contain cholesterol but oil is 100 percent fat. It may say cholesterol-free, but it has fat and calories.

Generally, oil-and-vinegar-type dressings have less fat per tablespoon than creamy, cheese, or ranch-type dressings. Check the Nutrition Facts panel for fat content of your favorite brands.

Fat-free does not mean calorie-free. Many fat-free dressings have calories from sugar, starch, or thickeners. Individuals with diabetes should carefully check the carbohydrate content of fat-free and reduced-calorie dressings.

To reduce fat and calories, use lower-calorie dressings or smaller amounts of regular dressings.

Thick dressings (like blue cheese dressing) can be thinned with plain low-fat yogurt, milk, buttermilk, broth, fruit juice, or water to reduce calories per serving. You also will use less because it takes less thinned dressing to coat greens.

Low-calorie dressings make great marinades for meat, poultry, or vegetables. The flavor permeates, but because they are drained off, they add virtually no calories.

Regular mayonnaise has 11 grams of fat and 100 calories per tablespoon; light mayo has 5 grams fat and 50 calories; fat-free mayonnaise has 0 grams of fat and 10 calories. Whipped mayonnaise-type dressings have 7 grams of fat and 70 calories; light dressings have 3 grams of fat and 40 calories; nonfat varieties have 0 grams of fat and 15 calories per tablespoon.

Look at the sodium level listed on the Nutrition Facts panel, if sodium is restricted. Salad dressings vary widely in sodium content.

Xanthan gums and EDTA are safe additives frequently added to bottled dressings to thicken them, maintain their consistency, and lengthen their shelf life.

Alternatives for salad dressing that contain no fat include fruit, herb, and balsamic vinegars, salsas, and fresh lemon or lime juice with seasonings.

Cream and Cream Substitutes

Look For

- Reduced-fat or fat-free coffee creamers; half-and-half for selected uses.
- Reduced-fat, light, or fat-free sour cream or sour half-and-half.
- Ultrapasteurized products, which stay fresh longer in your refrigerator.
- Instant real whipped light cream in an aerosol can with only 1 to 2 grams of fat per tablespoon, or light or fat-free whipped toppings found in the freezer case.

Shoppers Should Know

Half-and-half is a blend of milk and cream. One ounce of half-and-half (about 2 tablespoons) has 40 calories and 3 grams of fat. Adding it as liquid cream to coffee can add considerable calories and fat if several cups of coffee are consumed daily. Try substituting whole milk, evaporated skimmed milk, or powdered skim milk to boost calcium intake.

Sour half-and-half, also called reduced-fat sour cream, contains about 45 calories and 3 to 4 grams of fat (2 to 3 grams of saturated fat) in a 2-tablespoon serving.

Real sour cream has 6 grams of fat per 2 tablespoons. Sour half-and-half can be substituted for most uses without much change in flavor.

Fat-free sour cream has 35 calories and no fat per 2-tablespoon serving.

Whipping cream contains about 45 calories and 5 grams of fat per 1-tablespoon portion. One tablespoon yields about 3 tablespoons of whipped cream.

Cream in many recipes can be replaced with evaporated skimmed milk or whole milk.

Liquid nondairy creamers contain no protein or calcium. They are often substituted for milk and cream in cooking or used to lighten coffee, but they do not provide the nutrients found in milk. They contain varying amounts of sugar and some are flavored.

Powdered coffee creamers may contain saturated fat and sugar. Check the Nutrition Facts panel and choose powdered creamer containing unsaturated fats if you use this product often. Powdered skim milk is a nutrient-rich substitution for powdered coffee creamer.

Regular chilled nondairy whipped topping has only 1.5 grams of fat per 2-tablespoon serving, but all the fat is saturated. Light and fat-free chilled whipped toppings are fairly low in fat but contain small amounts of hydrogenated vegetable oils and/or saturated coconut or palm kernel oil to maintain their consistency. Because these toppings have little or no measurable fat, however, they are reasonable choices.

Frozen Desserts

Look For

- Frozen low-fat and nonfat frozen yogurts—desserts that are sources of calcium and other key nutrients—in cartons, bars, or individual cups. They are the most nutrient-rich frozen desserts.
- Frozen fruit or juice bars made with 100 percent fruit or juice are an excellent choice. Each bar counts as 1 serving from the Fruit Group.
- Low-fat ice cream with 3 grams of fat or less per serving. Fat-free varieties are also available.
- Low-fat frozen yogurt or ice cream bars coated with fruit sorbet.

- Fruit sorbets and fruit ices, which have no fat or cholesterol. Some provide vitamins C or A, depending on the type of fruit.
- Frozen fudge bars and pudding pops to provide extra calcium for less than 100 calories per serving.
- Ice milk and frozen low-fat milkshakes.
- Nondairy frozen desserts if lactose intolerant.
- Ice cream cups, sugar cones, or waffle cups to go with some frozen desserts.

Shoppers Should Know

Preportioned, single-serving items help curb the tendency to eat large portions.

Most frozen desserts fall within the Fats, Oils and Sweets Group. Frozen yogurt, ice cream, and 100 percent juice bars are the exceptions.

Frozen yogurt is a good source of calcium and other nutrients provided by that food group. One cup of frozen yogurt counts as 1 serving from the Milk Group.

Some frozen yogurts have as much fat and sugar as light ice creams. Check the Nutrition Facts panel.

Sherbet is a milk-based frozen dessert with less fat than ice cream but more sugar.

Sorbets and granitas are sweetened frozen desserts usually made from fruits but sometimes with herbs. They contain no milk or cream and are fat-free and cholesterol-free.

Premium ice creams can have up to 26 grams of fat per 1/2-cup serving.

Some premium ice cream bars with chocolate coating have 22 grams of fat and 300 calories per bar. Reduced-calorie chocolate-covered ice cream bars are available.

Ice cream candy bars have 140 to 200 calories per bar and 7 to 13 grams of fat. Some reduced-fat ice cream candy bars are available.

Sundae cones have 310 calories and 16 to 17 grams of fat. They have more calories and fat than a cone you fill with frozen yogurt or light ice cream.

Ice pops are colored, flavored water with added sugar.

Sugars, Syrups, Sweet Sauces, and Toppings

Look For

- Granulated white, confectioners, and brown sugar and honey to use in moderation.
- Molasses. Its intense flavor and sweeteners allow you to use a small amount and, unlike other sweeteners, it provides some iron and calcium.
- Fruit syrups or real maple syrup—very intense flavors—to use in small amounts.
- Light or lite maple-flavored syrup—for reduced sugar and calories. Some have butter flavoring.
- Individual sugar packets or sugar cubes for portion control.
- Sugar substitutes if restricting sugar.
- Chocolate syrup, fruit, or low-fat or fat-free caramel, butterscotch, or fudge toppings for use over ice cream or frozen yogurt. All are low in fat but high in sugar—calories vary.

Shoppers Should Know

Brown sugar is sugar crystals with a bit of molasses. It has 50 calories per firmly packed tablespoon and tiny amounts of calcium, iron, phosphorus, and potassium—not enough to make a nutritional difference. Dark brown sugar has slightly more molasses. Light brown sugar uses the term "light" to describe the color and flavor. It is not lower in calories, carbohydrate, or other nutrients.

Confectioner's sugar is pulverized granulated sugar with a bit of anti-caking agent. It is used for frosting and sprinkling on foods. It has fewer calories per teaspoon than granulated sugar, and it now comes in lemon, strawberry, and chocolate flavors.

Corn syrup and high-fructose corn syrup are made by processing cornstarch to a thick sweetener containing several sugars. Frequently used in processed foods, corn syrup contains 60 calories and 15 grams of carbohydrate per tablespoon. Light corn syrup has a bit of added vanilla; dark corn syrup has a bit of caramel flavor.

Pure maple syrup is the sap of the sugar maple tree boiled down to a syrup. Less costly maple-flavored syrup (pancake syrup) is corn syrup with maple flavoring.

It is against the law to sell raw sugar in the United States because it is unrefined and contaminated with yeasts, molds, and soil.

When a food is labeled "no added sugar," it means that there is no added table sugar or other sweeteners like honey, corn syrup, or fruit juice concentrate. The product may contain sugars that occur naturally in that food.

Reduced-sugar foods contain at least 25 percent less sugar than the standard product.

Sugar-free means a food contains less than 1/2 gram of sugar per standard serving of that food. Other terms meaning the same thing are no sugar, sugarless, and without sugar.

Cinnamon toast made with cinnamon sugar is an economical low-fat alternative to sweet rolls. Mix your own cinnamon with sugar for an economy blend.

Most butter-flavored pancake syrups are fat-free.

Natural fruit syrups have 210 calories and more than 50 grams of sugar per 1/4-cup serving.

Chocolate and strawberry syrups and fat-free toppings both have about 80 to 130 calories per 2-tablespoon serving—about 25 grams of carbohydrate from sugar. Regular hot fudge topping has about 140 calories per 2- tablespoon serving with less sugar but 4 to 6 grams of fat.

Marshmallow cream topping provides about 90 calories per ounce, 23 grams of sugar, and no fat.

Frozen strawberries, raspberries, or peaches can be puréed to make a sweet sauce that is lower in sugar than syrups.

Never give honey to infants, small children, or people with impaired immune systems. Honey can carry spores of botulism that are dangerous to those who have little resistance. Once swallowed, the spores can germinate, releasing toxins. Honey should not be put on pacifiers or in baby food, or added to tea given to individuals with impaired immune systems.

Jellies and Fruit Spreads

Look For

- Fruit preserves, marmalades, jams, and spreadable fruits.

- Fruit butters, such as apple, apricot, and peach butter.
- Reduced-sugar jams, jellies, and preserves, if limiting calories or carbohydrate.

Shoppers Should Know

Spreadable fruit is concentrated fruit with fruit juice used as sweetener instead of sugar. It has about the same amount of sugar and calories as jam or jelly—about 40 to 50 calories per tablespoon.

Contrary to what their name suggests, fruit butters contain no fat.

Fruit spreads and fruit butters on toast, English muffins, or bagels are a healthful, economical alternative to sweet rolls and doughnuts.

When using any fruit spread or fruit butter, omit or use less regular butter, margarine, or cream cheese to save on fat and calories.

Jellies are clear compounds of fruit juice, sugar, and pectin thickeners. Jams and preserves contain bits of fruit. Marmalades are made of citrus fruits and contain strands of the citrus rinds.

Reduced-sugar jellies, jams, and preserves have about half the sugar of regular ones, about 25 calories per tablespoon.

Artificially sweetened jellies, jams, and marmalades (including some light preserves) substitute artificial sweetener for sugar and contain a modified form of pectin that allows jelling to occur without sugar.

Combined Foods—Soups, Sauces, and Dips

Look For

- Vegetable, bean, chicken, seafood, and beef soups. Reduced-sodium or lower-sodium soups, if sodium is restricted.
- Split pea, bean, lentil, and barley soups. All are excellent sources of protein and fiber.
- Canned broth to be used to replace some or all of the fat in stirfrying.
- Low-fat dry soup mixes. They come in interesting flavors but are usually high in sodium.
- Vegetable broth, especially for vegetarians.
- Reduced-sodium sauces, if sodium is restricted.

- Canned or bottled gravies. Many are low-fat or fat-free and taste as good as homemade.
- Tomato-based pasta or pizza sauces with or without added vegetables or seasonings.
- Oriental sweet and sour sauces and hoisin sauce. They are high in sugar but low in fat or fat-free.
- Salsas and picante sauces.
- Fruit sauces such as cranberry sauce and mango chutney.
- Bean dips made with black beans or pinto beans.
- Prepared onion and other low-fat dips made from skim and nonfat dry milk. Two tablespoons contain about 30 calories and 8 percent of daily calcium needs.
- Low-fat, light, or fat-free chip and party dips.
- Light guacamole dip.

Shoppers Should Know

A standard serving of soup is 1 cup, about 8 1/2 ounces by weight.

Soups can be an excellent way to eat more vegetables, legumes, and grains.

Ready-to-eat hearty vegetable or chunky-style soups make a good entrée for a quick meal.

Condensed cream soups can be diluted with skim milk, water, or broth.

New England clam chowder (white) has more fat than Manhattan-style clam chowder (red).

Cranberry sauce or chutney with pork or poultry is a tasty alternative to homemade gravy; mint sauce works well with lamb instead of gravy.

Prepared cheese, pesto, and clam sauces are likely to contain considerable fat. Read labels carefully. Canned white clam sauce for pasta has more than twice the fat of canned red clam sauce. Check the Nutrition Facts panel.

Alfredo sauce is made primarily of butter, eggs, and cheese. Stroganoff sauce contains sour cream. Both are high in fat and, usually, sodium.

Bottled creamy sauces for chicken have 8 to 10 grams of fat in 1/2 cup. Cacciatore and sweet and sour sauces for chicken have 2 or less grams of fat per 1/2 cup.

Guacamole is made from avocados, which are high in fat—but the fat is monounsaturated.

Regular sour cream dips and seasoned cream cheese spreads are high in fat.

Prepared cheese dips vary in fat content. Check the label. Blend cottage cheese or reduced-fat cream cheese with shredded cheese and seasonings to make homemade cheese dip.

Prepared Entrées

Look For

- Frozen full meals with less than 400 calories, 15 grams of fat, and 800 milligrams of sodium. Among regular frozen dinners, sirloin, teriyaki chicken, roast chicken, sirloin tips, shrimp creole, sliced turkey, ham steak, and some pasta entrées are generally the lowest in fat. Short ribs, fried chicken, cheese-filled manicotti, macaroni and cheese, Mexican combos, and fish and chips are generally among the highest in fat.
- Frozen entrées with no more than 300 calories and 10 grams of fat per serving. Frozen entrées that usually meet these criteria include spaghetti or mostaccioli with meat sauce, sliced beef or turkey with gravy, chicken cacciatore, green pepper steak, sirloin tips,

chicken or beef teriyaki, chicken chow mein, shrimp creole, and any entrée labeled light.

- Whitefish or other cooked fish balls in broth. Each piece has 7 grams of protein, 60 calories, and only 2 1/2 grams of fat. Kids, even toddlers, often like this gefilte fish and fish balls.
- Canned turkey chili with beans, labeled 99 percent fat-free. It has only 200 calories and is high in fiber.
- Canned chicken in broth.

Shoppers Should Know

Check the Nutrition Facts panel to help you make wise food choices. Frozen meals and frozen and canned entrées vary widely in both serving size and nutrient content.

It's wise to compare serving sizes. Some frozen dinners are only 8 ounces; others are 19 or more ounces.

Most frozen meals do not contain a full serving of vegetables.

One standard serving of frozen pizza is about 1 (5-ounce) slice; 2 slices have twice the nutrients stated.

Each small single-serving beef or chicken pot pie (8 ounces) has 18 to 24 grams of fat.

Breaded or batter-dipped fried frozen foods are usually high in fat, calories, and sodium.

Adding a fresh green salad, bread, and skim or low-fat milk enhances the nutritional value of meals based on frozen entrées.

Canned pasta entrées vary widely in calorie and fat content. Read the labels and compare. Generally, pastas with tomato sauces are lowest in fat and calories.

Many canned entrées, such as ravioli and chilis, have more than 1000 milligrams of sodium per 1-cup serving. Read labels carefully if on a sodium-restricted diet.

Canned beef stew has about half the fat of canned corned beef hash (13 versus 25 grams).

Canned chili with beans has more fiber than canned chili without beans. But even vegetarian chili may not be low in fat; one brand has 20 grams of fat per cup.

If restricting sugar, sweet and sour sauces should be avoided. One brand of boil-in-bag sweet and sour chicken has 63 grams of sugar in a 10-

ounce package. One sweet and sour chicken frozen dinner has 66 grams of sugar.

Baked Desserts

Look For

- Baked desserts that provide Nutrition Facts on the label so you can make informed choices.
- Angel food cake, lady fingers, gingerbread, sponge-cake dessert shells, baked meringue shells, or other plain or low-fat cakes and baked goods to top with fresh fruit.
- Unfrosted or lightly frosted cakes.
- Small cupcakes, sweet rolls, and other single-serving desserts.
- Fruit-filled crepes and tarts—they usually have a smaller amount of rich filling than pies.
- Pumpkin or sweet potato pie—rich in beta-carotene and fiber.

Shoppers Should Know

Calories and nutrients are based on the portion size listed on the label. You may choose a larger or smaller portion.

Much of the fat and calories in pies is in the crust. Tarts, cobblers, and meringue- or crumb-topped fruit desserts usually have less fat than double-crust pies.

Think twice about any dessert that has more than 10 grams of fat or more than 4 grams of saturated fat per portion. Enjoy a small serving.

Words such as "homestyle," "all butter," and "premium" usually translate to high-fat, high-calorie.

Many fresh baked goods don't have a Nutrition Facts panel. Look at the first few ingredients on the ingredient list as a clue to probable fat content.

Enjoy small portions of high-fat favorite desserts occasionally. Balance high-fat desserts with plenty of fruits, vegetables, and plain grains in the same day or the next day.

Deli Choices and Carry-Out Foods

Look For

- Steamed, grilled, or roasted vegetables.
- Lean sliced roasted beef, turkey breast, pork, or baked ham.

- Grilled chicken breasts; rotisserie chicken. (Remove skin before eating chicken.)
- Poached or grilled fish, shrimp, or scallops.
- Surimi (imitation crab, lobster, or shrimp), made from seasoned pressed fish.
- Grain salads, pilafs, couscous, and rice mixtures.
- Italian beef, barbecued beef, and meat balls in marinara sauce.
- Pastas with tomato-based sauces.
- Turkey or other lean meats or veggies in rolled flour tortillas or in pita pockets.
- Low-fat tuna, crabmeat, and chicken salads.
- Black bean and other bean salads.
- Beet, potato, carrot, or cucumber salads without lots of mayonnaise.
- Raw cut fruits and vegetables.
- Vegetable and pasta salads with vinegar-type dressings. Excess liquid can be drained, which can't be done with creamy dressings.
- Ratatouille and other mixtures of cooked vegetables.
- Salsas and fruit or vegetable relishes.

- Fresh mozzarella cheese balls and feta cheese in water.
- Reduced-fat cheeses in slices or wedges.

Shoppers Should Know

Virtually all prepared foods are time-savers but command premium prices.

It's smart to ask how foods are prepared and if nutrient information is available. Because prepared foods seldom carry nutrition labeling, it is hard to know which are the best choices. Many stores have nutrition or ingredient information available even if it is not displayed. Ask the deli manager for product information.

Eggrolls, potato pancakes, and vegetable pancakes are usually deep-fried.

If buying fried food, buy it in larger pieces (chicken breast versus wing, larger pieces of fish). The percentage of fried surface is less—so there are fewer calories in the same weight of that food.

Mousses and pâtés are prepared with lots of butter or cream.

Most deli sausages are high in fat.

Order sandwiches on French or Italian bread, on whole-wheat bread or rolls, or in pita pockets. Croissants and focaccia add a lot of fat to sandwiches.

Some deli sandwiches, particularly large sub sandwiches, have 900 calories.

Portions of some single-serve items in delis are often very large. Realize that a 12-ounce stuffed potato is at least 2 servings, giant muffins about 3 servings, and over-stuffed sandwiches 2 servings each of meat and bread. Count servings from the Food Guide Pyramid and calories accordingly.

Beverages—Coffee, Tea, and Cocoa

Look For

- Plain or flavored coffee and teas.
- Coffee beverages (latte, cappuccino, etc.) made with skim milk.
- Decaffeinated coffees, decaffeinated teas, or herbal teas or grain-beverages, if you are sensitive to caffeine.
- Iced tea mixes, with or without sugar.

- Green tea. It contains protective substances that may boost the immune system and may help reduce the risk of gastrointestinal cancers.

Shoppers Should Know

Because they contain no nutrients, plain coffee and tea (unless sweetened) are not required to carry a Nutrition Facts panel.

Some instant, flavored coffees made from dry mixes contain about 50 calories and 2 grams of fat per cup. They also contain considerable amounts of sugar, unless sugar-free. Brewed coffees made from ground, flavored beans are calorie-, sugar-, and fat-free.

Dry mixes for flavored coffees sometimes contain coconut oil or hydrogenated oils.

Decaffeinated coffee is brewed from beans that are at least 97 percent caffeine-free.

Caffeine occurs naturally in coffee, tea, kola nuts, and chocolate. In moderation, it is a mild stimulant. Drip coffee contains about 130 milligrams of caffeine per 5-ounce cup; standard brewed coffee about 80 milligrams; instant coffee about 60 milligrams; and decaf about 3 milligrams. The amount of caffeine in tea depends on how long it is brewed. It ranges from 25 to 50 milligrams per 5-ounce cup. A 5-ounce cup of hot cocoa contains about 5 milligrams of caffeine.

Bottled cappuccino and other coffee-based beverages vary in nutrient values—read the Nutrition Facts panel.

Iced frosty cappuccino and similar drinks made from syrups may be promoted as fat-free. Some of them have about 250 calories per glass, all from sugar. Real cappuccino or latte poured over ice cubes have a fraction of the calories and sugar. Ask for skim milk in cappuccino and latte to boost calcium and for less fat.

Bottled iced teas and tea-based beverages come with and without sugar and in many flavors. Some iced teas have almost as many calories as soft drinks.

Bottled or canned prepared iced tea or instant tea from mix is far more expensive than tea made from teabags, which can be prepared and chilled in advance.

Soft Drinks, Sports Drinks, Water, and Flavored Waters

Look For

- Plain, sparkling, and flavored mineral waters, club soda, plain seltzers, sugar-free tonic water, sugar-free fruit drink mixes, and diet soft drinks. All have no calories.
- Water, juice, or sports drinks to replace fluid during and after physical activity.
- Caffeine-free colas and soft drinks if caffeine must be restricted.
- Regular soft drinks if extra energy or weight gain is needed.

Shoppers Should Know

Sweetened sodas and sweetened, flavored mineral waters have 130 to 210 calories per 12-ounce serving, all from sugar.

Corn syrup and high-fructose syrup are sugars used in beverages and are equal in calories to regular sugar. Some fruit-flavored sparkling waters contain a surprisingly high amount of sugar from these syrups.

Products containing noncaloric sweeteners indicate the type of sweetener used on the label.

Colas and some other soft drinks contain caffeine. Ginger ale, root beer, and most fruit-flavored beverages are caffeine-free.

Tonic or quinine water contains 90 calories per 8 ounces; diet tonic is calorie-free.

Sports drinks are blends of water, sugar, sodium, and potassium, often with artificial color and/or added flavor. Some are carbonated, and some are artificially sweetened. Unless exercise is sustained for one hour or more and the weather is hot, regular water will maintain hydration.

Buy the size of carbonated beverage you will use at one serving time. two-liter bottles cost less per serving but lose their carbonation once they are opened.

Beverages packed in "sports bottles" command premium prices.

Wine, Beer, and Liquor

Look For

- Wine, beer, liquor, and other beverages containing alcohol for adults who choose to enjoy them in moderation.
- Alcohol-free beer or wine.

Shoppers Should Know

The Dietary Guidelines say, "If you drink alcoholic beverages, do so in moderation." Moderate alcohol use is 1 serving per day of wine, beer, or liquor for women, 2 servings for men.

A standard serving is 5 ounces of dry white or red wine, 12 ounces of regular beer, or 1 1/2 ounces of liquor.

Alcohol-free wines and beers usually contain fewer calories than their alcohol-containing counterparts.

Alcohol is second to fat in calorie value. It provides 7 calories per gram but few or no nutrients.

Research shows that moderate drinking, particularly of wine, may increase lifespan, and may lower risk of heart disease in some individuals.

In some studies, moderate use of alcohol is linked with higher HDL or "good" cholesterol levels. Higher HDL may protect against heart disease.

Small amounts of alcohol can enhance the enjoyment of meals and promote relaxation, and may reduce blood pressure slightly.

Eighty-proof distilled spirits, such as Scotch, bourbon, and gin, contain 100 calories per 1 1/2 ounces. Gin, rum, vodka, and whiskey that are 100 proof (50 percent alcohol by weight) provide about 125 calories per 1 1/2 ounce jigger.

Liqueurs, which are sweetened alcohol-containing beverages, contain 150 to 190 calories per 1 1/2 ounces.

Most dry red and white wines have about 100 calories per 5-ounce glass; sweet dessert wines contain 90 calories in only 2 ounces.

Regular beer contains about 150 calories per 12-ounce bottle or can; light beer has 100 calories per 12-ounce bottle or can.

Children and adolescents, pregnant women or those trying to conceive, and individuals who plan to drive or do activities requiring good motor skills (such as using power tools) should not drink any alcohol.

Alcohol creates multiple health risks in anyone who consumes it in excess. People who are sensitive to alcohol, or who can not control drinking should avoid it entirely.

Alcohol interferes with the effectiveness of many medications. Speak to your doctor about potential problems if you take medicine and drink alcohol. With many prescribed medications, alcohol should be avoided.

Cook with wine you would drink—or use leftover wine. Cooking wines have added salt, used as a preservative, that changes their flavor.

When cooking with wine, liquor, or liqueurs, some of the calories and alcohol are burned off if there is prolonged cooking or very high heat.

Seasonings and Condiments

Look For

- A variety of herbs and spices to season foods.
- Buy small amounts of less frequently used dried herbs and spices.

- Fresh herbs for maximum flavor and color.
- Cider, balsamic, wine, or other flavored vinegars.
- Garlic, shallots, gingerroot, horseradish, and other seasonings that add bold flavor without fat or salt.
- Mustard or flavored mustards, which are low-fat and low in sodium, as a seasoning or marinade.
- Salsas, barbecue, Worcestershire, chili, hot pepper, mint, seafood, and other low-fat or fat-free prepared sauces and seasonings.
- Asian sauces including teriyaki, reduced-sodium soy sauce, and tamari marinades and marinade mixes.
- Salt-free herb blends and light salt, reduced-sodium soy sauce, reduced-sodium chili sauce, and similar products if sodium is restricted.
- Fresh lemons, limes, oranges, and tangerines—for their zest and juice.

Shoppers Should Know

Liberal use of herbs, spices, and condiments allows reductions in fat and (sometimes) salt without loss of flavor.

Dried herbs and spices should be stored in a dry, cool, dark place. They lose flavor with age or when exposed to heat or light. Replace herbs and spices that have lost their fragrance or changed color.

Grate the zest from citrus fruits (lemons, limes, oranges, and tangerines) and use the zest and juice to season vegetables, grains, sauces, and marinades. Small amounts of citrus don't count as a serving from the fruit group but add lots of flavor to foods.

Generally, sources of sodium in the diet are one-third from sodium added to processed foods, one-third from salt (sodium chloride) added in cooking or at the table, and one-third from the sodium that occurs naturally in foods.

Kosher salt is a coarser grind than table salt. It has 480 milligrams of sodium per 1/4 teaspoon compared to 590 milligrams of sodium per 1/4 teaspoon in regular salt. Many chefs prefer Kosher salt or sea salt for cooking.

Iodized salt contains a small amount of iodine, a trace mineral. Getting enough iodine used to be a problem for some people. Now, because food processing equipment is cleaned with solutions containing iodine, the tiny amounts needed are generally supplied by processed foods.

Ways to reduce or moderate intake of sodium or salt include: using salt sparingly, if at all, at the table; seeking lower-sodium choices by reading labels; and limiting intake of salted or high-sodium foods, such as most cheeses, frozen desserts, packaged mixes, canned soups, and salty condiments.

Baking Basics

Look For

- Pantry cooking basics including flour, baking powder, baking soda, yeast, flavor extracts, etc.
- Pure vanilla extract. It has a much better flavor and aroma than imitation vanilla flavor.

Shoppers Should Know

Cooking "from scratch" is generally less expensive and allows better control of the amount of fat, sugar, and salt used.

Flour is made from pulverized whole grains. All-purpose flour is wheat flour. The percentage of protein to starch varies among different types of flour. Bread flour is a bit higher in protein than all-purpose flour. Most all-purpose flour is pre-sifted.

Most flour has been "bleached" with safe chemicals to make it lighter and whiter; unbleached all-purpose flour is available.

In enriched flour, a few of the vitamins and minerals lost in milling have been replaced and some folate is added. It is still lower in fiber than whole-wheat or other less-refined flours.

Baking powder is a mixture of starch, baking soda, and salts. It is used as a leavening agent in baking. Introduced in the mid-1800s as one of the first convenience foods, it is high in sodium (about 350 milligrams per teaspoon). Reduced-sodium varieties are available.

Baking soda, when activated by heat and liquid, particularly mild acids like buttermilk, releases carbon dioxide, which leavens batters and doughs. Baking soda provides 475 milligrams of sodium per 1/2 teaspoon. It is also an antacid. Its alkaline properties intensify the color of green vegetables but destroy their vitamin C content so it should not be used in vegetable preparation. Baking soda is an excellent, inexpensive household c eaner that neutralizes unpleasant odors.

All yeast is dated with a "use by" date. The "use by" date indicates how long a product will maintain optimal quality after you bring it home. Dry yeast products do not require refrigeration. Compressed fresh yeast is perishable and must be refrigerated until used.

Chapter 5

Keeping Food Safe

America is blessed with one of the safest and most abundant food supplies in the world. Keeping food safe is a shared responsibility of farmers, manufacturers, distributors, retailers, the government, and, ultimately, consumers.

Eighty-four percent of shoppers say they are confident that supermarket food is safe—until there is a problem due to bacterial contamination, pesticide residues, or product tampering! But we shouldn't wait until there is a crisis to act. Most of the time, we could be more vigilant about protecting the food we buy and eat.

Safe Food for You and Your Family, another book in The American Dietetic Association's Nutrition Now Series, explores food safety issues such as the causes of foodborne illness; storing, handling, cooking at home; eating away from home; and the effects of food additives, pesticides, biotechnology, and other food processes.

Here are some shopping tips to help you make safe food choices:

- Shop at clean and responsible stores and markets. Check display cases, shelves, and floors for cleanliness. Permanent facilities, like supermarkets, are more likely than farmstands to implement regular sanitation and pest control procedures. Stores with a high volume of sales are more likely to have greater turnover and fresher perishable foods.
- Buy food in excellent condition, such as fruit without cuts or bruises. Bruised or wilted produce has passed its peak or has been mishandled.
- Look for "sell-by" and "use-by" dates on perishable foods like milk, dairy products, bread, fresh meat, and cold cuts. The sell by date is the last date that a food should be sold. Plan to use the item within a few days of that date. Choose items with the latest available "sell-by" date.
- The "use-by" date indicates how long a food will maintain its quality after you bring it

home. If the "sell-by" or "use-by" date has passed, don't buy the product.

- Anything you buy frozen should be frozen solid and tightly sealed without evidence of previous thawing. Plain frozen vegetables (like corn or potatoes) should be separated, not frozen in a solid clump. Packages that are oddly shaped or with evidence of frozen liquids around the edges are likely to have been thawed and refrozen.
- Select frozen and refrigerated foods at the end of the shopping trip. Don't choose them first and then spend another 40 minutes shopping. They will thaw in your cart.
- Foods in bulk bins, salad bars, or self-serve bakery areas should be held at an appropriate temperature and protected by covers, lids, or plastic or glass sneeze guards. Each food should have its own separate scoop or utensil.
- Eggs, cheese, fresh meat, and poultry should be sold from refrigerated cases. Open egg cartons to ensure the eggs are clean and whole. Avoid cartons with any cracked eggs.
- Canned goods should be in labeled cans free of dents, leakage, rust, or bulges.

- Fresh fish and shellfish should be sold from cases that are well-chilled, with clean, fresh ice. Raw seafood in the case should be separated from cooked shrimp or other ready-to-eat shellfish.
- All fresh fruits and vegetables should be sold from clean display areas. Bagged salad greens and fresh-squeezed juices should be displayed in refrigerated cases to preserve quality. Some stores have water misters to preserve produce freshness. Potatoes, onions, and winter squash should be stored in cool, dry areas. They don't require refrigeration. Tomatoes and bananas should be neither sold from nor stored in refrigerated cases. Handle fresh fruits and vegetables gently. Place produce in your shopping cart and grocery bags where it won't get bruised. Damage and bruising promotes spoilage.
- Roadside stands and farmers' markets can supply wonderful, fresh produce but be extra-careful to wash it well before eating it. Avoid buying shellfish, meat, poultry, or other highly perishable foods from temporary roadside stands or trucks. Buy fresh mushrooms only

from known purveyors or stores. Wild mushrooms can look edible but be poisonous.

- Never buy any wrapped or packaged product in a poorly sealed container. In addition to a potential mess and spillage, there is the possibility of product tampering.
- If you see insects or rodents or any evidence of them, alert the store manager and/or city health department. Don't buy food at that store.

Use these hints to transport and store food immediately after purchasing it.

- Ask the bagger to pack all frozen and chilled items together to keep them cold longer. Put all raw meat, poultry, and seafood together to keep them from leaking on other foods. Take all refrigerated, chilled, and frozen foods home immediately and store them in the refrigerator or freezer as soon as possible.
- Be sure all food is bagged for transport in clean plastic or paper bags or in washed cloth or plastic carriers. Do not allow food to touch dirty car or truck storage areas or seats where pets have been carried.

- Store produce loosely wrapped or in covered containers. Fresh fruits and vegetables are safe as long as they are firm and there is no evidence of mold, a yeasty smell, or sliminess. Don't wash fruits and vegetables before storing them in the refrigerator (except salad greens you are cleaning and crisping). They will stay fresh and firm longer if washed just before eating.
- Read the safe handling instructions printed on some packages, particularly fresh meat and poultry. Some foods contain bacteria that can cause illness if the product is mishandled, cooked, or stored improperly. The graphics tell you how to store and cook that food safely.
- Larger packages of fresh meat or poultry are often sold at a reduced price per pound. Divide large packages into meal-sized parcels. Wrap and seal them tightly in freezer bags, freezer paper, or plastic containers. Label packages with contents and date purchased. To maintain quality, repackage foods immediately after shopping when they are very fresh. Don't refrigerate food for several days before repackaging it for the freezer.

- Fresh meat and poultry covered with plastic film is not wrapped appropriately for freezer storage. Use freezer paper, foil, or plastic wrap to overwrap the original packaging material.

And don't forget to:

- Thoroughly rinse poultry and seafood in cold running water before cooking it. Scrub the shells of shellfish with a scrub brush. Use a separate cutting board for raw fish, poultry, meat, and seafood—one that is not used to cut produce and other foods you will eat raw. Don't let raw juices of poultry, meat, fish, or eggs touch other foods. Wash your hands before and after handling these foods. Also wash cutting boards, sinks, and utensils that have touched raw poultry, meat, and seafood with hot, soapy water and sanitize them after each use.
- Wash produce under cold, running water or in a colander to remove surface sand, dirt, insects, pesticides, and contaminants. Clean root and other firm vegetables and fruits with a vegetable brush or peel them. Use a chemical fruit and vegetable wash or a mild liquid soap to wash produce that may have been exposed to pesticides or bacteria.

- Discard any food that has evidence of mold or spoilage or that smells bad. The Department of Agriculture says, "If in doubt, throw it out." If you have just purchased it, return the food immediately for a refund.
- Check your refrigerator, freezer, and pantry and use existing stores of food first when planning menus. Periodically, clean out your pantry and refrigerator and discard foods that are very old (and of questionable quality and safety). Discard frozen foods with evidence of white, dry patches of freezer-burn or partial thawing.

Keeping food safe and maintaining a clean kitchen protect you and your family from potentially severe and sometimes recurring illness. Many people who have frequent gastrointestinal upsets or "flu" are victims of bacteria harbored in cutting boards, sponges, utensils, and refrigerators. Thorough cleaning with soapy water and a mild bleach solution should be a regular kitchen routine. The few minutes it takes is a good investment in protecting the health of everyone who eats in your home.

Index

acidophilus, definition of, 102

additives, 45, 53, 153

alcoholic beverages 4, 179-181

antioxidants, 72, 88

aspartame, 22

baked desserts, 170-171

bakery products, 43-48

baking, basic ingredients, 184-186

baking mixes, 48-50

bars, 58-60

  energy, 60

beans, preparing, 78

beef, 114-120

beer, 179-181

beta-carotene, 68

beverages, 174-181

blood cholesterol, 4, 13

Bovine Somatotropin (BST), 104

bread products, 43-48

breads, 43-48

butter, 144-146

buttermilk, 102

caffeine, 175-176

calcium, osteoporosis and, 20

calories, food labels and, 15

cancer, 3, 4, 21
carry-out foods, 171-174
cereal, 50-53
cheese and cheese products, 107-110
chips, 60-62
cholesterol, blood, 13
cocoa, 174-176
coffee, 103, 174-176
cold cuts, 130-131
condiments, 181-184
convenience foods 33, 36-39, 171-174
cookies, 58-60
cooking fats, 147-148
coupons, 28-30
crackers, 56-67
cream and cream substitutes, 154-156
custards, 111

Daily Values, 14-16
dairy foods, 98-112
deli foods, 171-174
desserts,
  baked, 170-171
  frozen, 156-158
diabetes, 3, 13
Dietary Guidelines for Americans, 3-4
dietary fat, food labels and, 16
dips, 164-166
dressings, salad, 151-153

egg substitutes, 49, 136-139
eggs, 136-139
entrées, prepared, 167-170

fiber, dietary, 13, 51
fish, 124-130, 193
flour, 44, 184-185
folate, 21, 47
Food and Drug Administration, 24
Food Guide Pyramid, 5-7
food labels,
  Daily Values and, 14-16
  dietary fat and, 16
  exempt products, 9-10
  sugars and, 16-17
frozen desserts, 156-158
frozen foods, 189, 191
  desserts, 156-158
  entrées, 167, 168
  fruit, 89-91
  vegetables, 73-76

fruit spreads, 162-164
fruits, 81-97
  canned and bottled, 91-95
  dried, 95-97
  fresh, 82-89
  frozen, 89-91

game birds, 120-124
game meats, 114-120
grains, 53-56
guidelines, dietary, 3-4

health claims, food labels and, 20-21
heart disease, 3, 4, 21
herbs, 69, 181-184
high blood pressure, 3, 4
honey, 162
hypertension, 3, 4
  sodium and, 21

ice cream, 156-158
ingredients, food labels and, 17-18
irradiated foods, 89

jellies, 162-164
juices,
  canned and bottled, 91, 92-95
  fresh fruit, 86
  frozen, 89, 90

kefir, 105
kidney ailments, 13
kosher symbols, 22

labels, food, 9-24
  Daily Values and, 14-16
  exempt products, 9-10
legumes, 132-136
liquor, 179-181

margarine, 144-146
meats, 114-124, 192, 193
  packaged, 130-131
milk and milk alternatives, 99-105
mixes, baking, 48-50

nut butters, 139-142
nutrient content claims, 18-21
nutrients, sources of, defined, 14
Nutrition Facts label, 10-16

nuts, 139-142

obesity, 3, 4
oils, vegetable, 149-151
omega-3 fatty acids, 127
organic food,
  dairy products, 104-105
  poultry, 123-124
  produce, 70, 87-88, 133-134
osteoporosis, calcium and, 20
overweight, 3, 4

packaging, 40
pasta, 53-56
pasteurization, 101-102, 138-139
pastries, toaster, 59-60
peanut butter, 139, 140, 142
phenylketonuria (PKU), 22
phytochemicals, 72-73, 88-89
popcorn, 60
pork, 114-120
portion sizes, 10, 12
poultry, 120-124, 192, 193
pretzels, 61
pricing, unit, 33-35
produce, 27, 63-97, 192, 193
puddings, 111-112
pyramid, food guide, 5-7

rebates, 29-30
recycling, 40
rice, 53-56

safety, food, 80, 117, 123, 129, 187-194
salad dressings, 151-153
salt, 4, 183-184
sauces, 164-166
  sweet, 159-162
seafood, 124-130, 193
seasonings, 181-184
seeds, 139-142
serving sizes, 10, 12
shopping from home, 39
shopping list advice, 25-28
shopping, money-saving advice, 25-39
shortening, 147-148
snack foods, 58-62
sodas, 177-178
sodium, 4, 13, 183-184
  hypertension and, 21
soft drinks, 177-178
soups, 164-166

soy products, 132, 134-135
spices, 181-184
sports drinks, 94-95, 177-178
spreads, 144-146
  fruit, 162-164
stroke, 3
sugars, 159-162
  food labels and, 16-17
  tooth decay and, 4
sulfites, 22, 96
surimi, 125, 128
syrups, 159-162

tea, 174-176
tofu, 132, 135-136
tooth decay, 4
toppings, 159-162
tortillas, 47

unit pricing, 33-35

veal, 114-120
vegetable oils, 149-151
vegetables, 63-80
  canned and bottled, 76-80
  fresh, 64-73
  frozen, 73-76
vegetarian diets, 13, 139

water, 177-178
  flavored, 177-178
weight problems, 3
wine, 179-181

yogurt and yogurt products, 105-107
  frozen, 155-158